Spiritual Exercises to Serve for the Annual Retreat of a Carmelite

Christian Meditations on God, Sin, the Baptism and Life of Jesus Christ, by a Leader of a Carmelite Convent

By Ecclesiastical Superior

of a Carmelite Convent

PANTIANOS
CLASSICS

Published by Pantianos Classics

ISBN-13: 978-1-78987-176-0

First published in 1919

Contents

Letters of Approbation

To the Most Holy Virgin Mary Mother of God and Queen of Carmel

Humbly prostrate at your feet, the least and most unworthy of your servants comes to beg you to accept the offering of this little treatise which has for its object the sanctification of a family of your Holy Order of Carmel.

Ever since I undertook to retrace in the Spiritual Exercises of a Retreat, the degrees which conduct these Religious souls to the perfection of charity, that is to say to the love of God and of man, carried even to contempt of self, forgetfulness of self, entire immolation of self, sublime end of their Holy Institute, you know that I have had constant recourse to your powerful mediation, while my eyes were ever fixed upon your admirable life. You are among all creatures the one who without any possible comparison has carried farthest the heroism of Divine Love; the only one who has attained the perfection of it, since you have immolated to its Divine object more than yourself in sacrificing upon Calvary the Emmanuel, the Man-God, your Son, by a sublime act of love comformable to that with which you gave Him to the world in Bethlehem.

Between these two prodigious, ineffable acts of your charity, your life was but one uninterrupted exercise of holy love. Therefore, it is in your Immaculate Heart that I have sought the rules and the holy rigors which the perfection of Carmel, of which you are the foundress, the Queen and the Mother, requires of her children,

Deign to complete your work by pouring down upon this writing your benediction, O Mother of Beautiful Love, in order that those who read it, and above all, that those who will use it for the purpose for which it is particularly destined, may draw abundant fruit for their advancement in the perfection of their holy state.

I beg this of you for the love of Jesus, your Son, Whom you saw so perfectly submissive to your will on earth, while you were yourself all lost, annihilated in His. Amen.

Advice Upon Prayer

As Methods of Prayer, when we come to the application of them, contribute sometimes to embarrass, or even to discourage beginners in this holy exercise, by the multiplicity of the acts which they prescribe, I have thought it well to analyze and at the same time, simplify these acts, in order to convince the most prejudiced, as well as the most discouraged minds, that nothing is more simple or more easy than meditation, and that if they but bring to it a sustained application, they will be able in a short time with the ordinary means of grace, to make their meditations well.

In effect, it is only necessary in this exercise that the just, whom Jesus Christ calls the children of light, should apply to the truths of Religion the same operations of the soul which the children of darkness make use of for their temporal interests. When the latter wish to undertake some affair, they commence by studying the nature of it, the advantages, and the inconveniences; then they take into consideration what means are necessary to succeed in it, after which they determine by reflection to reject or to apply themselves to it.

Therefore the Christian or the Religious soul, who wishes to undertake seriously the important affair of her salvation or of her sanctification, represents to herself some holy truth, draws the consideration which naturally flows from the subject, makes the application to herself, and determines by reflection to reject vice and to embrace virtue.

Meditation is then only a serious reflection upon some truth of Religion, in order to draw practical consequences from it; and to succeed in this, it is only necessary to apply to a spiritual subject, the three powers of the soul, which are the memory, the understanding and the will.

The memory recalls the subject upon which we wish to meditate — be it something learned from a recent lecture, or a remembrance of some truth of Religion, for example, some circumstance in the life or the Passion of Jesus Christ. The understanding by examining all the details, and by the consideration which it draws from them, endeavors to penetrate the truths which are their consequences. Thus in the example cited, a soul will take some one of the virtues of Our Saviour, His sweetness; His charity; His patience; His humility; and then making the application of these considerations to herself, she will try, by comparing these virtues with her faults and defects, to understand the extreme need which she has of the help of grace to get rid of her imperfections.

Here commence the acts of the will; for at the sight of her misery and the perfection of her Divine Model, the soul enters into sentiments of confusion, of regret, and of repentance, which she expresses with so much the more compunction as she will have become more penetrated with them.

Then follow holy desires, fervent prayers, loving colloquies with Jesus, Mary and the other holy personages who have entered into the subject of her prayer. She takes at their feet fervent and efficacious resolutions, imploring them to grant her the grace (or to obtain it for her) to be faithful to them.

Then she should recommend to God her particular needs, renew her petitions to obtain the virtue most necessary to her, or the correction of her predominant passion, represent to Him the general needs of the Church, and of those persons for whom she wishes especially to pray. We find a great number of persons who, imagining themselves to have little aptitude for reflection, believe it a duty to neglect the considerations of which we have spoken, that is to say, the operations of the memory and the understanding, to pass immediately to those of the will, which are pious reflections or aspirations.

But the greater number fall into a grave illusion, and perceive not that the acts of the will are but the fruit of the considerations which they previously made, and when not willing to take the pains to make reflections and thus overcome the first difficulties, their pretended affections are vain and sterile, and their prayer pure idleness. It must be admitted that there are souls who from the first time they commence to give themselves to the holy exercise of prayer show a great facility in producing these pious aspirations and in uniting themselves to God by acts of the will alone, without any preceding reflections, but as this facility is the effect of a particular grace, it should not be lightly supposed in beginners: it will always be more sure to prove them first, and afterward, it will be very easy for the Mother Prioress, or the one who has the direction of the Novices to recognize if the prayer of these souls is produced by grace. It will suffice to examine the fruit which they draw from it, that is to say, the change which is operated in their conduct. But the great and we may say the one obstacle to progress in prayer comes from a defect in what is called the remote preparation, that is to say, the habits of mortification and recollection.

It is necessary then that the soul who aspires to establish in herself the reign of God by prayer, should keep her senses so closed to exterior objects, and to the impression of creatures, that she can habitually retire within herself during the course of her daily occupations, and this she will easily do, if to the mortification of her senses, she adds care to produce frequent aspirations, and renews the offering of her actions through love. As to the proximate preparation, this consists in a great purity of intention, that is to say, to propose to herself as the unique end of her prayer, the glory of God with perfect indifference as to the means by which He wills to unite Himself to her. The soul thus disposed is prepared for aridities or consolations, asking nothing but the good pleasure of God. The immediate preparation consists in putting one's self in the presence of God, and invoking the light of the Holy Spirit.

First Day

First Meditation - The Retreat

"And Jesus was led by the Spirit into the Desert."— Luke IV, 1.

FIRST ACT
To Place One's Self in the Presence of God. (1)

I come, O my God, to converse with Thee, I seek a place where Thou wilt be alone with me, a throne where Thou mayest reside through love, awaiting Thy well beloved to hear and to answer them, and Faith teaches me that this throne is my heart. I enter then within myself; I descend into this interior sanctuary of my soul, there I find Thee and I commence by annihilating myself before Thee, filled with confusion and sorrow at the sight of my profound misery and numberless sins. I wish to detest them sovereignly, to regard myself as the most unworthy and the most culpable of Thy creatures; yet notwithstanding this, I pray Thee to efface them, and to suffer me in Thy adorable Presence, all unworthy as I am, and to permit me to entertain myself with Thy Divine Majesty. I will do this with confidence because I am clothed with the merits of Thy Son, Our Lord Jesus Christ, and I address my prayer to Thee in the same spirit in which He prayed to Thee while on earth.

SECOND ACT
To Represent to One's Mind the Subject of Prayer

I prostrate myself humbly before Thee, O Divine Solitary, perfect model of souls in retreat. I follow Thee into the desert. I come to adore Thee, to contemplate Thee, and to unite myself to Thee, in order to have part in the spirit of that profound solitude in which Thou didst live for forty days and forty nights, to merit for us those graces which have peopled the deserts, and have sanctified the inhabitants of them. Grant me grace to share in this Retreat, in the lights, the sentiments, and the affections which Thou didst have in Thine.

Speak to my heart, fill me with Thy holy unction, discover to me the obstacles with which I have until now opposed Thy Divine inspirations; teach me how to overcome the devil, and to render Thee entire master of my heart, in order that I may draw from these holy exercises, the principal fruit which I should propose to myself, that is to say, the amendment of my life, a result without which the best sentiments can be counted as nothing.

The Second Act varies with each Meditation.

To Invoke the Light of the Holy Spirit

my God, I implore Thee to come to my aid, that I may draw from this meditation the lights and the fruits which are most appropriate to my wants. Without Thee I can do nothing, absolutely nothing: Thou hast said, "Without Me you cannot have even one good thought, for you know not what you should ask, or how you should ask it". Give light to my mind, O Lord, and the impulse of Thy grace to my heart, in order that for Thy glory, and in view of Thy pure love, I may find in this prayer, a remedy for the wounds of my soul, strength to overcome its weakness, and constancy to put an end to its uncertainties and levities.

FIRST POINT - Importance of the Retreat

I have now entered into the solitude of the Retreat, profound solitude, happy solitude! I shall live separated, not only from the world since I have left it and no longer belong to it, but from the commerce of all creatures, of those even whose company is advantageous to me at other times, because we are united by the same Rule for one common end of sanctification.

To-day, God wishes to find me alone! It is upon the solitary soul that He is accustomed to lavish His most precious favors. It is in Retreat that He discovers to the soul of a Religious, the secrets which He hides from the children of the world. There He touches her with lively compunction at sight of her past sins, which she has known until now but imperfectly; there He discovers to her their greatness and their multitude, at the same time that He enlightens her upon her actual infidelities and upon the principal obstacles which she has opposed again and again to her advancement in virtue.

The exercises of a Retreat are a picture of the different degrees through which a Religious soul must pass to arrive at perfection, a faithful mirror where she can see her faults clearly, and also her negligence in the practice of the means which the Rule furnishes her for her sanctification. In effect, in the first part of the Retreat, after having meditated attentively upon the end for which God has created her, having naturally thought of death, which will decide the important affair of her salvation, and being well penetrated with the rigors of the judgments of God, and the chastisements reserved for sinners in hell, the soul comprehends all the malice of sin, and detests it more and more. She then enters into the design of working to purify herself by penance, and to practice the virtues of which Jesus Christ has given her the example. This first part of the Retreat corresponds with the "Purgative Way".

Then commences the Second Part, a picture of the "Illuminative Way", thus called because the soul finds in the different mysteries of the life of our Saviour, not only the model of all virtues, but also the motives for them, and the lights and helps to practise them; the effects of this contemplation being to produce in the heart which applies itself to it, a grace corresponding to the truths which it considers in its prayer. This assiduous meditation excities in the soul the love of her Divine Model, a love which produces conformity to Him and which unites her to the object of her contemplation.

The Third Part of the Retreat is the picture of the 'Unitive way", of which the Religious soul can feel the foretaste, and by attending with fidelity to the good resolutions which she will make, she will become truly established in it, and this is the end of her vocation.

"Alas, the earth is made desolate with extreme desolation, because there is no one who thinks in his heart", for if we think always of our last end, we shall never sin. Whence comes so much relaxation which is found in certain Religious Orders? Why even in holy communities under the strictest rules do we find so many tepid and imperfect souls? It is because they have neglected to lay a solid foundation to their perfection by the attentive consideration of their last end, and wishing to leave too soon the exercises of the purgative way, if they have ever so much as seriously entered it, they have abandoned the practice of mortification, of doing penance for their sins, and of correcting their faults, to throw themselves with temerity into a search after imaginary virtue, and a prayer replete with illusions. Is it not from a want of serious consideration upon the fundamental truths of salvation that I myself should attribute the little fruit which I have until now drawn from my ordinary meditations, and especially from my Retreats, in which I have produced only superficial reflections, and deluded myself by sentiments of piety which soon vanished, leaving me in my habitual sterility?

Oh! Lord, open the eyes of my soul and I will consider the wonders of Thy Law, and the secrets of eternity. "Give me intelligence and I shall live". May this Retreat be not like preceding ones. Grant me the grace to be so entirely penetrated during it with the fundamental truths of salvation, that I may preserve the salutary impressions of them the rest of my life.

SECOND POINT - The Means of Profiting by the Retreat

There is yet another cause of the little fruit which we draw from the Retreat, the exercises of which are so proper to make a soul advance in perfection, and which have sanctified so great a number. It is that so few on entering the Retreat seriously propose the amendment of their lives; so f ew understand that without this real and lasting change, we cannot attain the true end of these holy exercises. In effect, the fruit of the Retreat consists not in consecrating a more considerable time to prayer; to communicate daily; to live in silence, in recollection, and separation from creatures; to conceive good sentiments and pious ardors; to read much and to write our resolutions; but it consists in changing — in becoming better. We would be able to say to a person entering the Retreat what Samuel said to Saul in announcing to him the choice which God had made of him: "The Holy Spirit will take possession of you, and you will be changed into a new man"; but if in terminating these holy exercises, or in a short time after, I am subject to the same weakness, if I am as little generous in overcoming myself, as little recollected, and as unmodified as before this solitude, no matter what might be the sentiments of fervor which accompanied it, it will have been for me only a loss of time, and an abuse of grace.

To attain then the end of the Retreat, which I now understand is the amendment of my life, it is necessary first, to neglect nothing to make it well. It is necessary to commence by regulating the exercises, determining in advance, the subject and the time to be spent in each exercise, in order that I may never be uncertain about the employment of any part of the day. It is necessary to live not only in recollection and exterior silence, but still more in interior silence, which withdraws me as much as possible from useless thoughts, the remembrance of creatures, and all that is foreign to the great affair with which I am going to occupy myself. It is necessary in fine, besides the general change of life which I must propose to myself, to determine a particular object, without which these projects oi changing remain inefficacious, because they are conceived in a manner too vague and too little determined. Each Religious can know with the aid of her Spiritual Guide, what her predominant passion is, the virtue most necessary for her, and the principal obstacle to her advancement, and it is toward this point that she should direct all her efforts, having recourse to fervent prayer, and doing a holy violence to heaven, begging the intercession of the Blessed Virgin and the Saints to whom she has a particular devotion, and under whose protection she will have placed her Retreat. But a very essential remark to be made in terminating this meditation is that the life of a Carmelite should be a continual Retreat, and the spirit of the Rule being one of solitude and of death, she who commences her Retreat should enter it with the thought and the resolution never to leave it, so that she should be determined, after having employed in these holy exercises the ten days prescribed by the Rule, to continue to live in the same spirit of separation and of recollection, (of which she will have commenced to gather the fruit and to taste the sweetness), by preserving the holy habit of conversing with God in the midst of her occupation. This resolution is decisive and its execution will become the source of a multitude of graces and the principle of her sanctification. If, in effect, the most imperfect Religious sometimes experience so great a benefit from the Retreat, if they there receive so much light, if they are there so strongly drawn to virtue that, in a short time, they find their sentiments entirely changed, what will they not gather who persevere in these dispositions? But, alas! scarcely out of Retreat, our unmortified nature, as if in satisfaction for the fatigue of these holy exercises, now that they are terminated, hastens to free itself from this restraint, and to give itself up to its former liberties, having no longer any regard for the holy practices of recollection, of modesty, or of silence.

O my God, I recognize in this picture myself. I find there the history of the days which have followed my Retreats until now, I understand the cause of the little fruit which I have drawn from them. I did not enter them with a sincere will to be changed into another person, since I did not take the means necessary to operate this change, to become a true Carmelite, that is to say, a true Solitary, vowed to silence and separation from all that is not God. I believed that I had done enough for my perfection when I had devoted myself during ten days to this complete separation without thinking that, although less sensible out of the time of Retreat, it should be the habitual disposition of my heart and the ordinary state of my whole life. Oh, how I have deluded myself until now!

Who will give me the wings of a dove, that I may fly to the desert, with Jesus, never more to return? O Divine Solitary, hide me in the secret of Thy Face, may I dwell there unknown to all creatures, and may they never again find me. Bless these resolutions which I take at Thy feet of profiting so well by this time of salvation, and of being so faithful to the graces which Thou wilt grant me, that becoming a new creature, I may correspond to the sublime vocation of Carmel with which Thou hast favored me.

(1) The First and Third Preparatory Acts are not found in the following Meditations, but they should not be omitted.

Second Meditation - God is the End of Man

"God has made all things for Himself." — Prov. XVI, 4.

I come trembling to adore Thy Divine Majesty, O Immense, Eternal God, Infinite Source of all good, of all truth! Thou art my Creator, my Beginning and my Last End. I humbly come to supplicate Thee to make me comprehend, to make me relish and love this first and most important of all truths: that Thou hast created me for Thyself, and that my supreme interest consists in uniting myself to Thee by grace in this life, and by glory in the next.

If with the aid of Thy grace, I succeed in profoundly engraving in my heart, this fundamental truth, I will have acquired the principle, the basis of my salvation and of my sanctification. I supplicate Thee, O my Creator, to grant me the grace to be touched and convinced in a lively manner with this truth in commencing this Retreat. I acknowledge with confusion and sorrow that my sins and numberless infidelities render me unworthy to obtain this favor, but I hope for it from the infinite love which Thou hast for all Thy creatures.

FIRST POINT - God is my Last End

God exists: evident truth, eternal truth, necessary truth, because from it all others flow. The heavens and the earth proclaim it; the most savage of people have recognized it, while they disfigured it. Pagan philosophers have declared it. It is true that they did not draw from it the necessary consequence: they have believed that God exists, but that sufficed not for their salvation. It is necessary to believe with the Church in God, that is to say, we must recognize Him as our Last End, and direct to Him all the faculties and all the powers of our soul, "Because God has made all things for Himself".

Formerly God said to Moses: "I am Who am", that is to say, "I alone have being, I alone live from Eternity; all other creatures live but by Me, and for Me". Thus all creatures who have been gifted by Him with intelligence and liberty, and to whom He has been pleased to make Himself known, are obliged to live for Him alone, and to refer to Him, not only in general but even in particular, all their actions, their thoughts, and their words, without voluntarily withdrawing any from Him. It will not suffice them to believe that there is a God, it is necessary to believe that there is only one God, who alone has Being, who alone lives of Himself, and that I should live but for Him, and regard all things else as nothingness. This is a necessity, it is a law which creatures cannot violate without outraging their Creator, and doing themselves an infinite wrong. In this consists their interests, their glory, and their sovereign happiness in this world and in the next. It is the end of Man, it is the term of his creation. "Fear God and keep His Commandments", says the Holy Spirit, "because this is all man". Yes, it is the whole man, it is his perfection and his beatitude, since the excellence of any creature consists in attaining the end for which it was made. Admirable thought, astonishing thought, but most true, for it is the foundation of all Religion. This good God, who is love itself, this great God, father of all being, source of all good, of all joy, and of all glory, sovereign Bounty, ineffable Beauty, infinite Spirit, possessing in His simplicity all imaginable perfections, — infinite in number and in grandeur — wishes to be the End of man, that is to say, He has created man to make him a sharer in His eternal felicity. "I, Myself, will be thy recompense', said He to Abraham, "a recompense too great for the capacity of thy heart", because God is infinite.

O my God, what is man that Thou has't thus glorified him, and raised him to the equal of the angels? O beautiful truth, glorious truth, but terrible truth if I conform not my life to it! God has placed me upon earth, giving me His Commandments (a perfect expression of His infinite sanctity) in order to render me conformable to Himself, that by their faithful accomplishment I may unite myself to Him, in this world by grace and in the other by glory, thus securing for myself a happiness which will never end. But if unfortunately, I quit this world without having accomplished this condition, I shall be justly and eternally separated from God, my last End, and precipitate myself into hell, there to receive forever the terrible chastisement of my ingratitude and my injustice. To be united to God, behold the end of the creature, behold my end! To 'work for it with fervor and without relaxing is then my essential affair, my only affair, my first and last affair.

FIRST, MY ESSENTIAL AFFAIR. Although I shall have failed in all others, although I be despoiled of all things, lose my reputation, my repose, my health, even my life, if I succeed in this affair, all is gained, but if I fail, although I should succeed in all things else, all is lost.

SECOND, MY ONLY AFFAIR. God has not placed me in this world for any other interest. He has not created me to acquire here below fortune, talents, or a great reputation; to attract to myself the esteem or the affection of creatures. No, He ha? created me to acquire His love in this world, and His felicity in the next.

THIRD, MY FIRST AND LAST AFFAIR. It is in seeking and in obtaining the end for which God has created me, that I will find the plenitude of my felicity, and will repose in peace; while in the possession of creatures and all the joys which they are able to contain in themselves, I would find but anxiety, trouble, and emptiness, the entire world being too little to fill or to satisfy a soul created for an infinite good. It is then true my God that, "Thou hast made us for Thyself, and "that our hearts are agitated and cannot rest until they rest in Thee".

What have I done until now in this world. I who have so seldom sought Thee, I who have loved Thee so little, I who have placed my Last End in creatures, and lowered my ambition to the things of the earth? What have I done here below, O my God, my sovereign Beatitude? "O, too late have I loved Thee, Beauty ever ancient, and yet always new!" If I have loved Thee and sought Thee with but little eagerness and fidelity, Thou who art my Beginning and my End; it shall be so no longer. I desire to be entirely Thine, Thine without reserve and forever.

SECOND POINT - How to attain my Last End

When God created this universe with so much magnificence, He made it for man. It was for man that He extended the rich pavillion of the heavens, for him that He filled the sea, the earth, and the air with all sorts of creatures, providing with paternal bounty not only for his needs but even for his pleasures. He established him king of creation, and as God was the End of man, man in a way was the end of all other creatures, since God has made them for his use in order that they might aid him to glorify and to love his Creator. Such was the happy state of Adam in his innocence; he used creatures only in as much as they assisted him to elevate himself by love, even to the Author of all good. But by his sin, being turned from God, his Last End, he placed this end in creatures, who became then but snares for degraded man, and instead of using them to elevate himself to the One who had made them, he placed in them all his affections, and made use of them to forget and to outrage his Creator.

It is now necessary for the Christian soul who does not wish to fall into this culpable disorder, but on the contrary to attain the end of her creation, to use created things only in as much as they conduct her to this end, and to abstain from them if they turn her from it. Since, in consequence of the evils which Adam's sin introduced into the world, the use of creatures is full of sufferings

14

for the soul and for the body, it is therefore necessary, according to the admirable disposition of Divine Providence and the Infinite Wisdom of God, that we use the goods and the evils of this life to arrive at our Last End. To attain the possession of God is then the end, all things else are but means. Health or sickness, joy or sorrow, poverty or riches, the esteem of creatures or their contempt, their love or their hatred; what does it matter? All these things are but means, the one thing of importance, the one thing necessary is to arrive at my Last End, it is to unite myself to God in this life and in the next. Behold my end, I must at any price attain it! I should then be perfectly indifferent as to the means or the way by which God wills to conduct me to it; whether He makes me pass through aridities or through spiritual consolations; whether He permits that I be abandoned by those whose support seems most necessary to me, or that I receive their encouragement; esteemed by my Superiors or disregarded and left by them in oblivion; whether He calls me to serve Him in an office which is agreeable to nature, or in an employment for which I have a repugnance; whether by the practice of hidden virtues which escape the notice of men, or by acts the most brilliant; in fine, whether He grants me great peace of heart, or exercises me in the most cruel trials, or the most severe temptations; what does it matter, provided that by this I accomplish His holy will?

But for an end so noble, so sublime, so important, does indifference as to its means suffice? And if faith discovers to me that to arrive there, poverty is a more sure way that riches, sufferings than pleasures; if it reveals to me that the contempt of creatures is more advantageous to me than their esteem, solitude than the company of the world, tears, trials, temptations, and combats, than joys, satisfactions, or the approbation of men; should I hesitate to follow this path, straight and thorny, but more short and secure? Is not my choice already made? Has not Jesus Christ taught us these ways as the most sure and called them Beatitudes, saying: "Blessed are the poor, Blessed are those who weep, who suffer, ...who are meek," etc., because they have found the way to heaven, and are assured in advance of its possession.

O my God, what has been my illusion until to-day? I now recognize that the sufferings, contempts, contradictions, inconveniences, privations, and blame, which I have avoided with so much care and fled from with so much eagerness, are precisely what would have conducted me to Thee. Ah, if I had at least referred to Thee the use I made of Thy creatures! If I had offered to Thee ail my thoughts, words, actions and affections! If I had for Thy glory and my own salvation, consecrated entirely to this one end, the employment of my time, my work, my repose, even my eating and drinking, as Thy Apostle prescribes, I should be less culpable. But alas! Lord, when I used the life of Thy creatures and of myself, I had no regard for my Last End, I sought what would give me the most satisfaction, what would be most agreeable to my self-love. Behold the cause of my wanderings out of the right path, and of the numberless sins which I have committed. C my sovereign Lord, grant me the grace in this Retreat to be so deeply penetrated with the important truth that

Thou art my First Beginning and my Last End, and that my supreme interest consists in living for Thee alone, that henceforth I may not have any other care or desire.

Third Meditation - On the End of the Religious Life

"Listen my daughter and see, lend an attentive ear; forget thy people and thy father's house, and the King will greatly desire thy beauty."— Ps. XLIV, II.

Behold me humbly prostrate at Thy Feet, O Jesus; my Lord and my King! Thou hast caused me to hear Thy voice, and I have listened; Thou hast invited me to follow Thee, to quit the world, to abandon my father's house, and Thy grace has given me the strength to respond to the call. But the first step suffices not for Thy love, or for my obligations. It is necessary now that I render myself worthy of the choice which Thou hast made of me for Thy spouse; it is necessary that I render my life and my sentiments conformable to Thine; that I love what Thou hast loved, and despise what Thou has rejected. It is necessary in fine that I understand the infinite value of my vocation, and above all the inestimable advantages which I find in it, of being able to arrive more surely and more happily at the end for which Thou hast created me. Thy grace will finish the work which it has commenced: I expect this of Thy infinite mercy.

FIRST POINT - End of the Religious Life.

After being convinced of this important truth, that God is my Last End, and that my sovereign beatitude consists in uniting myself to Him in time, that I may be united to Him in eternity; I have concluded that I ought to make every effort without ceasing, to refer to this great and unique affair all the actions and ail the thoughts of my life.

But ah, how difficult it is for those who live in the world to fulfil, in its full extent, this obligation! Either they are so much taken up with the interest of this world, or they are so engaged in temporal affairs, or they are so held back by the ties of flesh and blood, as scarcely to be able to raise themselves above themselves, to think of eternal things, and to refer to this thought the goods or the evils of life. In a heart filled with solicitude and love for created things, there remains but little place for the love of the Creator, or little care to please Him, and to attain perfection which is, notwithstanding, the greatest and most desirable good in the world.

But God must have adorers in spirit and in truth; it is necessary for His glory and the edification of the Church that there should be in it until the end of time, generous souls who, bidding an eternal adieu to the world, renouncing all the pretentions and all the hopes of earth, and severing all the ties of nature, have no other ambition than to please Him, and to attach themselves to

Him by ties the most binding and the most indissoluble. The Divine Master, in His Gospel, has not only traced the precepts which all are obliged to accomplish in order to be saved, but He has also transmitted the counsels for those {souls who should feel the desire of imitating Him more particularly and following Him more closely, in order to -arrive at a higher perfection, and thus merit the grace of a more intimate union in this world and a more glorious recompense in the next, Now this state of greater perfection is the Religious State, to which God by a signal favor, calls a certain number of privileged souls, and to which He has called me, notwithstanding my sins. After having prevented them by His grace, which alone could in spire them with so generous a design, He aids them by His inspirations to triumph over the obstacles which the world, the flesh, and the devil offer to prevent them from accomplishing it, and conducts them if they are faithful, to the end of their vocation, which is their sanctification in this world, and in the next to a more abundant participation in His glory and eternal happiness.

The Religious life at first sight appears to have no other end than that of the Christian life. To possess God in this world by grace and in the next by glory, is the end of both; but we can say, nevertheless with truth, that the Religious life has a more particular and a more excellent end than the common life, because the soul who embraces it, having burst all earthly ties, renounces forever by the vows of Poverty, Chastity, and Obedience, all her goods, her body and her will, and the employment of all the moments of her existence, not only in general but in particular. She belongs no longer to the earth but to heaven, no longer to time but to eternity, no longer to herself but to God. Thus by her profession, she takes God for the only end of all her thoughts, her words, and her actions, even the most indifferent and natural. Therefore while the Christian in the world is obliged to make great efforts to acquire a dominion over nature, and to elevate to the supernatural state by offering them to God, the thought, words, and actions which compose her life, because they are ordinarily employed in the interests of the world, the Religious soul produces supernatural works as it were, naturally, unless selflove comes in to corrupt them, thus interrupting the holy habits of grace. The Religious life is then an anticipated Paradise where the soul possesses God in advance. It is the treasure hidden in the field of the Church, of which the Lord has discovered the price to a certain number of privileged souls, who have sacrificed all with joy, to assure themselves of its possession.

O ineffable grace of the Religious vocation, by which the soul walks more surely towards its End, where she works more efficaciously, and enjoys by anticipation, while here on earth, the life of the Angels! O precious pearl of the Gospel, to whose price all the goods of earth are but vile dust! O life of Carmel! Religious life pure and immaculate! "Where man lives more purely, falls more rarely, and rises more promptly, walks more securely, receives the dews of divine grace more copiously, reposes more tranquilly, dies more happily, merits to be purified more promptly, and to be recompensed more abundantly". What thanks should I not render Thee, O my most amiable Sav-

17

iour, for having called me to a Religious Life where I can, even in this world, unite myself so intimately to Thee, that I can live Thy life, and my conversation need be no longer with men but with Angels? Is it not the end of the Rule of Carmel to lead to this divine union, the souls who wish to bear its yoke? Ah! If I had profited by these precious advantages, I should now be more advanced in Thy holy love, and I should not have to regret the abuse of so many precious graces, and the loss of so much time, which will never return. But by Thy mercy,

I may still repair it, Lord, and I will work with all my strength in order to arrive at the happy state, where all my thoughts, words, and actions shall have no other end but Thy glory and Thy love.

SECOND POINT - How I may Attain the End of the Religious Life

Consider now the means which are offered you to arrive, even in this world, at the enjoyment of your end, by the divine union. The first, without which all the others would be but weak helps, is an entire separation from the world. It was by this that our Holy Mother, St. Teresa, commenced her reform: this separation was the foundation of the new spirit which she established. She prescribed strict enclosure, closed grates, visits to the parlor very rare and very short, and she endeavored to banish from the conversation of her Religious, everything that could recall to their minds, persons or things of the world. The world is in effect "full of fools" who despising the true good, run after a phantom, who give to lies the name of truth, and to truth the name of lies. All in it, according to St. John, is the concupiscence of the flesh, the concupiscence of the eyes, and the. pride of life, because pride, love of riches and of pleasures is the impoisoned source of all the sins committed there. Now by the three vows of Poverty, Chastity and Obedience, the ax is laid to the root of the tree, and on the day of her profession, the Religious soul cuts it down by one single stroke, and henceforth it will be easy for her to retrench the branches, which may still be able to grow upon the mutilated trunk. Disengaged thus from the flesh and the world, a stranger to its interests, and its affections; losing the remembrance, even the names of its pleasures and affairs, this privileged soul has but one pleasure, one affair, which is to labor to enrich her soul and to embellish it in the eyes of God.

To this first benefit of her profession may be added the means, so efficacious and so numerous, which the Rule furnishes her for despoiling herself of her faults, acquiring virtue, and attaining thus the end of her vocation. Silence almost continual, profound recollection, universal mortification, the habitual practice of mental prayer; frequentation of the Sacraments, pious lectures, public and private corrections, charitable admonitions, the company of the holy spouses of Jesus Christ, who by their good example excite, without ceasing, a generous emulation for perfection, — what abundant means, what facilities, what riches! After considering all these means of sanctification, the Religious soul reflects upon the loving attractions of grace which accompany practices so holy, and upon the precious and continual inspiration with which God pursues those who have contracted them, she asks herself how shall she be able to return thanks for the inestimable gift of her vocation! But what on the contrary should be her confusion and her sorrow, if she has not gathered from them the fruits which God has a right to expect from her?

Ah! Lord, when I consider all the advantages of the holy state to which Thou hast deigned to call me, and the great facility I find in it, to fulfill all my obligations, I feel a lively sorrow for having profited so little by them. Thy infinite wisdom and Thy ineffable goodness have delivered me for all the preoccupations of this life; Thy amiable Providence by the charity of my Superiors, provides for all my wants without my having to think of them for a single instant. Like the little birds of which Thou hast spoken in Thy Gospel, I sow not, nor do I reap, I gather not into barns, yet Thy paternal hands nourish and cloth me. I have no anxiety for the past, to which I have bid an eternal adieu, or for the future of which Thou hast taken upon Thyself the care; I have but to fulfill each day the task prescribed for me, and this only for Thy holy service.

And notwithstanding all this, I have robbed Thee of what belongs to Thee, seeking myself, and succeeding only too well in finding myself where I should have found Thee alone; stopping at the creature, when all should have been given to the Creator. Thou hast delivered me from all the solicitudes and embarrassments of the world, but the devil, seconded by my bad nature, knows how to create fears, anxieties and desires without foundation, to turn me from Thy holy service. Ah, Lord grant me in this Retreat the grace to overcome these obstacles so frivolous, yet so fatal to my weakness. Thou hast burst my bonds, I will sacrifice to Thee a sacrifice of praise, and I will call upon Thy Holy Name.

LECTURE - Perfection

I have understood in the First Meditation of today, that beatitude consists, for all reasonable creatures, in attaining the end for which God has made them, and that this end obtained is their perfection. I have seen at the same time that man is made for God; and his happiness and his perfection cannot be found except in his union with God, a union which is commenced in this life by grace, and completed in the next by glory. There will be accomplished his consummate perfection, and to speak more exactly, his only perfection, because in this happy state, he will be perfectly united to God, his Beginning and his End, without fear or danger of ever being able to separate himself from Him.

But there is question here only of that perfection which we can attain in this life, and which consists in a certain disposition of the soul to produce, besides those works which are of precept, those also which are only of counsel, and to practice them in a manner pure and spiritual. This perfection increases in the soul, in proportion with its union with God; and its progress will be so much the more sensible, as divine charity will have extended its dominion over a greater number of its thoughts, actions, and affections, animating all its virtues by transforming and in some sort divinising them. Perfection then supposes the faithful practice of virtues, in the midst of which shines charity, which is the queen and which gives them motion and life, at the same time that it gives value to their actions.

According to the Seraphic Doctor, St. Bonaventura, perfection consists in fleeing vice, doing good and suffering the adversities of this life, and all this in a manner the most generous that is possible to us; that is to say, a perfect soul, not only abstains from grave faults, but even from those which have the appearance of evil, that she does good with fidelity, generosity, and facility, and that she embraces sufferings with joy, knowing that there is incomparably more love, and consequently more perfection in accepting tribulations, because it is the will of God Who sends them, than in practicing some other good works which we ourselves choose; according to the words of the apostle, St. James: "Patience has a perfect work." After these reflections, it is easy to see that perfection is not the work of a day, but a serious undertaking which requires great courage and a strong resolution. Because of the double consequence of original sin, our perverted will finds itself considerably weakened, and our corrupt nature tries without ceasing to draw us far from the difficult path which displeases it; while the demon, jealous of the glory of God and our own advantage, employs all kinds of snares and even violence to draw us from it; and little by little, if we give way to our laxity and natural inconstancy, we shall soon find ourselves very far from the end which we had proposed to attain.

Let us then resemble a hardy navigator, who having discovered land fruitful in all kinds of riches, pursues his route with ardor until he reaches it, struggling with courage against the waves and contrary winds, and repulsing the powerful enemies who oppose his enterprise. Yes, whatever be the labor and the efforts which we must employ to acquire perfection, it is of so great a price and procures to those who attain it so much happiness, even in this life, that all the sacrifices which it requires bear no proportion to the advantages which it gives. By means of this divine perfection, the soul here below is put in possession of God Himself, to whom she is united by ties of the most ineffable friendship, and she enjoys the sweetness of a profound peace. If she must share with the other children of Adam, the sufferings and privations attached to their condition here, these evils lose for her the greater part of their bitterness, because love sweetens them and makes her come out victorious from these trials, enriched with the inestimable prize of patience. But a very consoling truth for the Religious soul, who on entering her Retreat proposes the acquiring of perfection as the end of these exercises, in order to commence to enjoy the precious advantages attached to it, is that it suffices that she be resolved to labor for it during her whole life, that at present she but enter resolutely into this holy undertaking, and never abandon it, notwithstanding all obstacles; notwithstanding even her infidelities. The first fruit which she will gather from her labor, (and it is precious enough to repay her superabundantly) is the assurance of her perseverance, in as much as it is possible to be assured of this grace, which God without doubt is not obliged to give to any one, and which is a pure gift of His love. In effect, as I have seen, there is much to hinder fallen man in the practice of virtue, because his natural inclinations violently draw him down to base and terrestrial things. In the execution of his good desires, he remains always much behind the end at which he has proposed to arrive; if he wishes to keep strictly to the exact requirement of the law without being willing to do more, it often happens that he transgresses the law. In the same way that an arrow directed to an end will not reach it, because of its own weight which always tends downward, if the one who aims it does not look above the mark, thus the human will should be directed to acts of the most eminent virtues in order to succeed in those which are of necessity. This is why our Divine Master, Who alone possesses the science of the human heart, presses us in the Gospel, to make every effort to enter by the narrow gate, and exhorts us without ceasing to follow the straight way which alone conducts to life, presenting us with nothing less than the sanctity of God Himself, as a model of the perfection which we should strive to attain; "Be ye perfect as your Heavenly Father is perfect." But the counsel of our Saviour is not relished nor understood by Christians of the world, and they should attribute to no other cause their want of perseverance in observing the commandments of God and of the Church. They imagine that to secure their salvation, it suffices to keep the rigorous practice of the precepts, without making any effort to advance in virtue. They neglect pious practices, make light of small faults, and very soon lose the inestimable treasure of grace, without even being aware of the immense loss which they have sustained.

The Church, faithful depository of the Spirit of her Divine Spouse, has established or approved a state of perfection in favor of those of her children who wish to apply themselves in a special manner to acquire this divine science. This is to be found in the Religious Orders, where she teaches, (as in some institutes they learn human sciences and the mechanic arts) by means of method and exercise. The Religious soul has then the means to arrive at perfection, and she is obliged by the sanctity of her state never to depart from this great end; and as there is no day of her life on which she is not obliged to be perfect, so there is none on which she is dispensed from laboring to become so. The moment she abandons this work, she sins against the spirit and the essential duty of her state. She is powerfully aided because each Religious Order, approved by the Church, offers in its rules and in the spirit which animates it, the means which should conduct the souls who embrace it, to that perfection which is proper to them, and which is the end of each institute. The Rules and Constitutions are not then matters of indifference which each one is at liberty to observe or to disregard, because by them, the Religious Orders are distinguished one from the other; and they present to the members of each, the way which they should follow in order to arrive at that perfection which God requires of them.

If then, it is true that each point in particular of the Rule does not bind under pain of sin, it is impossible, however, that the neglect which goes so far as to despise one of these points, or the tepidity which will dispense with their observance in general, does not constitute a veritable sin, which can be of fatal consequence to a Religious soul. We understand by this the evil and the danger of tepidity and negligence in the practise of the duties of the Religious life. What a disorder to see in this state, which is a state of perfection, souls without love for virtue, without zeal for their spiritual advancement. And, nevertheless, we meet with this disorder but too often. Thus, while we sometimes meet in the world, and even in the state of marriage, persons raised (notwithstanding the dangers of the world and the occasions inseparable from their state) to the most sublime perfection, there exists in the most holy Communities sheltered from the perils of the world, and surrounded by means of sanctification the most abundant, souls relax and pusillanimous, remaining in a state of stagnant idleness, without wishing to make the least effort to advance in virtue. It is to such souls that Jesus Christ addressed these words: "They (the people of the world) will themselves be thy judges', and ye will prepare for yourselves by the abuse of so many graces, a judgment much more severe than theirs.

But there is in regard to perfection another abuse opposed to the one we have just been considering, and which is not less dangerous. Into this presumptuous souls fall who wish to take their flight toward the very heights of the Holy Mountain, before they have wings (if it be permitted to speak thus), that is, to aspire to sublime prayer, extraordinary states, speaking only of ecstatic love and supernatural delights, thus mistaking for true virtue the means which lead to it. Perfection has degrees through which it is necessary to pass in order to arrive at perfect love. These degrees are the purgative way and the illuminative way; it is by them that the soul reaches the unitive life. It is necessary then, before all things and it is the first step in the career of perfection, that the soul be purified from her past sins by a sincere repentance; that after having discovered her secret vices, the disorderly inclinations of her heart, and her faults of character, she should labor generously to correct them, and to cause the death of nature by following the Spirit of Jesus Christ.

It is in the first period that she should, with the aid of those who direct her, study her predominant passion and the principal obstacles which oppose her progress in virtue. When she has labored during a considerable time to do penance and to amend her life, she will be enlightened by Him, who is the only true light, and meditating upon the virtues of Jesus Christ, she will strive to conform her life to that of her Divine Model and to be filled with His sentiments and His virtues. Moreover, this entire Retreat is a picture of these three states of perfection, and one of its principle fruits for the Religious soul is to make known to her the way which she ought to follow in order to arrive at the possession of this perfect Charity, of which we shall speak in the last meditation of the last day.

Examen Upon the Lecture

Have I a great esteem for perfection, regarding it as the hidden treasure, the precious pearl of the Gospel, for the acquisition of which I would be ready to sacrifice all? Second, have I a sincere and constant desire for my own perfection? Have I not abandoned it for a considerable time without caring about what I was losing and that it was one of the principal obligations of the Religious Life? Third, has not indifference for my spiritual advancement caused me to neglect the means of sanctification attached to the holy practices of the Religious Life, above all, the mortification of my senses, silence, recollection, the use of ejaculatory prayers, a careful preparation for Confession and Holy Communion, and particularly fervent and constant prayer? Fourth, instead of having recourse to my Superiors to find out my faults, and to take the means of advancing in virtue, have I not yielded to my repugnance to these openings, and have I not shown resentment and discontent when reproved or warned of my faults? Fifth, have I not sought to raise myself or to pretend to sublime gifts of grace without exercising myself for a long time in the practice of mortification and contempt of self?

Second Day

First Meditation - On Death

"The death of the wicked is very evil."— Ps. XXXIII, 22.
"Precious in the sight of the Lord is the death of His Saints.'"— Ps. CXV, 5.

Being well penetrated with the fundamental truth that Thou, O my God, art my Sovereign Good, my Last End, to Whom my entire life with all its interior and exterior acts should be directed, I come into Thy holy presence to represent to myself the supreme moment which shall terminate it. I come to transport myself in spirit to the moment of my death, which will decide the important affair of my destiny, and to consider if I shall be put forever into possession of my Sovereign Beatitude, which is Thyself, or if I shall be irrevocably condemned to pains, terrible and without end, which accompany the loss of Thee.

I understand, O my Lord, that nothing is more important for me than to transport myself now to my deathbed, in order that when I leave this Retreat

I may see the necessity of forcing myself to become such as I shall wish to be found at that decisive moment. Deign, O my God, to bless a meditation so important.

FIRST POINT - Terrible Is the Death of the Sinner

Death is the separation of the soul from the body, the rupture of all the ties that bind us to the earth, that attach us nearly or distantly to persons, to the affairs, and to the interests of the world. It is an eternal farewell to all the creatures of this earth; an adieu to the light of day and to the darkness of night; to the riches of nature, and to all the objects which surround our senses, and which compose this vast universe. We tremble at the thought of the terrible catastrophes which must precede the last judgment; no one would wish to be a witness of the last scenes of the world, such as they are described by the Prophets and by Jesus Christ Himself. Nevertheless, all these events shall take place for me at the hour of my death, because for me the sun will be eclipsed, the earth will tremble and open its bosom to engulf me, and my soul must go forth alone into an unknown region, where shines a light very different in brilliancy from that which now enlightens us. There all ideas are changed, all illusions dissipated; there the riches of earth have no value; nobility, science, reputation, honors count as nothing there: in a word, the money of this world is not current in the other, because there only the knowledge and love of the Creator is esteemed; there only those actions are counted which are done for Him. Behold why the death of the sinner is so terrible, he has done nothing for God, nothing for himself! "Fool," said Jesus Christ in the Gospel to the rich man, who had commenced to enjoy in advance the great riches which he had amassed: "Fool, this night thy soul shall be required of thee, and to whom then shall thy riches belong?" "Thus," continues our Saviour, "will it be with those who have not sought their treasure in God."

St. John in the Apocalypse, describing the events which are to precede and accompany the final judgment, tells us that he perceived an Angel, standing upon the sea and upon the earth, that is between time and eternity, "raise his hand to heaven and swear by Him who liveth and reigneth forever and forever, that henceforth there should be no more time." "No more time!" That is to say, the duration of the ages, which had been given to men to gain life eternal, is terminated. "No more time!" That is to say the years of grace are completed, man's career is forever closed to combat, to trial, and consequently to merit. "No more time!" That is to say, there remains but an unchanging eternity for punishing sin and recompensing virtue. Ah! this terrible sentence will be passed upon me at the hour of my death, and it shall be immediately executed. Is not this a consideration most proper to make me understand that death is truly formidable? Yes, at the hour of death, there will be no more time for me. This life is as a day of labor, which should be consecrated to meriting the salary promised to those who employ it well.

"Work while it is day," says Jesus Christ, "because the night cometh (death) wherein no man can labor." Now the end of time, the evening of this day is death. Then shall cease for me the means so numerous, so multiplied, which have been given me to reach my Last End, and particularly those which are attached to my vocation: means so efficacious that they would have secured my sanctification, had I but made use of them. In fine, death is the time of the harvest, when we shall gather what we have sown during life. Ah! what a cruel and disconsolate thought this will be for the tepid and negligent Religious, who finds herself at the last hour with empty hands. She will cast a last sad look upon the long years which she has passed within the solitude of her Monastery; she will reflect upon the graces so precious and so abundant, which she has received there, and which, alas! she has deplorably abused. She will desire but a little time to repair that which she has so unhappily lost, but the sentence, passed upon all men that they can die but once, is instantly executed for her. She must submit to it; she must bid an eternal farewell to that holy and happy solitude, where she found the sad secret of living so unlike a solitary; farewell to those silent cloisters, where she observed neither silence nor recollection. Farewell to that holy cell whose precious retreat she has loved so little. Farewell to the sacred tribunal of Penance where she should have purified her soul, and acquired a new life and new strength. Farewell to that mystic table of the Lord, where she was nourished with the Bread of Angels, reserving all her earthly inclination — to that sacred tabernacle, chaste delight of faithful spouses, but which she approached with a frozen heart and an inattentive mind. All the sources of grace are forever closed against her. Never shall it be given her to unite her voice to the sacred canticles which ascend day and night from the holy place, where she listened to the word of God and assisted at the august Sacrifice. Sad thoughts, useless regrets!

In vain, to calm her fears and to appease her terrors, are the Divine mercies recalled to her. Alas! are they who seek thus to reassure her reassured themselves? The priest is at her side, he presents to her the image of Jesus crucified, but can she render to herself the testimony of having conformed her life to the Divine Model? She has received from his hands the Bread of Life, which should be the happy pledge of her entrance into her heavenly home; but her dispositions in preparing for the Holy Eucharist being ordinarily so imperfect, perhaps even doubtful, how can we hope that in the trouble and agitation inseparable fiom the hour of death she can be better prepared? The oil of the last combat has flowed upon her members....But it effaces only the remains of sins already pardoned, and supposes a victorious soul, who awaits this last succor to secure her trimuph.

O my God! what folly, what criminal negligence to await the last hour to prepare myself for death! Should not the Religious Life, above all that of Carmel, be a preparation for that supreme moment? Ah! Lord, Thou hast shown me that death is most terrible; that it is the end of time and the beginning of eternity — the end of that precious time, which has been purchased for us at the price of the Blood of Jesus Christ, and of which each moment should be employed in gaining eternal goods. If, until now, I have not known its value, I now discover it by the light of death. If, until now, I have profited so little by the graces attached to my holy state, I will no longer abuse them, because very soon, O my God! I shall be called before Thee to render an account of the five talents of my vocation, and it is not for two or three that I must account, but for five! for "Unto whom much has been given, of him much shall be required." What have I done until now? My profession of Carmelite, the sanctity of my habit, and the practices of the Religious life cannot reassure me, since these should be new motives of fear, when I remember the terrible sentence passed not only upon the bad servant, but even against the idle one: — "Let them be thrown into exterior darkness, where there shall be weeping and gnashing of teeth." It is not the long years in the cloister that Thou countest, O Lord! but a truly holy life, be it ever so short; because the just live a long time in a few days. Grant, O Lord, that I remember often my last end, and that I keep in mind the eternal years.

SECOND POINT - Precious in the Sight of the Lord Is the Death of the Just

After having considered the sad sight of a tepid Religious on her death bed, let us now see her die whose life has been conformed to the sanctity of her obligations. The situation is the same, the circumstances are the same, both having lived together in the same Monastery, worn the same habit, followed the same exercises, exteriorly; but what a difference between them when we consider the dispositions of their souls. What a contrast in their sentiments, their fears and their hopes! What a difference in the feelings of those who assist at their last moments! Those who assist the first, retire full of inquietude, sorrow and uncertainty about her eternal welfare. On the contrary, those who assist the faithful Religious carry away impressions the most sweet and most favorable of her eternal happiness. They withdraw with regret from her bed of death, their hearts filled with consolation, and all embalmed with the perfume of the Religious virtues which they have inhaled. Although the features are so changed on that pale face, they find imprinted there the peace of God, which surpasses all understanding. In those eyes almost closed, in those few words scarcely heard, they can read the assurance of her eternal happiness, which the Holy Spirit makes her feel in advance. Ah! the true Religious dies not: death is for her but the commencement of life, the end of combats, the ceasing of trials, the last act of the dying life to which she has vowed herself.

In effect, the Religious life, and especially the life of Carmel, is the faithful accomplishment of the words of Saint Paul: "They who belong to Jesus Christ have crucified their flesh with its vices and concupiscences." "You are dead and your life is hidden with Christ in God." By her profession, a true Carmelite is dead to the world, not only being separated from it by her sacred engagements, and a stranger to its pleasures and its affairs; but she loses even the remembrance of the persons and things of the world, and comports herself in their regard as if they did not exist. She is dead to the goods of the world by voluntary poverty, dead to its affections by mortification of the heart; and to this renunciation of exterior objects, she joins a constant abnegation of her entire self. Her will and her judgment are annihilated by the practice of a generous and universal obedience; modesty and guard of her senses favor a habit of recollection, and cause her to live the life of God, a life unknown to men and praised by Saint Paul in these words: "You are dead and your life is hidden with Christ in God." What is death able to effect upon such a creature, except to sever the last feeble tie, which retains her upon earth, and to leave her soul at liberty to fly to Him, Whom she has loved!

The devil is there also, it is true, like a roaring lion foaming around her bed of pain, now become an altar where the victim of charity is consummating her sacrifice; but he dares not approach it, for he finds there nothing that belongs to him. He trembles in seeing there all the Religious virtues which she has loved and practiced, — obedience, chstity, humility, penance, solitude and silence, ranged around as a valiant guard, like the one which day and night stood, sword in hand, around the bed of King Solomon. It is to such a death that we may apply in a particular manner these words, or rather these magnificent promises of Jesus Christ: "I am the Resurrection and the Life, he who believes in Me, although he be dead, shall live." How precious in Thy sight, O my God, is the death of the just. "Blessed are the dead who die in the Lord, their good works shall follow them." O how well the faithful Religious now understands the austere life which she so generously embraced. If she could have any regret, doubtless it would be not to have done more for that most happy eternity, whose glory already appears to her infinitely surpassing her feeble sacrifices. O how well she now recognizes the value of mortification, of silence, of recollection, and the merits of trials and combats generously sustained.

"O my God, may my soul die the death of the just!" May I die the death of Thy Holy Spouse Teresa, our Mother! Love burst the ties which bound her, and her beautiful soul flew like a pure dove to Thy bosom, leaving all who witnessed her precious death penetrated with admiration. O may my soul then die so precious a death, may it die the death of many other worthy daughters of our Holy Mother, and imitators of her virtues! But, O my God, in order to die their death, I must live their life; and until now, I have lived my own, a life all natural, full of actions which had self-love for their motive, instead of being animated by Thy holy love.

But it shall be so no longer, O my Saviour, if I have lived until now as a foolish virgin, without taking care to keep my lamp filled with the oil of charity, I wish henceforth to live by Thee and for Thee alone, in order that, dying in Thee, I may possess Thee eternally. Amen.

Second Meditation - The Particular Judgment

"We must all be manifested before the judgment-seat of Christ, that every one may receive the proper things of the body, according as he hath done whether it be good or evil."— II Cor. V, 10.

I come trembling to prostrate myself at Thy feet, O my Lord, Jesus Christ! I adore Thee as the Awful Judge, before Whom I must appear when I leave this world at the terrible hour of death. Then Thou shalt have no more regard but for the rigorous rights of Thy justice, because the time of Thy mercy shall have passed. But since that time has not yet come, O my Saviour, thanks to Thy goodness, and as Thou hast even granted me this Retreat, which is doubly a time of mercy, I wish to profit by it and to anticipate to-day that terrible judgment, by judging myself in advance and citing myself in spirit before Thy dread tribunal. Make me feel at this moment all the rigor and all the extent of the rights of Thy Justice, in order that, being penetrated with a salutary fear and after the example of the Holy Fathers of the desert, I may live in continual expectation of that day.

FIRST POINT - "After Death, the Judgment."

After having meditated upon death, it is important to examine what it is that renders death so terrible, and to consider the decisive moment of judgment which follows it. Now, as this judgment is passed by God Himself, that is to say, by the Sovereign Monarch of the universe, Whom nothing can resist, from Whom nothing can escape, it is impossible to understand it in all its rigor. He is a judge enlightened and incorruptible, as He is powerful and dreadful. He has no need of satellites to drag the guilty to His tribunal, of witnesses to convict them, or of chains to keep them. He is God. He will not allow Himself to be moved by tears; He cannot be won by presents; He is deaf to all considerations foreign to His Justice; He laughs at the eloquence of human discourses. He is God, — God alone with His Justice, "Whose depth is an unfathomable abyss," says the Prophet, while His scrutinizing eyes count the grains of sand on the sea shore....And the soul appears before this Judge. Alone, also!....Alone with the good or the evil which she has done while in the body. All things else, talents, beauty, greatness, courage, friends, goods, parents, protectors, she has left on earth, not being able to bring any with her when she presents herself before Jesus Christ. She brings only the sins of which she is guilty and the virtues which she has practised; and these sins and these virtues shall be examined with rigorous justice. The time of life has now passed and with it the time of mercy. During the time that she lived upon earth, God had no regard to His justice, supporting with an infinite patience all her iniquities, ceasing not to pursue her with the attractions of His love, soliciting her by His grace, and offering her until the last moment a generous pardon. But to-day, unhappily for this soul if she has despised these invitations, abused these graces, and rejected these mercies, the hour of justice has sounded. "Call Me," says God by the mouth of His Prophet; "Call Me without mercy." "It is terrible to fall into the hands of the Living God," of the Just Judge, when one has despised the treasures of His infinite goodness, of His patience and His long suffering. What shall I do, what shall I say, when God shall stand to judge me, and when He shall demand of me the goods He has confided to my care, saying: "Render an account of thy stewardship"?

Alas! Lord, I tremble to think of myself as this unfortunate soul. I see myself, scarcely out of the prison of my body, and already standing before Thee as my Sovereign Judge. Hopelessly I look around me. Time has finished, my Eternity has begun. No longer can friends console me, nor protection defend me. I implore Thy mercy, but the time of mercy has passed. "Sad situation," says Saint Bernard, "for a sinful soul in the presence of God, weighed down by mortal agony: above, an inexorable Justice; below, the horrible chaos of hell which awaits her; on one side, the multitude of her sins which accuse her, and on the other, a troop of demons who claim her; within, remorse which tears her; outside, the world escaping and passing forever from her sight."

But, O my God, the time of justice has not yet arrived for me. Thou hast spared me until this day, to breathe the sweet air of Thy mercy. Thou hast granted me the grace of this Retreat, a time of mercy and of salvation by excellence. Suffer me, then, to say with Thy Prophet, "Enter not into judgment with Thy servant, O Lord, for in Thy sight shall no man living be justified." I implore Thy goodness and I hope for a favorable sentence. Teach me how to judge myself, since Thy Apostle assures me that if I judge myself I shall not be judged.

SECOND POINT - What Shall the Judgment Be?

I shall conclude from the preceding consideration that the rigor of the judgment which shall be exercised upon the soul at the moment of its separation from the body, exceeds all that I can imagine, since the Judge is God, Who possesses an infinite exactitude in the appreciation of faults, an infinite precision in the examining of consciences, an infinite justice in the application of punishment. This examination, this appreciation, this sentence, requires not a considerable time, for the soul invested all at once with the brightness of the light of God shall see herself entirely as she is, not only her sins, but her least imperfections, her abuse of the graces of God; and the consequences of all these faults will appear to her in an instant. Nothing can escape her: neither the sins of her youth of which she has lost the remembrance, nor the faults committed in the indulgence of her passions, and of which she has stifled the salutary remorse. She shall be judged upon the least thought she had formed in her mind; each word that had escaped her lips; all her affections, her desires, her hatreds, her repugnances; upon all her steps, actions and the undertakings which had filled her entire life. Nothing shall be omitted, since, according to the testimony of Jesus Christ Himself, we shall render an account for every idle word.

This account will extend to all the gifts of nature and of grace; it is Jesus Christ Who again assures us of this in His Gospel: "Render an account," says the Master to His unfaithful servant, "Render an account of what I have confided to thy care."

Yes, render Me an account of thy body and all its senses, of thy soul and all its faculties, thy hands, thy feet, thy eyes, thy mouth, thy ears — how hast thou used them? Thy understanding, thy memory, thy will, to what hast thou applied them? How hast thou used riches, beauty, credit, nobility? What use hast thou made of My creatures; the light of day, the darkness of night, fruits, plants, animals — in a word, of all the beauty and riches with which I have clothed the universe for thee? Render Me an account!

But what of the gifts of grace? General graces, the inestimable graces of the Incarnation, of Redemption, of Vocation to Christianity! The soul will understand then their infinite value and the important obligations which flow from them upon her. She shall then see the continual and particular succors that were given her by which to profit. She must render an account of all the inspirations of the Holy Spirit, and of the manner in which she has corresponded to them; of the trials, afflictions, spiritual aridities, as well as of the consolations and interior lights, because all have been measured out to her with equal wisdom for her salvation. The exterior means of sanctification will not be forgotten in this examination: Exortations, Lectures, Confessions, Communions. And that incomparable grace of her Religious Vocation, with all the means of salvation attached to it! The Holy Vows of Obedience, Poverty, and Chastity; happy separation from the world, examens, private advice, public corrections, prayer, the Divine Office, and all the holy means afforded by the Rule of Carmel for divesting one's self of imperfection and acquiring all the virtues! Religious souls, "Render Me an account of all these great talents confided to thee," a rigorous account, a decisive account, a prompt and definite account! But this is not the end of the examination, already so severe! This soul must answer to the Judge, not only for her own sins, but also for the sins and faults which she has caused others to commit; for the examples of relaxation and dissipation, of tepidity and sloth which she has given them. What a terrible examination for all, and especially for those who have care of guiding others, and who owe them not only good example, but warnings and corrections; because it is certain that in a community no one can sanctify herself alone, nor abandon herself to relaxation or be lost, without exercising a most malignant influence upon the other members which compose it.

But behold something more astonishing and more terrible yet, and it is the testimony of the Sacred Books: "God will judge even justice," that is, He will judge even our good actions, examining for what motive and under what circumstances they have been performed, and reducing their number to those which have been truly meritorious, not according to the opinion of man, but according to that of Truth itself. Oh! how we shall change our sentiments in the brightness of this Divine Light; how our illusions shall vanish! A crowd of works which we now judge as good will then appear but the fruit of human virtue; acts which we now consider holy, and habits which we esteem as virtues, will then lose their prestige; for they shall be found infested with secret vices, and soiled with the poison of self-love. When we put these pretended good works in the balance of our own estimation, they seem to be of great value; but when they are weighed by the Justice of God they shall be found worthless, and thus escape, leaving our hands empty. Not only souls of mediocre virtue, but even the most holy shall see a part of their good works, and the merits which they believe they had acquired, vanish thus. "Ah!" cries the Apostle, Saint Peter, "if, on the great day of the Justice of God, the just shall scarcely be saved, what must become of sinners?".

And this judgment, so terrible, will be succeeded by a sentence more terrible still. The sinful, and henceforth lost soul, who has already read with terror her doom in the irritated eyes of her Judge, shall hear from His holy mouth these frightful words: "Depart from Me, ye cursed into everlasting fire." Ah! Lord, I wish not to hear this terrible sentence. I will not hear it for this Retreat shall be for me a judgment which I desire to enforce upon myself, as severe if possible, as Thine. I shall treat my soul with the same rigor, with the same precision which I have just considered in Thee; I shall descend into the depths of my conscience, I shall question it, I shall examine not only my sins, but the sources whence they proceed. I shall consider the numberless graces which Thou hast bestowed upon me, I shall recall all the inspirations by which I have not profited, the precious time purchased for me by Thy Blood, and of which I have lost so much. I shall call to mind the bad example which I have given to the community. I shall forget none of my sins, none of my infidelities, Lord, in order that, by weeping over them now, I may merit to hear from Thee, "Come ye Blessed of My Father" — "Come good and faithful servant, enter thou into the joy of thy Lord." Amen.

Third Meditation - The General Judgment

"Then shall the king say to them that shall be on his right hand: Come ye, blessed of my Father, possess you the kingdom prepared for you from the foundation of the world.... Then shall he say to them also, that shall be on his left hand: Depart from me you cursed, into everlasting fire prepared for the devil and his angels."— St. Matthew, XXV, 34, 41.

I adore Thee, O Sovereign Judge of the living and the dead, My Lord Jesus Christ, Who, at the last day, shall cause to appear before Thy dread Tribunal all the nations of the earth. I represent to myself that solemn moment, when appearing upon the clouds of heaven with great power and majesty, Thou wilt send Thy Angels to order the dead to arise from their graves and to come to judgment. I see even now the sad separation of the good from the bad. I hear the happy sentence which Thou shalt pronounce upon the first, and the maledictions which Thou shalt cast upon the last, which will receive an eternal and irrevocable execution. How terrible and awful! How important and profitable these truths, to make upon my mind salutary impressions! Deign to grant me the grace to profit by them, O my God!

FIRST POINT - All Men Shall Be Judged at the End of the World

As it is very necessary for me to meditate upon this truth, it is important that I have a profound knowledge of it, and to conceive a lively and sincere faith in it. I will then consider that of all the dogmas of our Holy Religion there is not one more explicitly taught in the Holy Books, in the Old as well as in the New Testament, and upon the authority of the Church, as the one which I now consider: "That God has reserved a day upon which He shall judge the universe in His Justice." This divine teaching corresponds at the same time to the need that we feel of a great and solemn Reparation for the scandals, the injustice, and the disorders of which this world affords us a spectacle.

In the Old Testament, the Prophets have left the most terrible descriptions of this great day, at the same time that they represent to us in the most magnificent terms the advent of the Sovereign Judge. In the New, Jesus Christ Himself addresses His disciples arid the people who follow Him, at several different times, concerning the Last Day. He retraces it in the lamentable catastrophe of the unfortunate Jerusalem; He instructs them concerning the signs of terror which are to precede it; He describes to them the order and the principal circumstances of it; and goes so far as to refer to the words by which the Judge shall pronounce the sentences and the motive which He shall assign for them. In fine, to make known this important truth more clearly, He consecrates to it an entire parable, which is regarded as the most instructive and the most important of all His parables. It is that of the cockle, thrown by the enemy of man into the field of the father of the family, and which is allowed to grow together with the good seed, until the time of the harvest. "The field," adds Our Saviour, "is the world; the good seed, the children of the Kingdom; the cockle, the children of the wicked one. But the harvest is the end of the world, and the reapers are the Angels. Even as cockle is gathered to be burned by fire, so shall it be at the end of the world. The Son of Man shall send His Angels to gather out of His kingdom all scandals and them that work iniquity, and cast them into the furnace of fire, where there shall be weeping and gnashing of teeth."

"The just shall shine as the sun in the Kingdom of their Father"; "Those who have ears, let them hear."

After the example of their Divine Master, the Apostles ceased not in their Epistles to propose to the faithful the second coming of Jesus Christ as a most pressing motive for being vigilant and firm in the Faith. Saint John, in his

32

Apocalypse, has left us a most magnificent picture, at once touching and terrible, of the imposing scenes which shall precede, accompany and follow this grand event. It is in watching and prayer that we should await it, but it is necessary also, for the glory of God and the interest of Jesus Christ, that we desire it. "The Spirit and the Bride (the Church) say: Come," and those who hear say: "Come."

How can we consider the disorders which reign in the world, the contempt which most men have for the Divine Law, and their forgetfulness of their Loving Saviour, without being pressed with the desire of seeing that day on which Jesus Christ will seize the reins of His power and receive from His Father the investiture of His Royalty, a glorious, immutable and eternal Royalty, which He Himself has taught us to pray for in these words: "Thy Kingdom come." And as the world, not content with ignoring its Saviour and rejecting His grace, has dared cite Him before its tribunal at the time of His Passion, so God has established this Divine Mediator as Judge of all men, in order that He may judge the world, which has been guilty of the audacious sacrilege of judging Him.

At the same time God will avenge His Divine Providence, outraged by the blasphemies of the impious and the murmurs of His ungrateful children. This Day, in effect, shall be the day of His manifestation. This is why it is called the Day of the Lord, by excellence; for it shall not be formed by the light of the sun, but by that of God Himself, the true Sun of Justice, Who shall discover to all the admirable wisdom by which He has ruled all the events of the lives of all people in general, and of each man in particular, in order to their eternal salvation, if they had been faithful. It is this resplendent light of the Eternal Truth which shall force all men to render homage to the infinitely wise and merciful ways of Divine Providence, and all, whether just or sinner, elect or reprobate, must cry out in one voice, "Thou art just, O Lord, and Thy judgments are true." This day is necessary in order to make known solemnly the judgment which each soul has submitted to at the moment of its separation from the body, and to cause to appear the sovereign justice and wisdom of God in all these Divine Judgments, according to the words of the Prophet: "Judge between My vineyard and Me, and see if there is anything which I could have done for her and have not done."

Thus it is that the glory of God claims a day and a place where the generations of all peoples which have passed successively upon the earth must appear simultaneously, in the presence of their Creator, to cast themselves upon their faces before His Sovereign Authority, and to render a last and brilliant homage to His infinite perfections. After this supreme reason for the last and General Judgment, it is easy to explain the awful signs which go before, and the terrible catastrophes which precede, accompany and follow it.

These great events, the earth trembling to its centre like a drunken man, the sun refusing its light, the moon shrouded in a veil of blood, the stars falling from heaven, the furious sea breaking all its bounds, and, in fine, a devouring fire, are not only sent as terrible warnings to render men attentive to the great things which are to appear, and by which the justice of God menaces them, but, above all, to purify the earth from all works of iniquity.

And I, Lord, what can I say, what can I think when representing to myself this Last Great Day? Should I desire it? Should I fear it? Should I make it the subject of my prayers, because it will put an end to sin, be an entire defeat to the demon, the manifestation of Thy glory, the commencement of Thy reign and the triumph of Thy faithful servants? Or should I apprehend it because of my sins, my infidelities, and the resistance which, until now, I have made to Thy merciful inspirations? Ah, Lord, I fear it because of my sins, but I desire it because of Thy glory; and I shall force myself to be of the number of those to whom Thou dost address these consoling words: "When these things shall happen, lift up thy head, because thy redemption is near at hand." I will say with the Spouse, being myself Thy spouse, all unworthy as I am of it: "Come, Lord Jesus, come."

SECOND POINT - How Will This Judgment Take Place?

After being well penetrated with the truth, and the sovereign necessity of this Great Day, for the good of my soul I shall endeavor to represent to myself its principal circumstances.

First — The Coming of the Sovereign Judge

Immediately upon the given sign, the Angels shall sound their trumpets towards the four quarters of the globe, and in a voice like unto thunder, or the voice of great waters, cause to be heard among the tombs these formidable words: "Arise, ye dead, and come to judgment." The heavens shall open and the souls of the blessed shall descend and clothe themselves with their bodies, as with a vesture of glory and immortality; while, at the same time, hell will open her immense gulf and vomit forth her victims — wicked and unfortunate souls, who, constrained by an all-powerful Hand, shall re-enter each its own body, now become hideous and flaming, thus adding to their preceding evils the torture of those members which were the instrument of their sins. Behold this immense multitude, composed of all the peoples of all the generations which have inhabited the earth since Adam, without excepting a single one, whether just or sinner.

Led by the Angels, they come trembling before the Throne of the Sovereign Judge. Already He is seated upon the clouds of heaven, the Immortal King of Ages, to Whom, according to the faithful promise of the Eternal Father, is reserved a reign without end, and Who has received the privilege of judging the living and the dead. He is more brilliant than the sun, and is surrounded by innumerable legions of the Celestial Militia. The demon is under His feet, as the pitiless executor of that Justice of which he is the first to feel the effects. He waits — His terrible look interrogates this immense multitude.

What a terrible moment! Where shall I be then, O my God? What shall I do? Fear and terror penetrates my bones when I represent to myself this terrible hour, when the thunders of Thy judgment shall pass over my head; when Thou wilt come to discover the secrets of all consciences, and, opening the Book where all is written, Thou shalt seat Thyself to judge the world. Ah! Lord, imprint deeply in my soul a fear of Thy judgments.

Second — The Manifestation of Consciences

The Light of God, that light which envelopes every soul on leaving the body, shall shine at this moment upon this vast multitude which it shall illuminate on all sides — discovering all the thoughts, the words, the actions, the sentiments of each, with a million times more clearness and evidence than the sun shining at midday upon a vast field, illuminating all its parts, enlightening all its paths, and distinguishing all its objects, from the leaves of the trees to the smallest weed of the meadow. Thus shall be accomplished the words of Jesus Christ: "There shall be nothing covered which shall not be revealed, nothing hidden which shall not be seen on that Great Day." Each soul shall see clearly, in this Divine Light, the different ways and the ineffable means by which Divine Providence has willed to conduct her, and how, by her fidelity or her resistance, she has gained or lost the One True Good. Her crimes, her malice, her sins without number, she shall then see in the presence of God; and all other souls shall see them with her, and the confusion of the others shall diminish nothing of her own, for there shall be, in that Day so full of bitterness, place for the sorrows and the shame of all men. This prodigious and instantaneous brightness shall be the glory of the just, in discovering to all eyes, their combats and their victories by which they have triumphed over sin and established in their purified souls the empire of grace; and it shall cause such sorrow and such confusion to sinners that, according to the Prophet, they shall seek to hide themselves in the holes of the rocks, in the depths of caves, saying to the mountains, "Crush us," and to the earth, "Swallow us up." This manifestation of souls shall be more evident by the very state of our resuscitated bodies; for, as Saint Paul teaches us, those of the elect shall shine in their glory, and their beauty shall resemble the stars of heaven, shining with different degrees of light, and bearing character proper to the virtues which have distinguished them and to the combats which they have sustained; while those of the reprobate, hideous and deformed, shall portray the horrible variety of their sins and their vices, and show the frightful character of their perversity. O Day of Excellence! Day of Truth! Day without shadow! Day of God! There shall be then no longer illusions, no longer lies, no more dissimulation. The shameful nakedness of the earth shall be revealed to all eyes. We shall see the nothingness of its riches, its grandeurs, the dishonor of its cupidity, its voluptuousness, its pride. And all these shall proclaim that God alone is, that the supreme happiness was in His service, the sovereign unhappiness to offend Him.

Alas! O my God, this knowledge, so clear, shall then serve only for Thy Justice; it shall be useless for confounded and reprobate sinners. But since I may yet profit by it, Oh! may I make use of it to dissipate the illusions of my self-love and to destroy the false pretexts of which my laxity makes use to dispense me from the efforts which the practise of virtue requires.

Give that light to my soul now, in order that it may not turn to my confusion on the Last Great Day.

Third — The Sentence of the Sovereign Judge

It is then that Jesus Christ, the Sovereign Judge of the living and the dead, shall eternally separate the good from the bad. By His orders the Angels, like the shepherd who, in the evening, separates the sheep from the goats, shall distinguish in this vast multitude all those who bear the sign of the elect and who have combatted under the standard of the Cross, and separate them from sinners who have imprinted upon their foreheads the character of the beast. These are ranged on the left, the first on the right. The Supreme Judge, turning to those on His right, shall say in a voice full of goodness: "Come, ye Blessed of My Father, possess the Kingdom which has been prepared for you from the beginning of the world." Then, turning towards sinners with a look of anger, He shall cry out: "Depart from Me, ye cursed, into everlasting fire, which has been prepared for the devil and his angels." Thus will be accomplished the last part of the parable: "Then the reapers shall gather the good grain into My barn, but the bad they shall throw into the fire to be burned."

In effect, the ministers of Divine Justice shall seize and precipitate the infernal troop of confused, desperate and unhappy reprobate souls into the abyss; while the Angels are inviting the elect to ascend with them into heaven, to add glory to the triumph of Jesus Christ and to live eternally under the scepter of this glorious and peaceful King in the Heavenly Jerusalem. O, where shall I be on that Great Day of Thy Justice, O, Jesus, my Saviour! Shall I be on Thy right with Mary, Thy Most Holy Mother, Thy Holy Apostles, Virgins and Martyrs? Or shall I tremble on Thy left, struck with anathema and confounded? Shall I hear Thy sentence of benediction or of malediction? Shall I be among the wise virgins who will joyously enter with Thee to the nuptial banquet, or shall I be among the foolish virgins to whom Thou wilt say:

"I know ye not"? What terrible words, O my Saviour! Nevertheless, I know that Thou hast warned me of them, because, on that Great Day, many shall believe themselves Thy servants, who will even have performed brilliant acts, yet to whom Thou must say: "Depart from Me, ye workers of inquity, I know ye not!" Ah! Lord, it is now that I must separate myself from sinners, from languishing and idle souls, from tepid and negligent Religious, if I wish not to be found among such souls on the Last Day. I beg this grace of Thee. Amen.

As in a royal garden, where grows a multitude of fragrant flowers, each having its own particular grace and perfection, some are distinguished from others by their beauty, brightness, brilliancy of color and the sweetness of their perfume, so in the Holy Church of God, among an admirable variety of Religious orders, each one having a perfection proper to its particular end, there are, nevertheless, some which rank above the others, because in them are practised a more sublime and far-reaching charity. Such, in particular, is the Order of the Most Blessed Virgin Mary of Mount Carmel. There will be no longer cause for astonishment at the beauty and grandeur of this Order, and and at the sublimity of the virtues which it requires of those who embrace it, if we consider that it has been founded by the Blessed Virgin Mary, as several Sovereign Pontiffs have declared in their authentic Bulls. The Holy Mother of God has adopted its members for her true servants and as her children of predilection. She has given them her habit, image of that beautiful love of which she is the Mother and the most perfect model, and which she expects them to practice in a manner constant and heroic.

In effect, the law of this Holy Order is a law of charity, but of a charity carried to the highest perfection, and in virtue of which a soul forgets herself entirely, immolates herself entirely for the glory of God and the salvation of other souls. Their model of heroic love is the Holy Mother of God sacrificing upon Calvary all her affections, and a million times more than herself, since she there sacrificed her only Son to the rigorous requirements of holy love, to satisfy the justice of God and to operate the salvation of mankind. After the glorious Ascension of Jesus Christ, this admirable Queen still afforded to her well-beloved children a perfect example of all the virtues proper to to them. She lived incessantly plunged in the most sublime contemplation; while, at the same time, she powerfully aided the Infant Church by the efficacy of her continual prayers, the edification which she gave it, and the part which her admirable zeal took in its sufferings, its combats, and its progress. This spirit of zeal and of charity, joined to contemplation, with which this Holy Mother inspired her first servants of Carmel, who were already heirs of the pious traditions and sentiments of the Prophet Elias, became henceforth the particular spirit of this Holy Order.

But as in the course of ages, it began to decline from its first charity, God raised up our Holy Mother, Saint Teresa, to recall it to the primitive spirit, and to the end for which Divine Providence had destined it. That we may have no doubt concerning the spirit and the object of this Institute, it suffices to remark that it was precisely on the occasion of the evils which heresy and increasing scandals caused in the Church, that Our Lord pressed His Holy spouse to reform Carmel. He willed that in opening these houses of penance and of prayer, she should establish a more severe discipline and a greater separation from the world, in order to form chosen souls who would become instruments of His mercy, by calling down upon sinners greater abundance of grace through their prayers, their austerities, and their immolation of self.

The Daughters of Saint Teresa should then unceasingly reanimate in their souls, this spirit of zeal and devotion, continually immolating themselves by a life of abnegation and prayer; applying without relaxation to sanctify themselves, less in view of their own interest than in that of God and their brethren, completely forgetting themselves, so to say, for this noble object. It is thus that they will join the spirit of solitude and retirement to the apostolic spirit, and render still more vain and unjust the reproach sometimes addressed by the worldly minded to the Contemplative Orders: that they are useless to their neighbor, a reproach which can never be applied to true Carmelites, devoted to the most excellent of the spiritual works of mercy — that is, to prayer and self-immolation for their brethren.

The great means which this Holy Institute presents to those who aim at this sublime charity, is contemplation. It is in prayer and by prayer that the Solitary of Carmel is to establish in herself the reign of God. It is by prayer, if she is faithful to her vocation, that she will attain the Divine Union — her perfection, consequently, her end. Behold why some Patriarchs of the Order of Carmel have taught that prayer is the end of their Institute. A Carmelite is then an instrument of prayer, a vase of prayer. A Carmelite without the spirit of prayer is a body without a soul, she merits not the name of Carmelite.

Thus it may be said that all the Rules, Constitutions, and pious customs of Carmel, and above all the spirit in which they should be followed, tend to one end, which is to dispose souls for prayer, to make of them Contemplative Souls. Profound solitude, even to living in one's cell as in a desert; separation from the world, even to the avoiding of a word, a sign which recalls to mind the least of its habits, its goods, its pleasures; avoidance of the parlor, pushed even to disgust, even to seeing rarely and with necessity persons united by the ties of blood; silence almost continual, interrupted but seldom, and through piety or necessity; practices of modesty and of recollection which interdict even a look upon the countenance of a companion, or upon the work which occupies her; mortification constant and universal, which leaves no liberty to the senses, interior or exterior. How, with such practices, with Buch powerful means, if they are faithful to their observance, can they fail to arrive, and in a short time, at perfect prayer? It is true that great constancy, courage, and generosity are necessary, and that a relax and pusillanimous soul can never aspire to such a vocation. Thus Superiors should be as attentive in sending away from this Institute, souls of little generosity, as they are in dismissing those whose minds are wanting in rectitude and intelligence, which Saint Teresa calls a good understanding.

A peculiarity of this Holy Order which shows clearly that the Spirit of God is in it, is that it unites the advantages of the solitary life to the benefits of a community life, without having the inconveniences of either. The Solitary life is without doubt, the most suitable for establishing the soul in a holy communion with God, its separation from things of the world favoring a habit of recollection and facilitating holy thoughts; but on the other hand, an entire separation from creatures can give rise to many illusions, and expose one to most dangerous temptations. Let us add to this, that if a soul has the misfortune to fall there, she has no one to extend a helping hand to raise her from her fall; above all, she is deprived of good example and edification, of helps so advantageous as good counsel, encouragement, and the consolations which are to be found in a holy community; she is deprived of the occasions of practicing precious virtues, such as obedience, patience with others, humiliations. On the other hand, a community life has also its dangers and inconveniences which balance its advantages, if a soul is not animated by charity and submissive to regular discipline; because trouble, divisions, and jealousies will not be slow to form, and thus engender murmurs and antipathies which very soon make Religious Houses places where disorders abound, and where it is more difficult to be saved than in the midst of the world.

But the Spirit of God in dictating Rules so full of wisdom for the Order of Carmel, has placed such moderation in the intercourse of the Religious, that they communicate to fulfill the duties of fraternal charity, without losing the spirit of solitude, and their spirit of recollection and mortified life in no way injure charity; because this intercourse being accompanied by silence, modesty and mortification, these virtues avert its inconveniences and regulate its use. But this supposes that each Religious is animated by the spirit of solitude and recollection, of crucifixion and death. To maintain this two-fold life of solitude and charity, the Carmelites have two great devotions which they call the Mother devotions of the Order; these are a devotion to the Most Adorable Sacrament of the Altar, and to the most Holy Virgin. Behold the secret of their strength, their happiness, their support; from the Altar of Jesus where they imbibe without ceasing a new life, they pass to the Altar of Mary, there to seek new courage and assistance: behold the two great means, the two great treasures of Carmel's Solitaries.

To have in resume, a striking and perfect picture of the Holy Order to which I have the happiness to belong, it suffices to call to mind, and never to forget, the end of this Order — the love of God and our neighbor, carried even to the immolation of one's own interests, of one's entire self; its spirit — eremitical, and at the same time apostolic; its Mother devotions — love for the August Sacrament, and the most Holy Mother of God. The principal means to arrive at its perfection, means which in a way is the end itself of this Institute, is contemplation.

We must conclude from what we have just remarked of the perfection of Carmel, that it would be a great error to imagine that it suffices to wear its holy Habit and to follow its exterior practices, in order to belong truly to it, and to gain all the precious advantages attached to it. That which is most important is not the letter of its Constitution, but the spirit which vivifies them. One should without doubt, attach great importance not only to the observance of the Rule and Constitutions, but even to maintain the holy practices of the Order. But the more severe and rigorous the exterior observance of Religious discipline, the more difficult and painful it will be, if devoid of the spirit, which should animate it. It is necessary that the yoke of Rule should be to the religious soul what wings are to the bird; these wings like all material things have a certain weight; but notwithstanding this, it is by means of these that birds raise themselves above the earth, and take their flight on high. Thus it is that the Rule which is followed in the spirit which is proper to it, and the practice of which is animated by Divine love, far from being to the soul a heavy yoke, on the contrary, soothes, unbends, and charms it. The interior spirit is so essential for a Carmelite that if she be devoid of it, having nothing of her holy state but her Habit and exterior practices, she would resemble a ring from which the diamond that gave it its value is lost.

There are several Religious Orders where greater austerities are practiced than those of Carmel; but that which constitutes the excellence of Carmel is interior mortification, detachment from creatures, the spirit of solitude, the elevation above all created things, and the forgetfulness of all that is not God; the spirit of death to every care, affection, occupation and thought, foreign to the glory of God, and consequently, the gift , of prayer. Behold what constitutes a true Carmelite, what establishes her in the state of a victim devoted to the glory of God and the salvation of her neighbor; what makes of her an instrument of prayer, destined to call down by incessant supplication, the succors of heaven upon all the needs of the Church.

Examen Upon the Lecture

Have I a great esteem for my Holy State, and while honoring and esteeming all the other Religious Orders, since they have been raised up by the Spirit of God and approved by the Holy Church, have I had for that of Our Lady of Mount Carmel, a veneration and a love of predilection, since it offers in the Most Holy Virgin, who is its Foundress, its Queen, and its Mother, a model of the most sublime perfection, and in its Rules and Constitutions, the means of attaining it?

Have I understood well all it requires and all the perfection of that charity which should be practiced in it? Have I understood well that self-sacrificing love, which obliges me to labor for my perfection, even to attain the highest perfection of which I am capable with the aid of grace? This consideration made our Holy Mother, St. Teresa, regard as useless the vow which she had made, to do always what she believed to be most perfect; because a Carmelite, to be faithful to the spirit and end of her Holy Institute, should always choose by preference, that which is most comfortable to Divine love.

Instead of conforming myself to the holy rigors of Divine love, choosing what was most perfect, have I not inclined by preference to those things in which I found the most natural satisfaction, contenting my self with the assurance that there was no sin in it?

40

In order to acquire the perfection of our Holy Order, and the spirit of solitude, crucifixion, and death which it requires of its children, do I enter generously into the practice of a universal mortification and habitual recollection? To attain this, have I sought to augment in my heart a devotion to the most August Sacrament, and to the Holy Virgin Mary? In a word, have I not thought that to be a Carmelite, it sufficed to wear the Habit and to follow the exterior exercises without taking the pains to acquire the interior spirit and the gift of prayer, which is the soul of the Institute, while exterior practices are but its body?

Third Day

First Meditation - On Hell

"And these shall go into everlasting punishment." — St. Matthew, XXV, 46.

I adore Thee, O Incarnate Word, Thou who hast the key of David, Thou who openest to the elect and no man can shut, Thou who shuttest to the reprobate and no man can open! Ah! Lord, in order that I may not be among the number of those victims of Thy justice, whom Thou shalt shut up in the abyss, let me descend there to-day in spirit. I wish to contemplate there the place which my sins have merited. I desire thus to share in that grace, which Thou didst give to our Holy Mother, St. Teresa, when Thou didst in a vision full of horror, conduct her into that place of torment. This grace she always esteemed as one of the greatest which she had received from Thee, because by it, she understood the danger of infidelities, even the lightest. Grant that I may draw from it the same fruit.

FIRST POINT - What Is Hell?

St. Paul, raised up to the third heaven, where he had tasted ineffable delights, could say nothing except, with the Prophet Isaiah, that eye hath not seen, nor ear heard, neither hath it entered into the mind of man to conceive the greatness of the joy and happiness which God has prepared for those who love Him. Such would be, although in a sense very different, alas! the language of a reprobate soul if, appearing upon earth, it tried to explain the horrors of hell. The eye of man has not seen evils, torments and despair; his ear has never heard cries of rage, of fury, of sorrow and of suffering, gnashing and grinding of teeth; his heart has never felt agony, tortures, bitter ness, or despair comparable to the torments, clamors and agonies of hell. Because hell is the place where God exercises His justice, as heaven is the place where He satisfies His bounty; in one as in the other, He acts as God, that is to say,

41

with infinite love or infinite rigor. Just as in heaven, He places in the souls of the just an ocean of infinite glory and felicity, so in hell, He buries the reprobate in an abyss of desolation and suffering which surpasses all that we can imagine.

Hell contains in itself all evil, since in it reigns sin. which is essentially the sovereign evil; and because they who inhabit it are confirmed in sin, identified with sin, and as it were, become sin itself. Thus, if it were possible to accumulate upon one single person, in one single day, and in one single place, all that is most painful in bodily sufferings, all the torments invented by tyrants for their victims, by persecutors for the martyrs — fire, melted lead, devouring beasts, venomous reptiles, burning gridirons, and added to these, hunger, cold, fear, despair, persecutions and the hatred and the cruel insults with which victims have been tormented — all these evils, according to the testimony of the Fathers of the Church, especially St. Augustine, St. Chrysostom, St. Gregory and St. Thomas, are nothing, or at least very little, compared to those of hell; because not only are they all found there but united with them are an infinity of others unknown to man, and all are intensified in the highest degree.

These terrible evils are not confined to the place which the demons inhabit, neither to the air they breathe, as, for example, a closed furnace, or an atmosphere charged with pestilential vapors into which these unfortunate victims could be plunged; but, as in their proper place, they will be incorporated, identified with the reprobates themselves, in a word, they will possess them and be possessed by them. This possession is full and entire, that is to say, very different from the suffering which they endured on earth, where the patient neither suffers forever, nor equally, nor continually, nor everywhere, the evil which attacks him, while the reprobate must endure them all at once, in every part of their being, interiorly as well as exteriorly, and this without the least interruption, or the least alleviation. This possession is also perfect and entire, that is to say, eternal, because without this eternity the suffering of hell would not be a supreme misfortune and hell would not be hell. But they are to last always — this word "always" making the sovereign desolation of hell. 'Always' to suffer," cries out the lost souls, "never to cease!" "Always!" As long as God shall be God our torments shall never cease! To this desolate prospect of eternity must be added the most bitter remembrance, and the most poignant regret, at the thought of all the means which they had at their disposal for saving their souls when they lived on earth. They will recall the abundant helps which Holy Church offered them in the Sacraments, prayer, and the Word of God, and the many holy examples and charitable advice by which they did not profit. Ah! it is there that the worm of which our Saviour speaks dies not. But, above all, what shall be the despair of a Religious soul, in thinking of the many means of sanctification, of the grace of having been chosen, of other precious privileges, the contempt and the abuse of which shall add to her crime and to her unhappy eternity!

That which will put the finishing touch to all the evils and desolation of hell, and without which these evils themselves, all incomprehensible as they are, would nevertheless be susceptible of relief, is the awful certainty which the reprobates have of being always separated from God. The loss of God, — Ah! this is the sovereign evil! If, indeed, they could but conceive the faintest hope of seeing God for one instant at the end of each million of years, this sight, although so distant, would alleviate their torments. But, alas! the darkness which environs them being so dense, and the abyss into which they are plunged so profound, that never can the least ray of hope penetrate, nor one drop of the Blood of Jesus fall there. Who can explain this torture of a damned soul! A torture incomparably greater than all the others which she endures, as it is caused by the inconsolable regret of having lost forever the sovereign Good for which she had been created, which she could have so easily acquired — the sovereign Good which she has lost through her own fault.

In this present life, notwithstanding the light of Faith and the unction of grace, we can have but a very imperfect idea of the anguish of a lost soul at being eternally separated from God. In consequence of original sin, our understanding is so clouded and our will is so depraved that we forget that God is our end, and we seek it in the enjoyment of created things. But as soon as the soul is freed from the flesh which has held and weighed it down, it finds itself animated only with the instincts of its spiritual nature, and feels an immense need of light, of truth, of peace and of love. At the same time, it understands that God alone can satisfy it, and it flies toward Him; but, while the faithful and pure soul is received with love, the lost soul is violently driven back and cursed! Ah! who can explain the anguish, the agony, the torture of this unfortunate soul in the midst of the useless efforts which it makes to reach the Supreme Good, Who responds to its desires only by new maledictions. It is not love that thus transports it — it is the need it feels of possessing God, joined to a frightful inclination to hate Him and to curse Him. Horrible contradiction! Astonishing combat! which tears the soul and throws it without ceasing into new despair, into that "exterior darkness, where there is weeping and gnashing of teeth." "O, who will give water to my head, and a fountain of tears to my eyes, to prevent that useless weeping, and to deliver me from those eternal flames which burn, yet never consume!"

"Ah! Lord, turn not Thy face from me, and take not Thy Holy Spirit from me." Permit not that I separate from Thee here, that I may not be separated fiom Thee eternally. O my God, since hell is the sovereign evil because there is the reign of sin, Thy irreconcilable enemy, I detest it more than hell itself, because hell is less an evil than sin; I will weep over those I have committed, and I will live in the resolution of preserving myself from sin at all costs. Grant me this grace, O God, my Sovereign Good!

SECOND POINT - Should I Fear Hell?

It is infinitely important for the Religious soul to answer this question in the depths of her conscience, because it is generally Religious souls who imagine that this truth does not regard them; that it is not suitable for contemplative souls to meditate upon it, since they should have abandoned the imperfect way of fear, to raise themselves to God upon the wings of pure love. But if we interrogate upon this point the Doctors of the Church, the Fathers of the Desert, and the History of the Church, it will be seen how far these souls have been led into a dangerous delusion. From Judas, who was lost in the company of Jesus Christ, even to the last years of the last century, [1] when we have seen the terrible anger of God fall upon many Religious Houses, in punishment for the forgetfulness of their duties and their sacred engagements, how many Religious, solitaries, and persons consecrated to the Holy Altar, have left their holy state to follow the way of iniquity! Thus neither the holy habit nor their profession, neither solitude nor the high walls of their Monasteries could protect nor preserve them from the eternal damnation which they have merited precisely by the abuse of the graces of their vocation. This is why there was no practice more habitual with the Holy Solitaries of the Desert than the consideration of the severity of the judgments of God, and the rigor of the pains which He inflicts upon impenitent sinners.

But what! you say, a Carmelite to be damned! She who has quitted the world and made the greatest sacrifices for God; must she lead a life of crucifixion and death to end in hell! Angels in heaven have fallen, and the first man in the terrestrial Paradise, so many solitaries in the most profound deserts, so many Religious in the most austere orders have unhappily been lost; and shall I not tremble for myself? Shall I believe myself assured against all danger by my profession alone Ah! rather I should tremble more on account of the sanctity of my vocation, and the sublime perfection to which I am called in the Holy Order of Carmel, as this shall be for me matter for a more severe judgment and a more rigorous chastisement if I abuse so great a grace.

But how can one damn herself in Carmel? Alas! it is but too easily answered. How hast thou fallen from heaven, O Lucifer? It was pride — self-love which precipitated thee from it! Thus the first cause of our ruin is ordinarily a secret pride, which, becoming the principle as well as the motive of all our actions, causes us to refer all things to ourselves, to seek with avidity the esteem and affection of creatures, to seek or desire honorable charges, and suffer with pain to be forgotten or reprimanded, considering that we are injured when others are preferred to us. Then the demon, ever ready to profit by our vicious dispositions, drags us very soon to thoughts, murmurs and actions which become the source of the gravest faults and the most culpable disorders. Others are lost because of a pride more subtle and dangerous yet, as it is more hidden. Seduced by the illusions of their self-love, they are caught by the ruses of the demon, disguised as an Angel of light to deceive them. They believe that they are called to extraordinary ways; whether because they esteem these ways too much, or prefer them to the sure but humble way of faith; or whether it is because they despise the warning of their Superiors, they abandon the practise of humble and ordinary virtues, such as

44

obedience and contempt of self, to follow their pretended revelations and imaginary visions, which serve only to nourish their pride and lead them far from the beaten path of faith and obedience. Many others, in fine, according to the Oracle of the Holy Spirit, neglect small things, and thus fall, little by little, into grave infractions; or allow themselves insensibly to sleep in a fatal tepidity, which forces the Divine Spouse to vomit them out of His mouth.

St. Teresa gives us a terrible proof of the fatal consequence which infidelities can have for even the most generous souls, if they continue in them. This Holy Mother teaches us, in the thirty-second chapter of her life, that God had shown her the place in hell which the demon had prepared for her, and which her sins would merit if she persevered in her infidelities and her resistance to grace (yet, from the Bull of her Canonization, and from authors of her life, it is evident that she never fell into any mortal sin). "It seemed to me," she says, "that I found myself in a moment in hell, without knowing how I had been carried there. This lasted for very short time, but if I should live many years I do not believe it possible to lose the remembrance of it. The entrance seemed to be like a long, close alley, or rather like a low, dark and narrow oven; and the ground appeared to be like mire, exceedingly filthy, stinking insupportably, and full of a multitude of loathsome vermin. At the end of it there was a certain hollow place, as if it had been a kind of little press in the wall, into which I found myself thrust and close pent up. All that I have said might pass for delightful, in comparison with what I felt in that press; the torment was so dreadful that no words can express the least part of it.

"I felt a fire in my soul which I cannot express or describe, as it was in reality. All those other most grievous torments which I have endured by the shrinking up of my sinews, and by other ways, which, in the judgment of physicians, were the greatest which could be suffered in a corporeal way in this world, and some also, as I have said, which were caused by the devil, were all a mere nothing, in comparison with what I suffered there, joined with the dismal thought that all this suffering was to be without end or intermission. And even this is still nothing, if compared with the continual agony the soul suffers; that pressing, that stifling, that anguish so exceedingly sensible, together with such desperate torturing, discontent and disgust that I cannot express it. To say that it is a butchering or rending of the soul, is to say little; for this would seem to express a violence, used by some other agent to destroy her. But here she is her own executioner, and even tears herself to pieces. I saw not who it was that tormented me; but I seemed to find myself both burnt and cut to pieces all at once; and in so dreadful a place there was no room for the least hope of once meeting with any comfort or ease; neither was there any such thing as sitting or lying down. Thus was I thrust into this place like a hole in the wall; and these walls, which are also most horrible to the sight, press in upon their prisoner, so that everything chokes and stifles there. There is nothing but thick darkness, without the least glimpse of light; and yet I know not how it is, though there is no light, yet one sees all that can afflict the sight."

What a picture, O my God! painted by a soul who had herself felt all the frightful terrors which she describes. How after this can anyone dare say that no one has ever returned from hell to tell us of what passes there? How can I myself be able to sleep on in a mortal tepidity, reassuring myself on the lightness of my faults? If St. Teresa thus saw the place which would have been hers, if she had the misfortune to fall into the sins to which her infidelities might have led, had she not renounced them, should I not tremble now at the sight of my faults, my resistance to a multitude of Thy graces? Ah! Lord, I wish to delay no longer in giving myself entirely to Thee. I will do so no matter what it may cost me. I will recoil before no sacrifice, I will no longer resist Thy inspirations, that by this fear, which is the commencement of wisdom, J may arrive at the perfection of love.

[1] Eighteenth century. The author probably refers to the French Revolution.

Second Meditation - Mortal Sin

"Deliver us from Evil."— St Matthew, VI, 13.

I adore Thee, O my God, Who art sovereignly good and holy, or rather goodness and sanctity itself, — in a word, Sanctity by essence. "The heavens are not pure in Thy sight, and Thou hast found corruption even among the Angels." How, then, can I dare to present myself before Thy Divine Majesty, — I who am all covered with sins! But I throw myself at Thy feet, Lord, that Thou mayest enlighten me by Thy grace and make me understand the greatness of the evil from which Thou wiliest that I beg to be delivered. Thou dost detest it, Lord, because it is Thy supreme enemy: make me abhor it also as Thou dost, because it is also my greatest enemy. Dissipate the clouds which my sins have caused in my heart and my mind, in order that I may see clearly and feel deeply how "great an evil it is to have abandoned the Lord, my God."

FIRST POINT - The Injury Which Sin Does to God

God is essential Goodness: He is Love itself. He is the inexhaustible source of goodness and of love, and desires only to pour out His riches upon His creatures. Before the creation, and from all eternity, this communication took place in the Adorable Trinity, by the ineffable relations which the three Divine Persons have among themselves; and when God resolved to create man in time, He made him to His Image and Likeness, in order that he might enter into a participation of His Eternal Beatitude. God can do nothing but for His own glory, but this glory He places in the happiness of His creatures. Thus, as I have already seen, the end and the perfection of man consists in

46

being united to God by grace in this life and by glory in the next. The Creator has regulated all the laws which govern this vast universe to this end, so glorious and so advantageous to His privileged creatures. He has given them the Commandments, not as the arbitrary condition of the infinite glory which He has prepared for them, but as just and reasonable means for arriving at it, since the Commandments are the expression of His infinite Sanctity. He has prescribed them to man, ill order that preserving or re-establishing in himself, by their observance, the image of God, He may merit to be eternally united to Him. Nothing then is more beautiful, more admirable, or more just than the harmony existing among all the laws which govern the creatures of this vast universe, and the end which God proposed to Himself, when He drew them out of nothingness — man's eternal happiness. My Lord, and my God, I cry out with Thy Prophet: "How admirable is Thy name in the whole earth...What is man that Thou hast crowned him with glory and honor; and hast set him over the works of Thy hands?"

Who would now dare disturb an order so perfect, established for the glory of the Creator and the felicity of His creatures, a marvelous result of the eternal counsels, of the divine perfections, and in particular of infinite power, wisdom and love? What name can be given to the one who would try to prevent the Sovereign Master of the world from attaining the end of His works — who would deprive the Father of all Being from enjoying the complacency which He proposed to find in the happiness and the love of His children? This disturbance, this disorder is sin, the evil by excellence, because it attacks the Sovereign Good, because it attacks Him in His Essence, and wounds His adorable perfections in their exterior manifestations, in a manner so horrible, so unqualified, that if God, by His eternal and immutable Nature, was not beyond attack, sin would cause His death.

Sin, then, has no being; it is rather a non-being, since it is a violation of the Holy Laws of God, and attacks this God, Who alone has Being. — a violation so much the more culpable because it is committed by those in favor of whom these laws have been made — by man, who thus uses to outrage his Creator the very means given to glorify Him. These truths, which are so evident to reason enlightened by faith, are confirmed by the most formal teachings of Religion, teachings at which we should fear and tremble. In effect, I consider that God is Love; that He is Truth and Justice itself, that His mercies are above all His works, and by consequence, that the pains which He inflicts upon the culpable cannot be greater than their faults; that, on the contrary, knowing the frailty and imperfection of His creatures, whom He loves as His image, He shows, even in the chastisements to which He makes them submit, that His justice is tempered by His love. I am forced to admit that if God has inflicted upon sinners the greatest pains to which their nature is susceptible, it is because sin in His eyes is an infinite malice, a disorder, an evil without measure. Ah! what does Faith teach me here? It teaches me that the torments of hell are an assemblage of all evils, in an infinite degree, and that there may be a multitude of the reprobate guilty of but one mortal sin.

Again, what does Faith teach? That for a single mortal sin, a sin of thought, a sin committed in one instant, God precipitated into hell the most noble, the most beautiful of His creatures, the Princes of His Court, His friends in whom He took His complacency, in a word, the Angels — and that without any regard for their dignity, their beauty and their number. He condemned them to eternal and infinite torments, without giving them time to repent or the means to do penance.

But behold the Victim of the Justice of God, much more elevated, much more noble, much more worthy than all the legions of heaven — it is Jesus Christ. Has He not been condemned by His Just Father, as the Divine Saviour calls Him, to the torment of the Cross — that is to sufferings of infinite value, on account of the dignity of the One Who submitted to it in our name! We must then conclude anew, and tremble at the thought, that sin is an evil of infinite malice, since it was effaced at so infinite a price. How striking are these truths, O my God, which, until now, I have endeavored so little to comprehend. Where shall I find motives to reassure myself? Because, if Thou hast not spared even the Angels, if Thou dost plunge into hell each day a multitude of sinners who imitate them in their revolt, if Thou hast not spared Thy Only Son, what shall become of me?

Lord, all unworthy as I am, I beg of Thee this grace, give me light; grant today that I may understand that sin is the one evil, and that there is no other, because it attacks Thee, O my God! Deliver me, then, from the sins which I have already committed, and preserve me from those into which I am in danger of falling.

SECOND POINT - The Harm Which Sin Does to Man

If sin offers God an infinite injury, it is also for man a sovereign evil, because it separates him from God, his End and his infinite good in this world and in the next. God — as I have seen with admiration, thanks and love — God is the beginning and the end of man. The perfection of this privileged creature is commenced here by grace and is consummated in heaven by glory. Now, if man is faithful to grace, nothing can be an obstacle, nothing can deprive him of this supreme happiness. "If God is for us," says the Apostle, "who can be against us?" "What can separate us from the love of Jesus Christ; shall afflictions, or anguish, or persecutions, or hunger, or cold, or nakedness, or perils, or the sword? For I am persuaded that neither life nor death, nor any other creature, shall be able to separate us from the love of God, which is Christ Jesus."

The sufferings and evils of this life, far from being able to separate us from God, serve, on the contrary, if we support them with Jesus Christ and in His Spirit, to unite us more closely to Him, and merit for us a greater abundance of celestial glory. Tribulations and trials should, then, rather be called good than evil. Sin, on the contrary, is an evil unmixed with any good, an evil which is the source of all evil, because maladies, death, disorderly passions, all the sufferings of this life, all the plagues of the world, pests, wars, famine and hell itself come from it, as from a cursed father. But, above all, it is for man the greatest evil, because it separates him eternally from God, his Supreme Good, his perfection, his end; and, even in this world, reduces his soul to a state of such deformity that if a soul in mortal sin could be seen with our bodily eyes it would be the most hideous, the most frightful sight, ever given to man to behold. Moreover, sin, when mortal, plunges the soul into the most profound misery, into a complete and absolute indigence of all good. Whatever may have been his preceding good works, by this sin he immediately falls into disgrace with God; and not only is he despoiled of all merit and loses all right to recompense, but, as a tree struck by lightning, he is become sterile and incapable of producing any fruit for life eternal. Although this soul distributes all his goods to the poor, has faith enough to move mountains, and gives his body to be burned, according to the testimony of St. Paul, it profiteth him nothing. He is dead, his works are dead.

A soul in mortal sin is a profaned temple, a vine ravaged by storms and despoiled in an instant of all its fruits; it is a city, devastated by fire, of which there remains not a stone upon a stone. O unfortunate soul! like a sheep without a shepherd, wandering among the mountains, or like a vessel without a sailor or pilot, thou dost wander around the world, destitute of the favors of thy God and of the attentive cares of a loving Providence. Alas! thou dost possess no longer thy God, thou art the sad object of His hatred and His disdain, thou who wast called to love and possess Him eternally, and to find in this possession the entire satisfaction of all thy faculties. Thou hast lost this God. He is no longer thy God, or if He is still so, it is only because thou hast not yet descended into hell, where thy place is marked out. It is, then, a truth too certain that the sin called mortal, because it separates the soul from God, is the sovereign evil of man in this world, as hell will be his sovereign evil in the next; for hell is nothing else than the eternal reign of sin, and the eternal death of the soul in an agony without end.

It is here that the Solitary of Carmel should, in the silence of Retreat, recall, briefly however, in the bitterness of her heart, the sins of her past life, and, penetrated with a lively sorrow at having fallen into so great a snare as mortal sin, ask herself if her sorrow has ever been proportioned to the evil, and if she has ever thought of expiating it by penance. Above all, she should fear to fall into a very dangerous illusion by imagining that Carmel is a shelter from mortal sin, forgetting, alas! that she has brought herself into it with all her feebleness, her inconstancy and self-love — that the demon has followed her as a ravening lion, seeking to devour his prey. What such a soul should consider is, that not only can she fall into mortal sin, but that, if she has the misfortune to commit one, it will be much more grave than those of the same nature which she might commit in the world, because, belonging by her profession rather to heaven than to earth — the life of Carmel being an anticipated Paradise — she should be an Angel rather than a terrestrial creature. Her sin, consequently, assumes the character and the gravity of that of the

Angels. The sin of the rebel Angels drew its enormity from the fact that it was committed with full knowledge, in the midst of clear light, and notwithstanding the signal and continual favors which they had received from their Sovereign King, which marks it with a peculiar character of ingratitude and of felony. Add to this the terrible scandal, of which crime Lucifer was the first to become guilty, by drawing the other Angels in their horrible and proud defection. Therefore the Religious of Carmel cannot sin, without contemning graces and lights, the most precious and abundant, and abusing the most signal favors, thereby rendering herself guilty of infidelity, ingratitude and scandal. Ah! may she fear by thus participating in the character of the Angels' sin, to draw down upon herself their chastisement — blindness of mind and hardness of heart.

Lord, I will not say with the sinner spoken of in the Scriptures: "I have sinned and nothing has happened to me." On the contrary, I confess before Thee that when I sinned I offered Thee an infinite outrage, and at the same time drew upon myself a great unhappiness, for what greater misfortune, O my God, my Life, my All, than not to live for Thee! Ah! if this evil has befallen me a single time; if for one day, one hour, or even one instant of my life, I had remained in the state of mortal sin; I ought by tears of blood and the rudest works of penance to force myself to efface its stains from my soul. By separating myself from Thee, I have deprived Thee of the rights which Thou hast over my heart; of the complacency which, as Father, Thou desirest to take in Thy child; of the enjoyment as Spouse, of the reciprocal love of Thy spouse.

O sin! my enemy! my supreme evil! I declare thee eternal hatred. O God, my Sovereign Good! I promise Thee an eternal love, a fidelity without bounds. L.et me rather die a million times than offend Thee again; for this will be dying to live eternally. Amen.

Third Meditation - Venial Sin

"He that is unjust in that which is little, is unjust, also in that which is greater."—
St. Luke XVI, 10.

Since freedom from sin attracts the soul to Thee, O God of Infinite Sanctity, and since lightest offenses sadden Thy Holy Spirit, the Spirit of Purity; I come to-day into Thy holy presence to impress well upon my mind the powerful motives which should make me detest and avoid venial sin. Alas! until now I have not sufficiently considered its malice and its dangers — nor feared its terrible consequences, therefore my life is replete with faults which are called light. Ah! Lord, can I call light, faults which offend Thee and cause such prejudice to the soul? Grant me the grace to conceive on this subject sentiments more worthy of the holy state which I profess, and of Thy Divine Majesty, to which I have the honor of being consecrated.

Charity has two enemies, mortal sin and venial sin. The first not only wounds but kills, all its wounds are mortal. The second does not cause death, it is true, but it enfeebles the soul, it soils and makes it ugly in the sight of God, and disposes Kim to withdraw from it. If venial sin is not the capital enemy of God, and sovereign evil which mortal sin is, it is the greatest after it, because it is opposed to the Sovereign Good, whom it offends and displeases. Venial sin, being the enemy of God, cannot, according to all the Holy Fathers and Doctors of the Church, be called light, nor can it be compared with all other created evils. It cannot be compensated for by all the good that creatures may effect, because an evil of an infinite order cannot be balanced by a good of a finite nature.

These truths have been confirmed by the divine lights with which certain extraordinary souls have been favored. St. Catherine of Genoa teaches that venial sin is an evil greater than all the evils of the universe together, an evil worse than death and hell itself. And St. Catherine of Sienna says that even the slightest sin contains in itself, in a certain manner, an infinite malice. This doctrine is taught in the writings of this last Saint, which several Sovereign Pontiffs have praised as being all celestial, and which are conformable to the teaching of St. Thomas.

But that which should completely convince me of the evil of venial sin is the severity of the judgments which God has inflicted upon it in this world and in the next — chastisements which we might call excessive, if the offense did not possess that degree of malice and of gravity which we have just recognized in it. Moses, a man so dear to God, this servant so devoted and faithful, at the sight of the obduracy of the people of Israel, falls into a diffidence which seems very excusable; nevertheless he is condemned never to enter the Promised Land. After forty years of labors and of sufferings, he prays the Lord to retract this sentence, but receives only a refusal, and dies within sight of the land, whose entrance is closed to him. A slight vanity in David, on the occasion of the number of his people, caused the death of seventy thousand of his subjects. A vain complacency in Ezechias, who showed his treasures to the Babylonian Ambassadors, is punished not only by the loss of his riches, but by the desolation of Jerusalem and the leading away captive of the most illustrious families of the kingdom. An indiscreet look at the Holy Ark cost a great number of the Bethsamites their lives.

But what are these chastisements and the pains of this world in comparison to the torments of Purgatory, — torments which the Holy Fathers liken to those of hell, save the duration and the despair. If I descend in spirit into the expiatory fires, and ask myself who are those souls whom God keeps enchained in the midst of so much suffering, some for entire centuries, some until the end of time, I shall see that, alas! they are not souls of the impious or impenitent sinners; no, they are souls already victorious, they are the well-beloved spouses of the Only Son of God, whose place is marked in heaven, but in whom the Divine Eye perceives some trace of what we call light faults — venial sins.

After this reflection, it is easy to understand the teachings of all the Doctors of the Church, that if, even by one venial sin, a small lie for example, we could put a stop to all woes that desolate the earth — to war, famine, pests, inundations; deliver the human race from all anxieties of heart and mind, and from all the maladies of the body; convert all heretics, Mohomedans and Jews; snatch all the damned from the flames of hell; deliver all the souls from Purgatory; and secure the salvation of all the faithful, it could not be lawful for us to commit this sin — to tell this lie. This doctrine is especially that of St. Augustine and St. John Chrysostom.

The Sanctity of God obliges Him to pursue, and to punish the lightest offense with such rigor, that, to give us some idea of it, theologians say that if, by a supposition altogether impossible, the eyes of God could discover in the Sacred Humanity of Jesus Christ, or in the immaculate soul of Mary, the slightest trace of sin, the union of the Divinity and the Humanity of Our Lord Jesus Christ would be immediately broken, and the Holy Mother of God would be precipitated from her elevated throne where she reigns eternally, until purified from this stain, however light.

That which shows most clearly all the venom and the malice of venial sin, which so few Christians understand, is the impossibility of all creatures together, even the most perfect, to offer for it any reparation whatsoever. Yes, if I represent to myself an altar as large as the world, where there are to be immolated to the glory of God and in satisfaction for one single venial sin, the most noble among the celestial intelligences, the most holy among the Patriarchs, the Prophets, the martyrs, the confessors, and the virgins, supposing this expiation to be prolonged during entire centuries; all these reduced to their own value and dis-united from the merits of Jesus Christ, would be entirely impotent in effacing this pretended light stain of sin.

It is then not astonishing that the Saints, so penetrated with these great truths, had such a horror for the slightest faults that, rather than voluntarily commit the least sin, they would have precipitated themselves alive into burning flames. What is my confusion, O my God, to see how little I have until now understood the injury I have done to Thy Sovereign Majesty and Thy Infinite Sanctity by this sin so improperly called light! What is my grief for having committed it with such facility, for having taken so little care to testify to Thee my repentance, and so little pains to efface its stains by penance and virtue! Lord, it shall be so no longer! Should I have the misfortune to displease Thee again, may it be at least without reflection and deliberation, and may I at once testify to Thee my sorrow and confusion, and with Thy grace take the most efficacious means of not falling again.

SECOND POINT - The Effects of Venial Sin

The first effect of venial sin, which alone should suffice to fill us with an

52

eternal horror for it, is that it corrupts the most beautiful acts of virtue, it diminishes and even deprives them entirely of all of their merit, for, according to the Scriptures: "Dying flies falling into a precious perfume will corrupt all its sweetness." This truth is founded upon the words of Jesus Christ: "Take care that you do not your justice before men to be seen by them, otherwise you shall not have a reward of your Father Who is in heaven." Whence the Holy Doctors conclude that the best actions done through vain glory lose their merit; even martyrdom itself, according to St. Jerome, if endured to win the applause of men, would count for nothing before God.

Pause here, Religious soul, reflect upon this important teaching, and consider how easily you may lose all the merit and recompense of a life so full of sacrifices, immolation and holy practices. Yes, although I be raised to the highest contemplation, although I practise the rudest bodily austerities, although I acquire the purity of the Angels and the love of the Seraphim, and although my life be filled with acts of patience, resignation and sweetness; if these different acts of virtue be infected, however lightly, by any culpable thought or sentiment of self-complacency; if self-love seeks itself in them, or a desire of pleasing the creature insinuates itself into my heart, and I do not immediately reject it, this is sufficient; according to the part which my evil inclinations have taken in them: I have lost my recompense and the merit of my sacrifices. What a subject of confusion and regret that so many actions, which fill my days and ought to be works produced by grace and animated by a pure intention, are stolen from me by vanity, natural activity, love of ease and my own satisfaction — forgetting the good pleasure of God, which alone I should seek.

But a still more deplorable defect of venial sin is, that it diminishes the fervor of charity and in manner causes God to withdraw from the soul. To appreciate well these terrible consequences of an evil which is generally regarded so lightly, it is necessary to know that, however true it is to say that sanctifying grace cannot be lost by venial sin, we ought to remember, nevertheless, that such faults, committed habitually, through negligence or by a certain affection or inclination, weaken the soul, render it languid, and thus it becomes cold in the service of God, and experiences no longer in prayer that familiarity and fervor which it enjoyed when it was faithful. God, on His side, withdraws these sensible attractions, those secret graces, those particular inspirations with which He favors His friends. Thus is accomplished this double sentence of the Holy Spirit: "He who is unfaithful in small things shall fall little by little," and "Would to God that thou wert cold or hot, but because thou art lukewarm, I will begin to vomit thee out of My mouth." Behold, O my God, whither these venial faults lead the soul who takes little care to deplore and to avoid them — to coldness in Thy service, and, by consequence, to the loss of Thy favors, and to the subtraction of Thy graces and efficacious succors! What shall become of the soul thus destitute of Thy precious favors? She will fall into that fatal state which is called lukewarmness, a state so sad that, in one sense, mortal sin would be preferable to it.

53

But, alas! as a result of the unhappy facility with which venial sin is committed, this fall, or rather this invasion of mortal sin, is not long delayed; and it is the last and most terrible consequence of the habit or affection for venial sin. Thus the soul descends by degrees into the profound abyss of disgrace with God, where she sleeps and entombs herself without perceiving it, without understanding the horror of her situation, and without making any effort to free herself from it. If this unfortunate soul had fallen through the weakness of nature, or the ruse of Satan, into some mortal sin, she would have been instantly awakened by the very effect of the depth of her great fall; her sorrow and confusion would have served to raise her up more promptly, and it was in this sense that Jesus Christ has said to the tepid soul: "I would that thou wert either hot or cold," but because her death has been the last effect of a languishing life, which died out little by little, a miracle is necessary to resuscitate it to grace.

But, my God, what will it avail me to understand the malice of venial sin, the outrage which it offers Thy Infinite Sanctity, the injury which it does my own soul, and the peril to which it exposes my eternal salvation, if I do not entertain in my heart a profound aversion to all that can offend Thee, if I do not, according to the advice of the Apostle, take continual care to preserve myself even from the appearance of evil. I must confess, to my shame, that such has not been my past conduct. I have exposed my soul each day to a multitude of dangers. Provided I fell not into considerable infractions of Thy Holy Law, I counted as of little importance those continual infidelities by which I wounded Thy Eye so pure, which is kept fixed upon me. My words, my looks, my steps, my thoughts, and my desires are entirely according to nature, and I have not endeavored to render them conformable to Thy good pleasure. Therefore, who could count for one day my infractions of Thy holy will? Ah! if, even after having rendered myself guilty of these faults, I had deplored them and imposed upon myself some expiation; if, at least, I had felt confusion for them at the feet of Thy minister; if, in regard to the exterior, I had submitted, in presence of my sisters, to the expiations which the Rule permits; but, alas! I have shown in repairing these faults the same tepidity which I had in committing them. I have made of Thy tribunal of penance, and the public acknowledgment of faults, an excuse rather than a remedy for my infidelities.

Ah! Lord, St. Catherine of Genoa would have much preferred to throw herself into burning flames than to offend Thee in the slightest thing. I also take this resolution; I desire henceforth to be disposed to suffer and even to die, rather than to offend Thee deliberately. I will put a watch upon my eyes, my tongue and my heart, that they may not escape my care and follow after evil. I will entertain in my soul a great horror of sin; and if, notwithstanding all these precautions, I unhappily fall into some faults, I will deplore them bitterly until Thou dost pardon me. In fine, I will keep my heart in that purity which will permit me to contemplate Thee here below, in order to love Thee eternally in heaven. Amen.

Penance is one of the virtues most honored and practised in Carmel; it belongs essentially to the spirit of this holy Order. This virtue consists in a sincere sorrow for having offended God, joined to a firm purpose to offend Him no more, and to satisfy His divine justice. The spirit of penance is then the habitual disposition of bearing before God and nourishing in the heart regret for sin, and profiting by every occasion for making expiation. Thus the penitent soul, not content with accepting, in punishment for her faults, the fasts and abstinences of the Church and of the Order and the holy rigors of the Religious life, adds to them, with permission of her superiors, some particular austerities. She submits in the same spirit to trials and sufferings, interior as well as exterior, recognizing in them a loving Providence, which wishes to purify her by the fire of tribulation from the stains of her past sins. Thus it was that David, although he had received from the Prophet Nathan the assurance that God had forgiven his sin, he never wearied of testifying his regret, and feeling confusion before God. He repeats that his sin was always before his eyes, and that every night he watered his couch with his tears. He prayed to be purified more and more from his iniquity, and accepted with great submission and resignation the revolt of his son, the loss of his kingdom, and the most grievous outrages from his former servants, as the just chastisement of his crime. This spirit of penance has the double advantage of purifying us from our sins, and of rendering us more and more agreeable to God, while it nourishes a hatred of sin in our hearts and, at the same time, withdraws us from its possibilities.

We may say that the great cause of our little perseverance in grace, after receiving pardon for our faults, comes from the lightness of the penance which we receive, or which we impose upon ourselves. Thus it is much to be regretted and deplored that Holy Church has been forced to condescend to the weakness and the laxity of her children, and to relax her rights relative to the penances which she imposed upon sinners in the first centuries; because the rigor of her laws relating to penance made them feel the gravity of their faults and impressed, even on the just themselves, a fear and horror of sin.

It is not only the grievous sins of her past life that a Religious soul should strive to efface by penance and expiation; it is even her habitual infidelities which she should not pass over lightly. Happy the soul who knows how to humble and afflict herself before God for her slightest faults, and who offers Him some pain proportioned to each offense; she will attain in a short time a great purity of conscience, which will merit for her the most abundant graces.

This spirit of penance has also the advantage of increasing and nourishing in our hearts the precious and necessary virtue of humility, and of being thus the best disposition for prayer: because the greatest obstacle to this holy exercise comes from a certain presumption, a secret confidence in ourselves which arrests the flow of God's grace into our hearts, according to these words: "God resists the proud, but gives His grace to the humble."

The Religious soul who is habitually in this humble disposition has no difficulty at the commencement of her prayers, meditations, at the Holy Sacrifice of the Mass, and at Holy Communion to excite sentiments of true compunction, and God never fails on His part to be touched by her humble supplications.

Although the spirit of penance should never be dispensed with by the Religious soul, even if she has entered upon the exercises of the Unitive Way, it is most particularly suitable for the time of her Novitiate; and by the Novitiate must be understood the first four or five years from the time of receiving the Holy Habit, and during which the exercises of the Purgative Way should be insisted upon. It is during this time that one should make a general confession, and offer habitually, in expiation for all her sins, all the penances in use in Carmel, such as fasts, watching, austerities, etc., and, in general, all in its Holy Rule that is painful or difficult to nature.

It may appear at first sight that this spirit of penance is contrary to perfect love, and that the practices which it inspires are little favorable to souls called to a state of contemplation. To reply to this difficulty, or rather prejudice, we may cite the example of a multitude of Saints, in particular that of Saint Mary Magdalen, a patron and model of our holy Order, who united the most sublime prayer to the most austere penance. But it is sufficient to consider that the spirit of penance, far from injuring the exercise of holy love, serves but to purify the heart and to dispose it better for the flames of divine charity, just as wood, despoiled of its verdure and humidity, lends itself more easily to the action of fire. We must add that the remembrance of sins for which we have obtained pardon is a new motive for attaching ourselves to Him Who granted this favor, according to the comparison made by Jesus Christ when He defended this illustrious penitent from the unjust suspicions of the Pharisees: "The one to whom much is forgiven loves much."

Penitent love has a character of strength, sweetness, humility, generosity, and gratitude which is not always to be met with in innocent love, that is to say, in love which is not prompted by the motive of pardon obtained. To whatever degree of prayer we may attain, it is always necessary to present ourselves before God with sentiments of profound humility founded particularly upon a regret for the sins which we have committed — which we should always take care to express to Him and accept the salutary confusion which follows. It is true that, according to the intention of the Church, the practices of penance used in the Holy Order of Carmel have for their object to satisfy for sinners who never think of appeasing the Divine anger; but without excluding this motive, so holy and so charitable, the Religious soul should not stop here. She can well, she even ought to, offer herself to God, particularly at the Holy Sacrifice of the Mass, as a common victim devoted to His love and His glory; but the sentiment of confusion and sorrow for her own sins ought to lead her to look upon herself as a penitent, and to keep her habitually in humble sentiments of her misery and insufficiency. This act of humility, far from diminishing the value of her prayers and her sacrifices, will but add new value to them.

As to Penance considered as a Sacrament, it is unnecessary to refer here to its divine institution, the three parts which compose it, contrition, confession, and satisfaction, and the qualities which they should have, because no Religious is supposed to be so ignorant of the elements of Christian Doctrine. But it imports much that we entertain no illusion upon the dispositions necessary to receive with fruit this Sacrament, which is one of the marvels of Divine mercy, since through it God has given to man a power which seems incommunicable — that of pardoning the sins of a fellow-man. In frequenting this Sacrament it is equally important to preserve ourselves from an abuse too common in communities, as is signalized by great Bishops and skillful directors of souls — that of seeking in it rather the tranquility of the soul than its cure.

In effect, if frequent confession is a very holy and a very profitable practice, it can also be turned into an abuse by habit, when it degenerates into routine. We should descend into this holy piscina only to find a remedy for the maladies of our souls, new strength in order to triumph over our weakness, and an augmentation of sanctifying grace by being again bathed in the Blood of Jesus Christ. But, alas! how often we go there to seek a false peace and to calm the troubles of a conscience which God is secretly reproaching for its repeated infidelities and resistance to the inspiration of His love. Thus the tepid and negligent soul, accustoming herself to regard sacramental absolution as an infallible remedy for her spiritual infirmities, makes of it a support to maintain herself in her guilty negligences, in her dangerous attachments, for which she preserves all the affection, even while accusing herself of them. She leaves the holy Tribunal with that false peace to continue in the same way of infidelity and resistance to grace.

To understand well this disorder, and the pernicious consequences of this abuse, we must remember that if the Sacraments have an efficacy which is proper to them, because they contain a Divine virtue, their effects depend in a great measure upon the dispositions of the souls who receive them. Thus, for the Sacrament of Penance, it will not suffice to examine our conscience, to make an act of contrition, to confess our sins and to receive absolution; it is necessary that grace find hearts truly detached from sin, by a sincere repentance for it. and a firm resolution of not again falling deliberately. This is precisely what is often wanting to the souls of whom we speak, because, not having grave sins to confess and accusing themselves always of the same faults without ever correcting them, it is so much the more difficult to have true contrition, as these faults appearing so light they have more affection for them. For these souls there is, then, real danger of profaning the Sacrament, or at least of rendering it null and without effect.

It is to guard against this grave disorder that persons who ordinarily have but venial sins to confess, are counselled to add some grievous sin of their past life, because it is supposed, and with reason, that by this means the soul will have the contrition which is indispensable for the validity of the Sacrament. This is true of souls truly penitent who habitually reprehend and punish in themselves every offense against God, whether grievous or light; they have no difficulty in exciting contrition, it being the habitual disposition of their hearts. But it is not so with Religious who have little fervor, who have no zeal for their perfection, and who, being filled with sensible attachments, have no more facility in exciting sorrow for the grave sins of their past life than regret for their daily infidelities. To supply for this want of perfect contrition, they delude themselves by confessing a multitude of involuntary failings, of imperfections inseparable from human frailty, and exterior irregularities which have their place rather in a chapter of faults, because these avowals cost nothing to their self-love, while they drown in useless detail their real faults and pass lightly over the predominant fault, which is the source of all their disorders. A Carmelite, truly worthy of the name, need not fear to fall into the faults which we have just considered. Since she lives in the fear of offending God, and as she sincerely deplores the faults which escape her, and immediately imposes upon herself some expiation, she has no difficulty either in examining herself or in exciting contrition. Thus it is very justly said that a Carmelite should always be ready to go to confession, and her confessions are as simple and humble as they are short and easy. She does not charge them with useless recitals, vague accusations; she tells her faults clearly, making most prominent what is most guilty in her conduct and indicating the source of her habitual transgressions.

Examen Upon the Lecture

Have I understood that penance is a virtue essential to my profession; and that without its spirit I lose the greater part of the fruit and the merit of the practices in use in the Order of Carmel? Have I taken care to animate these works of penance with this spirit, accepting at Chapter the penances and corrections which have caused me confusion? Have I, according to my strength and with permission from my Superiors, added some particular penances to those ordained by the Rule? Have I accepted with resignation, and in the spirit of penance, the sufferings and trials, both interior and exterior, which have been sent me by Divine Providence? Instead of profiting by my examens of conscience, have I not waited until the time of Confession to enter into myself and to excite contrition for my sins and infidelities?

Note — Advice for the Following Meditation

The soul is now going to enter upon the second part of her Retreat, which corresponds to the "ILLUMINATIVE WAY." There she will be enlightened and illumined by the teachings of Jesus Christ and inflamed by the example of His virtues. But it is necessary that she examine beforehand, in the presence of

God, whether she has fulfilled well all the conditions of the First Part, which appertain to the "PURGATIVE WAY"; sufficiently excited compunction for her past sins; studied and recognized her predominant passion, her bad inclinations; and whether she has taken the most efficacious means to extirpate them from her heart. These means are prayer, vigilance and mortification. The soul should insist upon these essential points, and not allow herself to pass on to the following meditations until she has laid deep in herself a solid foundation of humility and penance.

Fourth Day

First Meditation - Imitation of Jesus Christ Necessary for a Religious Soul

"I am the way and the truth and the life." — St. John, XIV, 6.

Penetrated now, O my God, with these great truths of Faith — that Thou art my Sovereign Good, for Whom I have been created, and that Thou hast placed me in this world only to glorify Thee here, that I may possess Thee eternally hereafter — I come to beg of Thee a guide who will conduct me to Thy Heavenly Kingdom; for, alas! how can I, the degenerate child of a guilty parent, a traveler wandering in the midst of a world sown with snares and filled with enemies who seek my ruin, and finding in my own heart only inclinations to evil and to things of earth, how can I regain the path to my heavenly country, which I have lost? Behold! Thou presentest Thyself to me immediately; I hear Thy sweet voice saying: "Ye who seek heaven, come, I am the Way; ye who ask light to guide your steps, I am the true Light which enlightenest every man who cometh into the world; in fine, ye who desire to possess another heart, another life, Ah! I am the Life, the true Life." Ah! Lord, at this voice and these words, I recognize my Master, my Guide, and my Saviour, I adore Thee, O my Lord Jesus Christ!

FIRST POINT - "I Am the Way."

"He who followeth Me walketh not in darkness," sayeth the Lord, "because I am the Way, and no one can come to the Father except by Me." This admirable truth taught by our Lord Jesus Christ, that He is Himself our Way, our Guide, our Doctor, was known to the ancient people, and announced by Moses and the Prophets. "God will send you a Prophet like me, and like me taken from your nation, and you will listen to Him," said this holy Legislator to the Jewish people. And the Prophet Isaias addressed to them these solemn

59

words: 'Thine eyes shall see the Master whom God will give to instruct thee; thine ears shall hear the sweet words which He will address to thee, as, walking before thee, He will say: 'Behold the straight road, walk in it without turning to the right or to the left.'"

On the very eve of His death the Divine Master wished to recall to His disciples and to the whole Church the sweet and essential obligation of following and imitating Him, and of becoming entirely conformed to His sentiments and to His conduct. "I have given you an example," said He, "that as I have done to you, do you also." Saint Paul unceasingly recalls this precept and makes it the foundation of his sublime doctrine. "Be ye followers of me, as I also am of Christ." "Clothe yourselves with the Jesus Christ, after you have been despoiled of the old man;" and he adds that God has predestined to eternal glory "those whom He has foreseen would be conformed to Jesus Christ, and in whom He has found the image of His Son," making this, our conformity with Jesus Christ, the essential condition of our predestination.

But this conformity, this imitation, supposes a knowledge of the life, the mysteries, the doctrine and the intimate sentiments of Jesus Christ; or, rather, it is nothing else than a loving knowledge and imitation of Jesus Christ, according to the words of our Divine Saviour; "Eternal Life, O Father, consists in knowing Thee and Him whom Thou hast sent!"

In effect, we see the human race, in consequence of the sin of our first parents, plunged in the most profound darkness and sleeping in the region of the shadow of death. Not only had it lost the way to its true country, but it had lost even the remembrance of it, even the desire for it; it was then necessary to create a new way, a new communication, between heaven and earth, and this mysterious way, this chain is Jesus Christ.

It was to render this imitation more perfect, to facilitate this obligation, that the Religious Life has been instituted. Not content to conform herself to Jesus Christ by fidelity to His precepts, the Religious soul makes profession of embracing, after His Divine example, all that will raise her above the common life; that is, His obedience, His poverty, His chastity and His unreserved devotion to the glory of His Father and the salvation of souls. Aspiring to the glorious title of Spouse of Jesus Christ, she understands well that she cannot succeed in pleasing Him except in rendering herself conformable to Him by the assiduous practise of the virtues most dear to His Heart; applying to herself the very letter of these words of Saint Paul: "Jesus Christ is my life, and for me to die is gain."

O my God, how little have I considered, how little have I fulfilled until now the strict obligation which I am under of following and imitating Thee, and consequently, of knowing and of studying Thee. What I know of Thy Life and Thy Mysteries is only what I have been taught in my childhood, or what I have heard in the instructions and lectures which the Rule and the charity of the Superiors have provided for the Community. But what have I learned by my own efforts? What knowledge have I acquired of the Mysteries of Thy Infant Life, Thy Public Life, Thy Suffering Life, Thy Glorious Life? What care have I taken to meditate upon the "Law of the Lord," Thy Holy Gospel, those words so full of light, those actions all Divine, from which I should have learned so many admirable lessons? Ah! Lord, I blush at my negligence, I am penetrated with sorrow at my little zeal in studying Thy Life, and my little ardor in imitating it! Grant, that by Thy grace, it shall be so no longer! Remembering that I am Thy spouse, I shall take the greatest care to please Thee by conforming myself to Thee.

SECOND POINT - "I Am the Truth."

In order to penetrate well the sense of these admirable words of our Saviour, it is necessary to represent to ourselves the profound darkness which the sin of Adam had spread over the earth. Man, having lost the Divine light which showed him God as the Sovereign Good, sought in vain this good in the enjoyment and love of creatures, and placed his end in them, whence sprang innumerable errors and crimes; evil was called good, lying truth, and man, despising the true good, ran blindly after the shadow. He blushed not to raise altars to his own vices, which he deified, offering to them a sacrilegious incense. If some men seemed to rise above others, and to practise a certain kind of virtue, it was nearly always but a semblance — plants without root, because they ordinarily had for their principle only a more subtle and guilty pride. It was in the midst of this dense darkness that the true Light arose and shone with such sweetness upon all men coming into the world. From His first appearance at Bethlehem, Jesus Christ, Truth itself, discovered to all eyes the falsity of the goods, the pleasures and the glory of earth, by taking for His portion poverty, sufferings and humiliations. Henceforth all ideas are changed, all errors dissipated, and there are no longer any but the wilfully blind, who cannot see the folly and the vanity of earthly things.

But there are to be no bounds to the happy influence of this Truth; Jesus Christ will show in what true virtue consists, upon what principle it is supported and what motives it proposes. "The Word was made Flesh and dwelt amongst us," and "we have seen Him full of grace and Truth." He sought in all His actions, His words and His thoughts, only the glory of His Father.

Jesus is, then, not only the perfect model of all virtue, the type of all perfections — He is the principle. Saint Paul says: "Strip yourselves of the old man and put on the new, who, according to God, is created in justice, holiness and truth." "Have in you the same sentiments which are in Christ Jesus." There is, then, no other source of virtue for the Christian, and particularly for the Religious soul, than the interior of Jesus Christ. It is also the faithful mirror in which we ought to consider ourselves unceasingly, in order to discover our spiritual defects, and after having recognized them, correct them. Jesus is, according to Saint Teresa and all masters of the spiritual life, the most worthy object of our contemplation. The secret of this holy exercise consists in a great part in casting upon Him looks of love, in order to engrave in ourselves the likeness of His virtues.

My God, my Sovereign, should I not attribute my little advancement in religious perfection to the ignorance in which I have lived, until now, of the necessity there is for every Christian to imbibe Thy virtues, and to seek the principle, the grace and the practice of them in Thy Divine Heart? Yes, Lord, in Thee alone is virtue, amiable; in Thee alone, above all, is it true; and with Thee it is easy; because Thy grace sustains me by the interior look which contemplates Thee, rendering me capable of all the sacrifices which it imposes and causing me to cry out with Thy Apostle: "I can do all things in Him Who strengthens me."

THIRD POINT - "I Am the Life."

I am the Living Bread which came down from heaven; he who lives by Me shall never die." O words worthy of being received with ineffable transports of joy and thanksgiving! I can live the true life, not only that which I have in common with vile creatures, with animals and insects, but the very life of God; and I am assured that it is not within the power of any creature to deprive me of it. It is not enough, then, to imitate and to follow Jesus from afar, to have some of His sentiments, some of His virtues. We are called to live His own life; that is to say, He should dwell in us in such a manner that we abandon to the Divine Master the whole conduct of our interior; it is He Who ought to act by our hands, see with our eyes, speak through our mouths, etc. This is expressed by these words of Saint Paul: "I live now not I, but Jesus Christ liveth in me." It is toward this that all my prayers, all my Communions and all the exercises of the Life of Carmel should tend — that I live no longer my own life, but the Life of Jesus Christ, my Celestial Spouse.

Behold the whole economy of Religious perfection; behold the road which I should follow to attain it; it is to attach me to my Divine Model, to nourish me with His doctrine and example, and to live His Life. This was the art of all the Saints and their habitual study. It was in this rich mine that they found all their virtue, all their science. Ah! my God, grant me the grace during the days of my Retreat, which I am to consecrate to the meditation of the principal Mysteries of Thy Divine Life, to attach myself so strongly to the contemplation of the virtues of which Thou hast given me so many admirable examples, that they may be for the remainder of my life the principal object of my application, my study and my love.

May I understand, Lord, that I cannot be a true Carmelite, worthy of the name and of the habit which I wear, until I become filled with Thy Spirit, a faithful imitator of Thy virtues, and transformed in Thee, because it is thus that I shall be despoiled of my miserable life and live Thy Divine Life, and I may say with the Apostle: "Jesus Christ is my life." O my God, for so great an undertaking I cannot count upon myself, upon my resolutions, upon my own efforts; but permit me, Lord, to count upon Thy assistance and upon the grace of my vocation, which requires of me such perfection.

Second Meditation - Advantages and Qualities of the Imitation of Jesus Christ

"Therefore as we have borne the image of the earthly man, let us also bear the image of the heavenly."— I. Cor. XV, 49.

Since the seal of my predestination, O my Saviour, depends upon my conformity to Thy Divine Interior, I humbly come and prostrate myself at Thy feet, to supplicate Thee to make me appreciate more and more the advantages attached to the zeal which I ought to show in following Thee, imitating Thee and conforming myself to Thee in all things. Lord, teach me the secret of this science, so sublime; teach me by what means, by what way I may attain this Divine knowledge. An Angel is lost in heaven, and the first man falls in the terrestrial Paradise for having conceived, through foolish pride, the design of becoming like unto Thee. It suffices not, then, to wish to imitate Thee, O my God; it is necessary that this desire, this imitation, be inspired by Thyself, animated by motives agreeable to Thee, and clothed with the qualities required by Thy Infinite perfections.

FIRST POINT - Advantages of This Imitation

When God said in the beginning: "Let Us make man according to Our Own Image and Likeness," "He made him," says Saint Ambrose, "according to that of His Only Son, Who is the image of His substance." That image being effaced by the sin of Adam, this Son r the Eternal Word of the Father, becomes Incarnate, in order that man, by imitating Him, might re-establish in himself this first resemblance. Our beauty, our happiness, our glory are then attached to the re-imprinting in our souls the image of the Son of God. The more we approach to the Divine Original, the more right shall we have to the benevolence of our Heavenly Father, Who, perceiving in us the resemblance of His Son, will regard us with love and load us with His favors, saying, "This is an image of Him in Whom I have placed all My complacency." Can I be insensible, O Divine Father of my Lord Jesus Christ, to the signal honor, to the supreme happiness of attracting Thy regard, and of becoming an object of Thy Divine complacency? May I hasten, O my God, to efface in my soul the impure remains of "the image of the earthly man," to imprint there "the image of the heavenly man."

But it is not only the benediction and the favors of the Heavenly Father which I shall draw upon myself by the care I take to render myself conformable to His Only Son; I shall give to this Divine Son Himself an honor and glory by which He cannot fail to be touched. In effect, by my application to retrace in my soul the traits of this Divine Model, I recognize that Jesus is the pattern of the highest perfection; that all virtue and merit consist in approaching Him as nearly as possible; and that it is only by imitating Him that

63

I can render myself worthy of the great recompense which He has promised me. O my Divine Model, how I should redouble my efforts and my application to follow and to imitate Thee, since I see that i can thus render Thee some glory, and draw upon myself the most abundant graces.

We should add that the soul who is attentive in retracing in herself the life and virtues of Jesus Christ, thus gives Him the highest testimony, the most certain proof of her love, because love tends toward union, and this union, so desirable, with her Heavenly Spouse, cannot take place except by a resemblance and entire conformity to Him. By making this imitation the principal object of her attention and her efforts, she will show Him that she desires above all things to be united to Him, and to possess Him without division. How can her Saviour, Who is so sweet and so tender, be insensible to this care so attentive and this zeal so pure and so generous? Will He not accord her new and precious favors, and draw nearer to her in proportion to the efforts which she makes to unite herself to Him? Ah! Lord, inflame me with this holy ardor! "Draw me and I will run in the odor of Thy perfume!"

In fine, this assiduous care of the soul to imitate Jesus Christ attracts to her His Divine Spirit, that same Spirit Who was, in the Man-God, the principle and the source of all His actions. What would be all my efforts, my zeal in rendering myself conformable to so perfect a Model, if I did not attract within myself this same Spirit, to guide me and to aid me in this holy undertaking — this Spirit of light, of fire, of celestial unction, Who will regulate all my steps and Who will give to all my actions a value and a supernatural grace? It was by the effects of this indwelling of the Holy Spirit in their souls that the Saints, becoming other Christs, have produced such marvelous fruits of sanctity in the Church and gained so many souls to God. O Divine Spirit, create in me then, by Thy Almighty Power, a new heart, a heart like unto the very Heart of Jesus, entirely devoted to His glory.

But, O my Divine Saviour, Thou desirest this change to be the fruit of my labors, of my constant efforts; grant me then, I implore Thee, an ardent zeal, so attentive in following Thee that it may become the most pressing need of my heart. Thou hast warned me that I cannot belong to Thee unless I possess Thy Spirit, and this Spirit will not dwell in me unless I am conformed to Thee. Ah! Lord, then I shall apply myself to know Thee and to imitate Thee. Ah! Have I not cause to blush in seeing the children of the world captivated by a foolish love of creatures, or by ambition of the honors of the world; consuming themselves with cares and attentions, even to making themselves slaves of other men to satisfy their follies and their passions? And I, until now, have had no ambition to please Thee, no assiduity in paying homage to Thee, the Sovereign King and Spouse of my heart! Ah, what confusion, what regret I feel! I wish to repair my past insensibility and infidelity by a conduct the very opposite.

First — It should be affectionate: that is to say, it should have its source in the love of our Lord Jesus Christ, in a desire to please and to honor Him. Without this love for the Master, the disciples will soon weary of listening to and following Him; whereas hearts sustained by the affection they bear the one who instructs them will triumph over all difficulties inseparable from labor and study. Now I understand that the imitation of Jesus Christ is a science, which, like other sciences, can be acquired only by study. This study in the beginning, requires more effort on the part of the disciple^ because ordinarily love is then more weak and imperfect; but in proportion, as he advances in the knowledge of his Model and the contemplation of His adorable traits, his love becomes inflamed, his desires increase, his zeal is enkindled, and he applies each day with a new and greater ardor to conform himself to and be more closely united with Him.

Ah! I recognize, my Divine Redeemer, that my little care and application in contemplating Thy life, and in imitating Thy virtues, come from the weakness and imperfection of my love; but to-day I understand fully, the obligation which a Christian, and much more a Religious, is under of living a life entirely conformable to Thine. I wish to delay no longer this holy undertaking; may I be sustained by Thy grace and fortified by the hope of finding thus the source of true love.

Second — This imitation ought to be attentive, assiduous and persevering. It ought not to be superficially and at intervals, that the Religious soul should study the Divine Model and unite herself to His dispositions; she should do so with continual care, applying herself to enter into the views, sentiments and the intentions of Jesus Christ, keeping Him ever present in the centre of her heart. Thus will her union with her Divine Spouse become easy and constant.

This habitual application to unite ourselves to Jesus Christ is a good little relished, and appears very difficult; nevertheless it is the essence of the perfection of Carmel. Indeed, the true perfection of man is not in the beauty of his body, neither is it in the regularity of his features, but in his interior — in his soul; it depends upon the purity and sanctity of his disposition, according to this sentence of Scripture: "All the beauty of the King's daughter is within." The Holy Spirit says, "All," not a part, to make us understand that all the perfection of our actions depends upon the motive which produces them and the spirit by which they are animated. Now, as all the actions, thoughts and words of Jesus Christ have been animated by the most perfect motives, our continual care ought to be to get rid of the low, base, mercenary manner in which we generally speak and act, to enter into the dispositions of the Holy One, Who lives in us. Alas! O my Jesus, perfect Mirror of pure souls, to dispense myself from this holy obligation I offer the excuse of the inconstancy of my will, the levity of my mind and my many occupations; but I ought, rather, to acknowledge my tepidity, my little zeal for my own advancement, and my little attention in observing the holy practices of recollection, of silence, especially interior silence, and of abnegation. Ah! may it be so no longer.

Third — This imitation ought to be universal, that is to say, it should extend to the interior as well as to the exterior, embrace all the actions of my life, extend to all my occupations and to all my relations with God and with my neighbor. This union with the interior dispositions of Jesus is necessary in my Religious duties — the Holy Sacrifice of the Mass, prayer, recitation of the Divine Office, that they may become efficacious and truly worthy of the One to Whom they are offered; in my different relations with my Superiors and Sisters, in order to become penetrated with that respect which my Divine Model had for those invested with authority, and that charity which embraced all men, particularly those by whom He was surrounded; before and during work, rest, sleep and meals, in order to purify by the motives so pure, so noble, which animated the Divine Master, that which is vicious or too natural in mine. It suffices not that this conformity with Jesus be in the interior only; the imitation of the Divine Model should extend also to the exterior. If the disciples of those pretended sages of antiquity carried their docility to the teachings of their masters, even to servile imitation of their gestures, and their unworthy and even ridiculous manners, how comes it that I, who recognize in my adorable Saviour the most beautiful among the children of men, do not force myself to resemble Him, since this great honor is permitted me? The Holy Gospel and tradition show Him to me full of meekness and of grace in all His movements. His walk, His features, the modesty of His eyes, the tone of His voice — all in Him was admirable, and is worthy of being imitated, yet I do not conform myself to Him interiorly or exteriorly — I, whom He designs to call His Spouse, and who make profession of living only for Him!

O my God, all this appears difficult to me, this care and application are fatiguing. Ah! it is because I am loveless. But I feel the need of loving Thee, O my God! Therefore, I wish to unite myself to Thee, and it is this great favor which I supplicate Thee to grant me in this Retreat — that powerful and victorious grace which will raise me above myself, and make me undertake the most difficult things in order to attain to the perfection of Thy love.

Third Meditation - The Reign of Jesus Christ

"I have been established King upon the Mountain of Sion, there to publish His holy Law."— Ps. II, 6.

I adore Thee, O true King of the Heavenly Sion, Whose reign shall have no end. I am one of Thy conquests, because my soul is the price of Thy Precious Blood. And now, generous Conqueror, Thou hast called me to share Thy eternal reign; but to merit this priceless favor it is necessary that in this life I succeed in establishing in my soul the reign of Thy grace. Thou requirest more, because of the holy state which I profess — because, not content with establishing Thy reign in my heart, Thou wishest that I labor to establish it in the hearts of all men; Thou desirest that I identify my interests with Thine, and, filled with zeal for Thy glory, I contribute by my prayers, works and sacrifices to the destruction of the empire of Satan, and to the extension of Thine. Grant me the grace, O my Saviour, to enter thus into the particular spirit of my vocation.

FIRST POINT - Jesus Christ Is Our King

The Son of God, in becoming man, is destined by His Eternal Father to become the King of a new people. But this people being still struck with anathema, and groaning under the slavery of the Prince of Darkness, it was necessary that, before reigning over them, He should deliver them from this anathema by paying the debt which they owed to Divine Justice and by triumphing over the infernal powers. This admirable work He has accomplished by His Cross upon Calvary; this brilliant victory He has gained by His death. Man has been reclaimed and the demon overcome.

But the number of this people will not be complete, nor the Kingdom of Jesus Christ solemnly established, until the Last Day, when His Heavenly Father, after "having put all His enemies under His feet, shall establish Him King over the Mountain of Sion" — the Holy Nation which shall form the Church Triumphant. This Heavenly Jerusalem is then to be built slowly as a city, that is by the people, who will form it, little by little, in the course of centuries, from the militant Church — the souls who have chosen Jesus for their King and have established His reign in themselves. This truth is conformed to these words of Saint Paul: "Your life is hidden with Christ in God," and "When Jesus Christ, your life, shall appear on the Last Day, you shall appear with Him in glory." This Divine Redeemer, after having consummated His victory upon the Cross, has charged His faithful servants, who are filled with His Spirit, to go forth throughout the whole world, to gather its precious fruits, and to establish His reign in souls. Such have been the Apostles, the Martyrs, the Doctors; such also are Apostolic men, Religious Orders, holy virgins — the first have established the reign of Jesus Christ by their blood, the others by their preaching and their doctrine, while the greater number do so by their prayers and perpetual self-immolation.

Among these privileged souls shine in the first rank "the children of Elias." Heirs of the zeal of the Holy Prophet, the Solitaries of Carmel have for their peculiar mission, to contribute by their prayers and penances to the extension of the reign of Jesus Christ in souls, to the triumph of the Church in her combats against heresy and schism, to the conversion of sinners, the sanctification of the just — in a word, to preserve to the utmost of their power all the interests of God. It was this zeal which burned so brightly in Saint Teresa, their Mother, and which she has left them as the principal spirit of the Reform which she established.

I will now represent to myself, in order to reanimate in me the spirit of my holy vocation, the King of Heaven, Jesus, going through the whole world, seeking and gathering among faithful souls those who are more particularly filled with true zeal for His glory and devotion to His interests. He requires that they be profoundly touched by the ever-increasing progress of sin and impiety, and give themselves to Him without reserve, to gain new subjects for His empire, snatching them from the cruel captivity of Satan^ He Wishes that they sacrifice without hesitation, in this glorious enterprise, all the pretensions of the world, their own interests, their liberty, their goods, and if necessary their reputation, their health, and even their life. He walks at their head, He has received the first blows on His Sacred Person; and during a life of thirty-three years He embraced and suffered courageously poverty, contempt, persecutions and opprobrium, and finally crowned His labors by a most cruel death. But in dying He has overcome death, and promises to those who are generous enough to pursue the course of His conquests that their combats shall be short, their victory certain, and their recompense eternal.

O Divine King of the Elect! I have heard Thy invitation; I have responded to Thy appeal. Behold me! now ranged under Thy banner, to undertake this holy enterprise and to offer some reparation to Thy Divine Heart, so pressed by zeal for the glory of Thy Father and the salvation of souls. I belong to Thee, since I combat under the standard of Mary, Thy Mother. It is to serve Thy cause, to immolate ourselves to Thy glory, that she has united us around her, and imposed upon us this law of love toward God and our brethren — carried even to the sacrifice of all our interests and all human affections.

But, alas! how poorly have I understood, how little have I appreciated until now the happiness of my holy state! My laxity, my indifference, and my resistance contrast sadly with the fervor and courage which so holy and noble a vocation demands; that fervor and courage which have so brilliantly distinguished the Holy Reformatrix of Carmel and animated so great a number of her worthy children! O King of my heart, henceforth, with Thy grace, I will walk in their footsteps!

SECOND POINT - On What Conditions?

Consider then, O Religious soul! O Daughter of Carmel! O servant of Mary! the conditions offered you to co-operate in the great enterprise of this Immortal King, Who calls you to follow in His suite. It suffices to bring to mind the means by which He Himself overcame the world and the devil, and by which he taught His disciples to conquer. It was by poverty, abnegation, contempt of honors, and the esteem of creatures, by sufferings, humiliation, crucifixion, and death. Hence only those souls who by these means live the life of Jesus Christ merit to become truly His followers and instruments in extending His Kingdom.

Jesus Christ wills not to be served by you in this enterprise in the same manner as He was served by the apostles, martyrs and doctors; He will not ask you to contribute to it by the shedding of your blood, by your words or by your writings; but He expects from you a concurrence which may be even more efficacious — that of prayer and self-immolation. You can labor with apostolic zeal, and address continual supplications toward the Holy Mountains to call down upon the militant Church that succor so necessary for it. You can be a secret martyr of charity by sacrificing nature to the requirements of grace. You can, by your silence, recollection, your spirit of mortification, and continual example of all Religious virtues, offer to the community in which you live a living sermon that will powerfully contribute to the advancement of the reign of God in the souls of your companions and through them, in those of the entire world.

But to attain this end, it is necessary that, first, you completely establish in your own soul the reign of Jesus Christ — that you be so filled with His Spirit as to love only what He loves, hate only what He hates, and seek only what He sought. It is not in your mind only that His law and His maxims should be found, but especially in your heart and in your whole life; it is necessary, in a word, that Jesus speaks, acts and lives in you. This is the Reign of Jesus Christ. You will in this way be the instrument of the prayer of Jesus, of His sacrifice, of His immolation, and you will draw down upon His Church the most abundant benedictions.

Now the means of arriving at an end so desirable are those of which the method is offered you in the last part of the Retreat. You will contemplate the Mysteries of the Infancy, the Hidden Life, the Public Life, the Suffering and the Glorious Life of Jesus, and participate each day with affection in the virtue and the graces which spring out on all sides from this Divine Source: insensibly the Life of Jesus will be formed in you; you will become another Christ, and you can say with the Apostle: "I live now, not I, it is Christ Who lives in me."

O my Divine King, how little have I followed this way so well-trodden by Thy Saints, which would have conducted me to the perfection of my state, to the summit of Carmel! I had Thee ever near me, and I needed but to cast my eyes upon Thee. Thou wert ever watching at the door of my heart, ready to enter to establish Thy Reign, and to make me live Thy life, and I cared not to call upon Thee. I have expected everything from my own labor and efforts, and behold why I "have worked all night and taken nothing." O my Saviour, I will henceforth listen to Thee, my Divine Teacher, for "Thou hast the words of Eternal Life."

LECTURE - Prayer

Prayer, as we have already remarked, is in one sense the end of the Order of Carmel, since it is particularly by this divine exercise that the soul who fixes her dwelling upon the Holy Mountain ought to raise herself, even to the Divine union. It follows from this, that prayer is also the great means which will enable this soul to attain the perfection of her sublime state. It is then sovereignly important not only that a Carmelite makes her meditations, employing in this holy exercise the time prescribed by her rule; but she should strive to become a soul of prayer, that she may be to the Church an instrument of prayer, like one of those golden censers spoken of in the Apocalypse which, being swung unceasingly by the hands of Angels, sent forth continually the incense of prayer consumed by the fire of charity. Such, according to the order of Divine Providence, should a Carmelite be: such is the function which she is called upon to fulfill. Saint Paul teaches us that all the faithful should be as members of one same body, and although they have different functions, all are necessary and contribute by their diversity to the beauty of the body. If then in the Church there are active members who represent its hands and feet; if others charged with the duty of teaching doctrine are as its mouth; and if there are others in fine to guard and watch over it as its eyes; what shall we say of those hidden souls who constitute the most intimate part of this mystic body, who speak not, nor act exteriorly, but who are charged to pay to God in silence and adoration a tribute of unceasing love, supplication and thanksgiving? Should not these latter be considered as the heart of the Church? Now, it is to the contemplative Orders, and to Carmel in particular, that these sublime functions belong. However, Jesus Christ alone is the prayer and the victim of the Church, and our prayers and immolations draw ail their value from His, our prayers and our sacrifices have value only when united to this Divine Mediator, and they will be profitable to the Church in proportion as this union is more or less perfect. Let us then conclude that a Carmelite, who wishes to attain the end of her vocation and to accomplish what the Church expects of her, should strive to become a soul of prayer, and to work without ceasing to render herself conformable to Jesus Christ, and to have one same Spirit with Him.

The tribute of prayer which she ought to offer each day is divided by the Constitutions into two parts: Vocal Prayer or Recitation of the Divine Office and Mental Prayer or Meditation. We shall treat of each separately. In the advice which preceded this Retreat, we have given an abridged method of this meditation; and as it is also treated of at length elsewhere (in the Direction of Novices), we shall not repeat it here. We shall content ourselves with simply recalling the obligation of each Religious to understand this method well, and to prepare each day the subject upon which she is to meditate, either by reading or making use for this purpose of the knowledge which she has already acquired of the Mysteries, or the virtues of our Saviour, or of some truth of Religion. She will put herself in the Presence of God, humble herself before Him, excite sorrow for her sins, and implore the light of the Holy Spirit.

But what is essential to repeat here, as it is the principal part and the most important point of prayer, is that we should always terminate by lively and efficacious petitions. It is not lightly, briefly and by routine that we should acquit ourselves of this duty, but it is necessary to stop and reflect deeply upon the requests by which we conclude our meditations. Why should we reflect and make considerations? It is to move the will by the sight of the great truths which we are examining, our particular needs and the virtues which correspond to them. The first effect of these salutary impressions ought to be to draw forth our sighs, to express our regret and to expose our miseries and our wounds, as did the blind man on the road to Jericho, who, hearing that Jesus was passing by, began to cry with all his strength: "Jesus, Son of David, have pity on me!" Jesus, touched by these penetrating cries, asked, with sweetness, what he wished. He replied with great fervor: "Lord, that I might see." There are a great many persons who neither advance in prayer nor make any progress in virtue, because they do not reiterate and insist enough upon the pressing petitions by which they terminate their prayers, employing in this exercise only a few short moments, while lively and persevering prayer addressed to God for the cure of their defects, the acquisition of some virtue, or a grace for salvation, is always followed by its effects, because Jesus Christ has said so.

Although each Religious should keep to the ordinary method of prayer and not force herself into the more elevated ways without a special attraction of grace, submitting herself in this to the judgment of those who guide her and who know her well; at the same time it is important for her to know that by simple fidelity to the Rules of her Institute, above all by the practise of recollection and by the spirit of solitude and universal abnegation, as has been said elsewhere, she will infallibly arrive, and even in a short time, at contemplation.

We must not attach to this word contemplation the idea of something extraordinary, for it is or should be ordinary to the Religious of Carmel. It is not a question of visions, ecstasies, ravishments and other states more to be feared than desired for, besides the fact that these singular gifts are not virtues, they can draw into grave illusions those souls who are not humble and well directed. By contemplation we here understand "a view of God and the things of Faith, of the Mysteries of the Life and Death of Jesus Christ — a simple, free, penetrating and certain view, which proceeds from love and tends to love." In this kind of prayer the mind reasons not, the acts of the will are almost imperceptible, and the soul, in a manner simple, clear, evident and certain, embraces and penetrates the supernatural objects which she contemplates; she touches and in some sort nourishes herself with them, by making them the object and the food of her love; thus she draws greater profit from a few hours of such prayer than in many years of ordinary meditation.

But as this prayer is altogether supernatural and a pure gift of God, it is necessary that the soul, in order to be capable of it, should be free from the least deliberate sins, from disorderly affections, from eagerness, and from useless cares and inquietude: because with these defects she, like a bird having its feet tied, makes useless efforts to fly upward. The Prophet longed for this divine flight of contemplation when he said: "Who will give me the wings of a dove, that I might fly away and be at rest in the bosom of my God?" Contemplation is, then, only a single glance of the soul who habitually walks in

71

the presence of God and who sees Him alone in all creatures; it is the simple and direct flight of the dove toward the only object of her love. It is easy to recognize, if we examine them attentively, that the prescriptions of the Rule of Carmel, with all that they require of abnegation, of death, of recollection, of silence, of mortification, have for their end the rendering a soul capable of this grace.

Whence comes it that there are so few souls, even in Carmel, who enjoy this light of contemplation, and so many to be found in the ways of imperfection, with inclinations and tastes all human and natural? The pious Author of the Imitation gives the reason: "Unless a man be at liberty from all things created, he cannot freely attend to things divine. This is the reason why there are found so few contemplative persons; because so few wholly sequester themselves from transitory and created things. A man ought therefore to pass and ascend above every thing created, and perfectly to forsake himself, and in ecstasy of mind to stand and see that no creature can be compared to Thee, because Thou infinitely transcendest them all."

Nature suffers and groans at this restraint, it is true. What! not one look, not one preoccupation, not one useless remembrance! What! to check without ceasing curiosity, preoccupation, levity, the desire of speaking, of questioning what passes before us — what is done, what is said! Courage, with perseverance, prayer and frequent turning to God, we shall not have to wait long to obtain from Him this mortification and recollection in which we shall very soon find our delight, and the soul will then have only disgust for all that hitherto occupied it. When we neglect in the beginning of our Religious life to contract these holy habits, the soul never being made to submit to the yoke of mortification, but trained in the sad path of imperfection, will hide under the holy habit of Carmel a heart all sensual and human. The prayers of such an unfaithful soul will be filled with distractions and disgust. Far from finding in them a powerful support, which will sweeten her labors and aid her in bearing the yoke of the Rule, she will experience only weariness, and these prayers themselves will be but a burden added to the other observances.

As for the rest, the whole life of a Carmelite should be but a remote preparation for prayer. This is why she should acquit herself of her duties with an interior spirit, because by never entirely going out of herself, she will have, as the Author of the Imitation says of an interior man, "no trouble in finding herself always ready to converse with God"; or rather, this Divine conversation will never cease for her, as we can say without the least fear of exaggeration, that the life of a Carmelite ought to be a perpetual contemplation. Now, contemplation being nothing more than a simple glance, free and penetrating, toward God, can a Religious who has left all things, who has bid an eternal adieu to the world, have any other pretention than the good pleasure of the One whom she is seeking in solitude? Is it not in His presence that she walks, that she works, prays and keeps silence; that she takes her nourishment and repose? With a little attention and fidelity to grace, disembarrassed as she is of all earthly cares, can it be difficult for her to put in practise the precept of the Apostle: "Whatsoever you do, whether you eat or drink, do all for the glory of God and in the name of our Lord Jesus Christ?" It can then be only by continual infidelity, that is by a voluntary neglect of all the practices and the spirit of her holy state, that she can render herself unworthy to obtain from God the gift of prayer (which is the particular gift of her vocation), and thus remain deprived of the virtues and the graces which she ought to acquire by this means.

It is then very important that she examine herself during this Retreat upon the following points:

Examen

Have I not neglected to instruct myself in the method of Mental Prayer, or forgotten that which I have been taught?

Is it not in consequence of this that I do not know how to put myself in the presence of God, by first annihilating myself, recognizing myself as altogether unworthy to appear before His Infinite Majesty, humbly begging pardon for my sins, and regarding myself as the most vile of His creatures?

Have I taken care to consider that I am incapable of even a good thought, and begged the light of the Holy Spirit?

Have I, then, serious reflected upon the mystery or the truth given as the subject of my prayer, and made the application to myself, recognizing how far removed I was from the model or the virtue proposed in my meditation, producing from these considerations sentiments of sorrow and confusion at the sight of my faults, and exciting a lively desire for the perfection of the object whose beauty I have admired? Have I especially insisted upon the last part of my prayer, 'devoting at least a quarter of the time allowed to beg of Our Lord, of the Holy Virgin, or my patron Saints, with great fervor and earnestness, the object of my supplications — such as the acquisition of some virtue or the extirpation of some vice?

Have I added to these, loving colloquies and fervent prayers for the Church and for souls? Above all, have I taken practical and particular resolutions, trusting in the mercy of God to accomplish them?

Have I understood well that the success of Mental Prayer depends particularly upon the remote preparation, that is to say, the habitual and assiduous care to recollect myself and to mortify my senses?

Is it not because I allow myself to be dissipated exteriorly and interiorly, and have but little regard for my rules of silence, recollection and mortification, that I am assailed during my meditations with thoughts, useless and foreign to this holy exercise? When I have been tried by spiritual dryness or interior desolation, instead of submitting myself to the Divine pleasure, and to this crucifixion, willingly making of prayer a most profitable exercise of abnegation and renouncement, and taking occasion to humble myself as being justly chastised, have I not abandoned myself to discouragement and sadness, not reflecting that such dispositions are but, the fruit of my self-love which I ought to reject?

In fine, have I had a great desire to obtain from God the gift of prayer, and particularly the light of contemplation, which is truly the precious pearl of the Gospel, given in Carmel to purchase heaven? Have I for this end made use of continual mortification of my sense, profound recollection, fervent aspirations and familiar conversation interiorly with Our Lord Jesus Christ, the Blessed Virgin and the Saints?

Fifth Day

First Meditation - Love and Devotedness of Jesus Christ in the Mystery of the Incarnation

"And the word was made flesh, and dwelt among us." — St. John 1—14.
"God so loved the world as to give His Only Begotten Son."— St. John III— 16.

I adore Thee, O my God, the Father of Our Lord Jesus Christ! I am ravished with admiration, thanksgiving and love in contemplating the infinite charity which Thou hast shown in giving us Thy Only Son, in order that, believing in Him, we might not perish, but on the contrary acquire Eternal Life. This inestimable gift has, so to speak, exhausted all Thy power, because Thou couldst not give us anything greater or more excellent; and it has also put us under an impossibility of thanking Thee otherwise than by returning it to Thee, giving back the One Whom Thou hast given with so much munificence, and ourselves with Him. This is what I pretend to do to-day, O my God, infinitely amiable; give me the grace to enter so entirely into this mystery of love that I can no longer refrain from loving Thee without division, and from giving myself to Thee without reservation.

FIRST POINT - A Mystery of Love

God could have treated guilty man as He treated the rebellious Angels; but by a judgment as impenetrable as it is adorable, while He made Angelic nature, thus debased, the object of His justice, He made human nature the object of His mercy, by drawing it out of the abyss into which it had fallen through its own fault. "This rehabilitation of man is more admirable than His creation," and the means which God has employed are so marvelous, that "so far as the heavens are removed from the earth, are His thoughts above our thoughts, and His ways above our ways."

When God, after having created the world, wished to form man, He said: "Let Us make man." The Three Persons of the Holy Trinity take counsel for a work of so much importance, for there is question of the creation of the King of the Universe, of the one, who in the name of all other creatures, ought to render to the Creator the just tribute of their gratitude, their adoration and their love. And when man, imitating the revolt of the Angel of Darkness, was ensnared in his ruin, God, notwithstanding the greatness of his fault and the blackness of his ingratitude, resolved to extend to him a helping hand. The Adorable Trinity again take counsel; the Son offers Himself to the Eternal Father to be given to man; the Father consents to make the gift of His Only Son; the Holy Spirit applies to this work the seal of His love, and the decree of the Incarnation is decided. O Work of Love by excellence — not only because it is made by the One Who is Charity itself, but because its fruits, its effects should fill man with glory and happiness, and oblige him to pay to God all the love of which he is capable! Without speaking of the glory which this work renders to God by reconciling His justice and His mercy (since mercy in the person of His Son is charged to offer to justice a superabundant satisfaction), let us consider here, this Masterpiece of God's love, only in relation to the advantages which it procures us.

The Son of God becomes man; He is made a child of Adam to the end that man might become God, or according to the language of Saint John, "in order that man may not only be called the child of God, but that he may be so in effect." "The Word was made Flesh," in order that, as our souls had become fleshy in consequence of original sin, our flesh in turn might become spiritual by its union with the Word made Flesh. Man was lost by wishing to be like to God, and now God has come to resemble man, in order that we may not only, without crime, wish to be like to Him, but that our highest merit and greatest perfection might consist in our conformity to this Word of Life. Thus the Son of God makes use of human nature, with which He clothed Himself as with a garment, to attract us to Himself "by the cords of Adam" (as He has said by the mouth of His Prophet, Osee), that is, by the charms of His Humanity. Like a shepherd who clothes himself in sheepskin that he may be better followed by his flock, He wishes that, in following Him under this exterior accommodation to our weakness, the path of perfection would seem less rough, and the virtues personified in Him appear more amiable and easy. In fine, He wished to destroy that fear which He knew man, so weak and sinful, would have in approaching His Divine Majesty, that fear which made the Jews tremble at the foot of Mount Sinai and say: "Let Moses speak to us, but let not the Lord speak."

"Great," says Saint Paul, "is the mystery of godliness which was manifested in the flesh, was justified in the spirit, appeared unto Angels, hath been preached unto the gentiles, is believed in the world, is taken up in glory."

But this Mystery of the Incarnation is more a Mystery of charity than a Mystery of glory, and if it merits our admiration, it merits still more our love. "Consider," says Saint John, "what manner of charity the Father has shown us in willing that we should not only be called the sons of God, but should be so truly." "For my beloved," continues the Apostle of love, "we are now the sons of God, but the affiliation shall appear one day when we shall see Him as He is." Ah! who would not be ravished with admiration when Jesus Christ Himself experienced this sentiment, and in a transport of love exclaims: "God so loved the world as to give," not His servant, not one of the princes of His court, but "His Only Begotten Son," and with Him He has given us all things!

And it is not a loan; He made man a perfect gift, entire and irrevocable. He is made man's own. Man can clothe himself with Him as with a vesture, he can nourish himself with Him as with a food of immortality; not only can he put Him as a seal upon his heart, and upon his arm, but he can change himself, he can transform himself into God and, presenting himself to the Father, he becomes also the object of His eternal complacency.

O Jesus, Word Incarnate, the Man-God, my Celestial Spouse, by what thanksgiving, by what praise can I acknowledge the charity of Thy Father, Who has given Thee to me, and Thy own ineffable love, which has made Thee enter into His designs by putting Thy Adorable Self at my disposition? Ah! I understand, Lord, that the only means I have of acknowledging this work of love is by applying to myself its precious fruits. Thou art clothed in my flesh that I might acquire Thy Spirit. Thou hast given Thyself to me in order that I might give myself entirely to Thee. Thou art made the Son of man, that I might become the child of God.

Ah! my most amiable Redeemer, all the glory, the advantages and the happiness are on my side. And notwithstanding this, how little have I tasted of its sweetness, how little have I appreciated this inestimable gift of Thy love! I am so much the more guilty, so much the more filled with confusion at the thought that one of the principal objects of my vocation to Carmel was to honor Thy Incarnation, and to extend in myself its marvelous fruits, by retracing in my own person Thy life of prayer, of annihilation, of immolation — causing Thee, by the crucifixion of my flesh, and the union of my spirit with Thine, to become Incarnate anew in me. Alas! I am far from this happy state! O Incarnate God! inflame me with Thy love. Put me as a seal upon Thy Heart, in order to soften the hardness and coldness of mine, "for love is strong as death."

SECOND POINT - A Mystery of Devotedness

On the part of the Word made Flesh, the Incarnation is a work of devotedness by excellence — for the glory of God, for the salvation of man. Saint Paul refers to this sublime act of the Son of God entering into the world and announcing Himself by these words so clear, and expressed before by the mouth of His Prophet: "Sacrifices and oblations Thou wouldst not; but a body Thou hast fitted to me. Holocaust and victims for sin did not please thee. Then said I: 'Behold! I come.' In the head of the book it is written of me that I should do Thy will, O my God." "Thy Law is engraved in the depths of my heart."

Behold, then, this grand act of devotion by which Jesus Christ substitutes His Sacred Humanity for all the victims of the Ancient Law. He declares that He belongs not to Himself; but that He is the Lamb of God destined to be sacrificed, to satisfy the Divine Justice, at the same time that He gives Himself to the human race, of which He constitutes Himself the Servant and the Victim. In the accomplishment of this work, He submits Himself without reserve to all that the Eternal Wisdom of His Father has appointed. What devotedness contained in this single act! It supposes not only the sacrifice of the entire will of the Son to His Father's good pleasure, but the sacrifice of all His particular views, however perfect they may be; the sacrifice of His judgment, His desires, His hopes. The first use which the Incarnate Word made of His faculties was to consecrate them, to immolate them in the service of His Father, for the salvation of the world. And such should be the first thought, the first desire, the first duty of a soul prevented by grace and enlightened by divine light — to devote herself, to cry to God from the depth of her heart, with Jesus: "Behold, I come to do Thy Will," and with Mary: "Behold the handmaid of the Lord, be it done unto me according to Thy Word." This shows clearly that devotedness to the interest of God to which are linked necessarily the true interest of man, the salvation of souls, the reign of grace in all hearts, is contained in that act of sovereign love to which all Christians are obliged; for there is no love without devotedness. "We cannot render worship to God," says Saint Augustine, "otherwise than by love, and it is evident that we do not love Him if we are not devoted to Him."

To think of one's salvation in view of one's own interest, to fear hell and to desire heaven in order to insure one's own happiness, is a good disposition, but not a very perfect one: this is to be devoted to self rather than to God. Although the interest of God does not exclude this, it should hold the second rank, while His interests ought to hold the first. We should seek the glory of God in the care which we take of the salvation and sanctification of our own soul, but if, until now, we have made so little progress in virtue, it is perhaps because the zeal which we have for our perfection is debased by the view of our own interest and our own glory; we labor at it through the effects of a certain ardor of character, an activity all too natural, which we throw into all our undertakings, while we tend not to God in a manner sufficiently pure and disinterested.

Alas! this pure devotion is very rare in the world among Christians, even the most pious. Engaged as they are in the interests of the world, they think that they do enough for those of heaven when they do not neglect them. Nevertheless, they ought to remember that the devotion of which they have made profession is nothing else than devotion to the interests of God. But this unreserved devotedness should be appreciated and practised by Religious souls. What a subject of astonishment and sorrow if it be not found in them! What, above all, in those who belong to the Order of Carmel, if their piety does not extend beyond the narrow and mercenary views which, perhaps, might suffice for other souls, but which are too far from the spirit of sacrifice, from the forgetfulness of themselves and their own interests; in a word, from that entire devotedness to God and souls which is their fundamental spirit. It was that of their Holy Mother, Saint Teresa; it was the end of her Reform, of her numerous foundations, and of all her labors; this spirit of devotedness breathes in all her writings, and accompanied her even to her last sigh.

As the Prophet Eliseus begged of his father, Saint Elias, his double spirit, I ask of my Holy Mother the gift of her's, which will make me say unceasingly: "To Thee, O my Sovereign Lord, be all honor and glory, and to me confusion and contempt." I will contemplate my Divine Redeemer, the only worthy Adorer of the Eternal Father, the only One who knows and comprehends His infinite grandeur, Who has counted as nothing all the labors of His life, all the humiliations and sufferings of His death, in order to glorify His Father, to conquer souls made to His own image and likeness, not thinking them too dearly purchased at the price of all His Blood. Ah! Lord, Thy sentiments and Thy conduct show forth all that which is low, egotistical and mean in mine; if I examine the secret motives of my actions, I will find very few are not actuated by the seeking of self or creatures, yet, Lord, Thou hast made all things for Thyself and for Thy glory, which is just and could not be otherwise; since, being the only source of all good, all glory must redound to Thee. Unhappy the creature who deprives Thee of any part of it, by seeking its own satisfaction, praise or anything else before Thee: it is unfaithful to Thy pure love. Ah! Lord, make me understand that Thou art all, and that I ought to have no other ambition than to add by my labors, my efforts and my sacrifices some rays to Thy exterior glory. Make me feel a spark of that pure zeal by which Thou wert devoured for the glory of Thy Father's interests, which never permitted Thee for one instant of Thy life to seek Thy own satisfaction in anything, but only the extension and glory of the Reign of Thy Heavenly Father.

Associate me, all unworthy as I am, to Thy life of devotedness, for the salvation of souls, with Mary, Thy Immaculate Mother, and with Teresa, Thy heroic spouse, that following their example in time I may merit to share their glory in eternity. Amen.

Second Meditation - Annihilation of Jesus Christ in the Incarnation

"I am nothingness in thy sight."— Ps. XXXVIII, 6.
"He emptied Himself, taking the form of a servant."— Philip, II, 7.

I adore Thee profoundly, O Eternal Word, annihilated in the virginal womb of Mary. Thou art truly a hidden God. What, Thou art the Light of the World, and hidest Thyself thus from the gaze of men! Thou comest to save them, they await Thee; Thou art eager to manifest Thyself to them and they ignore

Thee, yet Thou wouldst remain in the midst of them; Thou dost hide Thyself in profound obscurity and this obscurity will envelop the greater portion of Thy Life upon earth. What a subject of astonishment, what a mystery! Ah! may I become well penetrated with it from this day. Make me understand the important lessons which I receive from Thee at the first instant of Thy Incarnation. Give me a proper knowledge of Thy annihilation, which ought to be the first act of a creature: to humble itself, to annihilate itself, to confess itself unworthy of any favor, and incapable of any good without the help of grace.

FIRST POINT - Jesus Annihilated

The Apostle Saint Paul, and after him Saint John, wishing to speak of the prodigious abasement of the Son of God in the Incarnation, and not finding, in human language, words to express the infinite distance which there is between the divinity and the humanity, employ expressions evidently exaggerated or improper, the first saying that He annihilated Himself, and the second that He was made flesh when, in effect, God cannot possibly reduce Himself to nothingness, nor cease to be God, even when He clothed Himself in our humanity. But the Holy Spirit, in suggesting such expressions, wished to strike us, to touch us by the consideration of this astounding annihilation, and to make us draw from it the salutary fruit of humility.

The Son of God, the Eternal Word, by Whom all things in heaven and on earth are made, lowered Himself so far as to rank Himself among His creatures. He is made man, man poor and suffering, a son of sinful Adam; and, afterwards, He speaks of Himself as the Son of Man, recalling to us by this title so dear to Him, and so familiar to us, how much His love for us has debased Him. From the first moment of His existence in the womb of Mary, He seems to take pleasure in repeating to His Heavenly Father: "I am become as nothing before Thee." Who can understand the sentiments of humility with which the Holy Soul of Our Saviour was animated, and the ineffable acts of this virtue which He offered to God. Our minds, so naturally proud, can hardly comprehend that humility could be found in Jesus Christ, or at least, that this humility was real, after all that faith teaches us concerning the interior riches, graces, virtues and grand perfections with which the holy Humanity was ornamented and ennobled without the least mixture of imperfection, without any possibility of sin. Notwithstanding this, the humility of the Man-God was perfect, and established upon foundations the most solid and true. Without doubt, Jesus Christ was not ignorant that His Soul was enriched with all the treasures of science and wisdom, filled with all the gifts of grace; but he understood that His Humanity drew all its glory from a personal union with the Eternal Word. And it was precisely this knowledge which furnished motives of humility the most profound and the most perfect that ever has been or ever can be; it was in this that He found the subject of that act of annihilation, by which He rendered to God a glory so great.

Scarcely entered into the world, this Divine Redeemer was pleased to rec-

79

ognize that the predestination of His Humanity to the Divine Union was purely gratuitous, without any preceding merit on its part, and that all the treasures of nature and of grace, with which it had been gifted, were but the outcome of this vocation, admitting that in quality of man, He was only a creature called forth from nothingness, like all creatures, and that the glory of His existence with all the wonders attached to it, ought to be referred entirely to the Creator. It would be necessary to have another intelligence, but not a human intelligence, another tongue, not human, to understand and to relate the profound abasements, the prodigious acts of His holy soul, comprehending in the single glance of His contemplation the Being of God and the nothingness of the creature. Behold in what His humility consisted, because humility is truth.

After Jesus, the most humble, the most annihilated of beings is Mary, His Holy Mother. While, according to the testimony of Jesus Christ Himself, the rebel Angel was cursed and precipitated from heaven because he had not remained in the truth that God is all and man is nothing, Mary, on the contrary, remained so fervently attached to her nothingness that God filled her with His grace and raised her to Himself.

O my God, teach me that admirable science of humility which exercises so irresistible an empire over Thee. Teach me the secret of that annihilation which obliges Thee, so to speak, to abase Thyself to the soul which produces such an act, while Thou dost resist the proud. O my Divine Jesus, it is in Thy Sacred Heart, so humble, that I must seek this fundamental virtue; there Thou wilt teach me how to annihilate myself before God, particularly when I come into His presence for prayer. There, also, I shall learn to abase myself before all creatures at the sight of my sins, my profound misery and the corruption of my heart. And if I am faithful to Thy grace, this salutary confusion, this contempt of myself, will lead me to suffer patiently and to desire even to be despised and rebuked by all the world, as I deserve.

SECOND POINT

But, not content with annihilating Himself in spirit before God, as I have just contemplated Him, Jesus Christ annihilated in some sort His Will, by putting His Human Will under the direction of the Eternal Word. It was this dependence which He wished to make known to us by these words: "I do nothing of Myself. I do always the things which please My Father." Thus, then, notwithstanding the distinction of the two natures and the two wills, divine and human, which existed entire and without confusion, according to the teaching of Faith, the Sacred Humanity annihilated Itself morally but voluntarily under the action of the Divinity. The only use which It made of Its wisdom and infused science, with all the gifts of nature and of grace which accompanied them, and the only movement which It gave to Its will, was to annihilate them, in order to leave the Word the entire control of Its thoughts, words, actions and sentiments.

Thus all is annihilation in the Mystery of the Incarnation: annihilation of mind, annihilation of heart. And this is the remedy which the Divine Physician has applied to the wounds of original sin, to pride, love of self and esteem of one's own excellence, and He has considered necessary nothing less than the annihilation of the Son of God, to satisfy the justice of the Eternal Father and to cure the wounds of the heart of man.

Behold then the secret of your salvation and perfection: First, to humble one's self before God by a true contempt of self and a just appreciation of our importance for good. Second, to renounce all the movements of nature, to follow entirely the conduct of the Divine Spirit and the inspirations of grace. The more we approach this moral annihilation of Jesus Christ, the more shall we approach perfection. The most perfect souls, then, are those in whom there is less of themselves and more of the Spirit of Jesus Christ, as a consequence of their fidelity in renouncing the sallies of self-love and mortifying the inclinations of corrupt nature, to follow entirely the conduct of grace, according to the constant teaching of Saint Paul.

But this fidelity in humbling one's self under the hand of God, supposes a great spirit of recollection, and an assiduous care in watching over the heart, in order to be able to discern the impulses of the Spirit of God, from those of nature, and a great spirit of interior mortification in obeying one and resisting the other.

O my God! Alas! I have known humility only in name. I have believed that it consisted only in certain illusions of holy souls to hide from themselves the knowledge of their virtues and their merits, while I see now that humility of mind consists in seeing according to truth that we are nothing, and of ourselves can do nothing, and that humility of heart consists in acting according to this clear light. Thus, they seek neither the affections nor the esteem of creatures, because they merit them not, and they apply themselves constantly to forsake themselves by a perfect self-contempt, obliging God to succor them by this avowal of their indigence.

Such have not been my sentiments and my conduct, my God! I have been filled with a secret confidence in my own virtue, expecting to obtain perfection by my own efforts. I believed myself doing good works, when I but followed in all things my natural inclinations. O Divine Jesus, grant me to-day this powerful grace which will enlighten me upon my own nothingness! Imprint in my will a generous determination of seeking henceforth, by constant union with Thee, the desire and the strength to practise virtue.

I beg this grace of Thee, through the intercession of her who, though the purest, was the most humble of creatures, and found in this humility the principal source of all the blessings with which Thou hadst filled her. Amen.

Third Meditation - The Birth of Our Lord Jesus Christ

"And it came to pass that when Mary and Joseph were at Bethlehem, her days were accomplished, that she should be deliverd, and she brought forth her first-born son, ..and wrapped Him up in swaddling clothes, and laid Him in a manger; because there was no room for them in the inn." — St. Luke, II, 6-7.

I enter in spirit the stable with the shepherds, whom Thou invitest by the voice of Angels. I prostrate myself, O Divine Infant, before that manger which serves for Thy cradle. I adore Thee, O Desired of Nations! O my Amiable Redeemer! O my King! O my Master! I come to listen in silence, and to gather the admirable lessons which Thou givest me at Thy first appearance in this world. I unite my adoration to that of Mary and Joseph, humbly supplicating Thee to accept the offering of my heart and grant me in return a clear knowledge of the Mystery of Poverty which is shown in Thy Birth.

FIRST POINT - The Poverty of Jesus Christ in His Birth

I will first consider with the deepest recollection, and with the eye of faith, that touching picture which unfolds itself before me. An abandoned Stable, a frail Infant clothed in poor garments, and laid in a manger. Near Him I perceive a daughter of Israel, whose mien and visage full of modesty bear the impress of every virtue, but whose exterior announces only an humble mediocrity. Such is also that of the venerable old man, who accompanies her and who is but a poor artisan. Around them press the humble shepherds, called by the voice of the Angels.

Is this then, O my God, the One Whom Thou didst promise from the beginning of the world to our first Parents, the One Whom Thou didst show to Abraham, Whom Moses announced to Thy People, and of Whom the Patriarchs left the hope to their children as their most precious heritage?

Is this He, Whose glorious entrance into the world the Prophets have related in such magnificent terms, Whose victories, conquests and Eternal Reign they have described with so much pomp? Is this the strong God, the Angel of the Great Council, the Prince of Peace, the Father of the world to come? Can I, in fine, recognize in such signs the Mediator Whom Thou hast promised, the glorious King Whose throne is established upon indestructible foundations? Is this His palace, His court, His guard; are these the insignia of His Royalty?

Yes, respond the heavens, by the voice of Angels — yes, by these signs thou must recognize that God has accomplished His promises, that Christ, Our Saviour is born. It is voluntarily, it is by choice of preference, that He takes to-day Poverty as His portion. We should not attribute to the vanity of Caesar, who ordained the enrollment of his subjects, the journey of Mary and Joseph to Bethlehem; neither should we attribute their retirement into a stable, to the avarice and cruelty of the innkeepers, who repulsed them, because the birth of Jesus Christ in this place had been decreed in the Council of Eternal Wisdom. He should be born in destitution, deprived of all those helps which in like circumstances are not wanting to the most indigent families. And God, Who, in His Almighty Power, makes use for the execution of His designs, of the perverse wills of His creatures, so disposed all things that His Divine Son was born at Bethlehem, as had been announced by His Prophets, and that this temporal birth was marked with the character of the most abject poverty.

In order to become initiated into this Mystery, it is necessary that we recall to mind that the Creator, when He drew man forth from nothingness, had placed him in a Paradise of delights, with the intention of elevating him by the contemplation of creatures, and causing him to attain by the enjoyment of created goods to the possession of eternal riches. But Adam lost himself in this path; and creatures, instead of being for him a means of salvation, became in consequence of sin and the corruption of his heart, obstacles to the exercise of love. God then resolved to save him by an opposite way. Behold why our Redeemer gives us at His Birth a shining example in His obscurity, of perfect contempt of all created goods. And from that instant, that is to say, from the Crib at Bethlehem, to the Cross on Calvary, His life will be marked by a want of all things. When the time of His infancy and youth has passed, He will live painfully by the labor of His hands; in His public life, He will receive His subsistence from charitable souls. He has not whereon to lay His head; He will die despoiled of His garments, and be buried in the tomb of another. But if His first example is one of poverty, the first word with which He opens the promulgation of His new Law, is in favor of holy Poverty. "Blessed are the poor," He says! "Blessed are the poor," echoes through the Christian ages! And these words received in hearts prepared by the grace of the Redemption will change the face of the earth. Human wisdom had placed happiness in an abundance of temporal goods; it had for poverty nothing but contempt; and behold how Divine Wisdom discovers to those who are willing to hear Him, the falsity, the insufficiency and the danger of these goods, and the precious treasures hidden in the absence of all terrestrial things. Immediately we see following in the footsteps of their poor Redeemer, not only His Apostles and first Disciples, but a multitude of Christians of both sexes, from every rank of life, who with joy distributed to others their goods, esteeming Evangelical Poverty more than all the goods of the universe.

O Holy Poverty, precious pearl, hidden treasure, which Jesus has loved, which He made His companion during His whole life, and from which He wished not to separate in death! When wilt thou become the object of my ambition and my love? Without understanding the precious advantages attached to thy practise, should it not suffice for me to love thee, because thou belongest to Jesus, Who has espoused thee through love for me, in order to enrich me with eternal goods? Ah! if I possessed some part of the garment which He had worn, I would cherish it tenderly, kiss it with respect, and preserve it with love; and yet, when I wear this habit of brown, when I dwell in a cell despoiled of all ornaments, when I repose upon a poor bed and make use of the food of the poor, do I not truly possess the relics of the Poverty of Jesus, with which I am enriched? But, alas! there is wanting in these holy practises the faith which should elevate them, and the love which should give them value and cause me to seek them. And often, instead of cherishing these holy observances, I fear and try to escape them. Ah! how far am I from the spirit of my holy state, and the sentiments of Carmel's holy Reformatrix who, having had so much zeal for this precious virtue, has left us so many admirable examples of it. My God, I again beg Thee to grant me in this Retreat the grace of understanding and of practising the Poverty of Jesus.

SECOND POINT - Advantages and Practice of Religious Poverty

It is certain that one of the principal causes of the perdition of men is, according to Saint Paul, cupidity, that is, a love of earthly goods. Hence arises in us a crowd of useless desires, cruel thorns, as they are called by Our Saviour, which choke the seeds of grace, kill good desires, prevent us from thinking of celestial goods, from loving virtue, and from practising good works. Some pursue with inquietude these goods because they possess them not. Others put all their affection in the enjoyment and preservation of these deceitful riches which become for them a source of innumerable sins; because, from the time that man makes the things of earth the object of his ambition and his efforts, he forgets the care of his soul and his eternal destiny, and counts as nothing the violation of the Holy Laws of God and of the Church. Provided he satisfies his cravings, he puts the things of time before those of eternity, the care of the body before the care of the soul, and falls into the vice which Jesus Christ combats in His Gospel by these words: "Be not solicitous, therefore saying: What shall we eat, or what shall we drink, wherewith shall we be clothed? Thus the heathens seek. Seek ye first the Kingdom of God and His Justice, and all these things shall be added unto you."

According to this divine doctrine, the great Apostle, writing to Timothy, says: "Fly, cupidity, and adorn thyself with piety, which is the greatest of treasures to a heart which knows how to content itself with the little which it possesses. For we brought nothing into this world: and certainly we can carry nothing out. But having food, and wherewith to be covered, with these are content."

These words of Saint Paul are a resume of all the advantages of Religious Poverty; Holy Poverty, one of the most admirable inspirations of the Spirit of Jesus Christ, by which each member of a Religious family, having nothing of her own, is poor in effect. She has before God all the merit of renouncing the goods of the world, while, by the care of the Community, nothing is wanting to her of necessary or even useful things, and each one can truly say with the Apostle: "I am as one having nothing, yet possessing all things." The Religious soul thus finds herself placed in that happy state which Solomon begged of

God when he prayed to be delivered equally from extreme indigence and great opulence, because one is too often the source of complaints, murmurs, the forgetfulness of salvation, and a multitude of sins, while the other opens the door to all the passions by furnishing the means of satisfying them.

Blessed, a thousand times blessed, is the Holy Poverty of Carmel! It is here that the solitary soul, having no care but to make the praises of God resound day and night throughout her solitude and to enrich herself for heaven, resembles the little birds of which Jesus Christ speaks: they neither sow nor do they reap, yet they are nourished each day by their Heavenly Father. Her treasure is in her detachment. According as she curtails her own wants, as she becomes enamoured of the Poverty of Jesus Christ, and desires to bear His Livery — as a just recompense of the Divine Remunerator, she gathers more abundantly from His hand those celestial goods which fill her heart, according as He finds it empty of creatures. These precious advantages the Holy Spirit reveals to hearts which are His.

But Religious Poverty, however holy it may be in itself, has for each soul no reality or advantage, except inasmuch as it is voluntarily embraced by faith and practised with love. It is very necessary and indispensable to be penetrated with its spirit; otherwise the words of Our Saviour, "Blessed are the poor in spirit," the poor by their own will, are not applicable to us. Alas! some Religious souls have embraced Poverty by a vow, yet understand neither its obligations nor its value.

They have no love for it, they observe its practices badly, and consequently do not gather its precious fruits. If they do not go so far as directly to violate their sacred promises, by disposing of what they have the use of, or receiving what is given them by others, without the consent of their Superiors; at least they show this same disposition in the use of things, as if they really belonged to them, whether it be by attachment, by the complacency with which they use them, or or by the pain which they experience in giving them up, or lending them to others. Oh! how far removed from the examples of St. Teresa and all holy Carmelites are such sentiments, they were never so happy as when by some circumstance, fortunate in their estimation, they could suffer the want and the privation of the very necessaries of life. On the contrary, these Religious of whom we are speaking give way to secret murmurs when it happens that the Sisters charged with the care of providing for their needs have not satisfied their desires for clothing or nourishment, seeking always for themselves what is the best and most comfortable.

What is not my confusion, O my God, in contemplating Holy Poverty, so amiable in Thy Person, for which if I have not had a real repugnance, at least I have not loved as I ought, after the precious example Thou has given me of it during Thy entire life. The Order of Carmel contains a great treasure in Holy Poverty, with which I can acquire a multitude of spiritual goods, and yet this treasure has been for me, until now, a buried treasure. I was poor by my profession, in my habit, in my customs, but I was not poor in spirit and in truth. I was rich in those riches which Thou hast cursed, rich in desires, in a multitude of cares and thoughts which filled my heart with creatures, and, alas! this is why I behold it so empty of Thee and Thy Spirit.

Ah! Lord, grant me to understand the favor Thou hast done me since, being rich, Thou hast made Thyself poor to enrich me by Thy own indigence. Make me love Thy Poverty more than the world loves its opulence, that I may buy of Thee that pure gold, which is Thy Love, and which will insure for me the eternal possession of Thy Kingdom! Amen.

LECTURE - The Divine Office

The Religious of Carmel are bound to recite each day in Choir the Divine Office. Among the obligations imposed upon them, this is one of the gravest, the most holy and the most glorious. It is then very important to be penetrated during this Retreat with a high esteem for this holy exercise, and to understand that not only their perfection, but even their salvation, will depend upon the exactitude and the piety with which they acquit themselves of this duty.

Let us first speak of the motives which will make us conceive that respect and esteem which the Divine Office merits. Consider its antiquity, the greatness of the authority which imposes its obligation, the matter which composes it, the end for which it has been instituted and, in fine, the circumstances which accompany its recitation.

The practise of reciting the psalms and canticles by two choirs is so ancient in the Church that Saint Augustine says that the chanting of the Divine Office has not been established by any ecclesiastical law, but by the example of Jesus Christ and the Apostles. The Church has charged her priests and the Religious Orders to pay for her to God this tribute of prayer, imposed upon her by Jesus Christ. This is the sacrifice of the lips which she has ordained them to offer at stated times of the day and night, which takes the name of Matins, Lauds, Prime, Terce, Sext, None, Vespers and Compline, according to the hours at which they are recited. Thus, there is no hour of the day or night when the Church ceases to send up to heaven the precious perfume of her prayers. There is nothing so useful as this thought to make us understand and esteem the dignity of the functions confided to Religious communities. They should consider themselves as a deputation sent from earth to the Throne of God, by the authority of the Church, to pay in her name this tribute of praise and thanksgiving which she owes to her Sovereign Lord, and to present to Him the sorrow and the supplications of this desolate Mother, for the sins of her children, the cry of her distress, and of her needs, amid the perils and combats which assail her. It is like a continual sacrifice which the Religious are charged to offer to God — a sacrifice which joins to the merits of prayer that of obedience to the Church, thus becoming infinitely more precious and agreeable to God.

This admirable truth will acquire a new value in our eyes when we consider the matter which composes the Divine Office, the spirit with which it is

86

replete, and the circumstances which accompany its recitation. In effect, in the accomplishment of this holy exercise there is question of nothing less than the glory of God and the salvation of souls. It is to praise God, to exalt His grandeur, His wisdom, His infinite mercy; it is to beg of Him the sanctification of the just, help for those in tribulation and in temptation, and grace for the conversion of sinners, that this tribute of praise is offered each instant, and in order that God may receive it more favorably, the Church makes use of words which have been inspired by the Holy Spirit.

Moreover, the Holy Fathers have always recognized that the Psalms and Canticles which compose the different parts of the Divine Office are the voice of Jesus Christ and of His Church. For it is the Spirit of Jesus which filled the Prophets, which made them feel in advance the different sentiments of the Man-God, and express them in so lively and so touching a manner, not only those which the Messiah was to experience in His own Person, during the course of His life on earth, but also those which He was to feel in His mystical body, which is the Church, during the course of its duration; that is to say, until the end of ages. What a consolation, and at the same time what a glory for the Religious soul to be thus, in the recitation or chanting of these holy canticles, the organ of Jesus Christ, and as an instrument which He Himself causes to vibrate by His Holy Spirit, sometimes representing to His Eternal Father His sufferings, His labors and His death, and demanding of Him mercy for the sins of men; sometimes celebrating His victory over hell, the glory which He has acquired, and which He shares with His children.

Even the language in which the holy words are written and pronounced should inspire the soul with the most profound respect; for it is the unchangeable language of the Church, and of Faith. It matters little that one does not penetrate the sense of the holy words, provided that she understands well how to unite herself to the Spirit of Jesus Christ, Who is so perfectly understood by His Father. Know then, O Religious soul, that these words, thus full of the Spirit of Jesus as they fall from thy lips, are gathered by the Angels, invisible witnesses of thy prayers, and immediately borne to the Throne of God; and that the functions which thou fulfillest in this circumstance are in a measure those of the Divine Mediator, since it is in His Name, and by His Spirit, that thou speakest.

That which in fine especially enhances the value of the Divine Office is that it is a common and public prayer. This unanimous concert of voices and of hearts united in one same language, in one same thought, in one same love, and reunited in the Heart of Jesus, ascends directly to the Throne of the Lord and does Him a holy violence; as we read of the ten lepers, who, uniting their voices, cry from a distance to the Savior: "Jesus, our Master, have pity on us," and were immediately heard and their prayer granted.

After these considerations, and without recalling here the obligation which is imposed upon us under pain of grievous sin, of reciting the Divine Office, we understand that one of the first duties of a Religious of Carmel is to acquit herself of this obligation in a manner corresponding to its grandeur and its holiness. The first condition of fulfilling it worthily is to have a heart) pure and full of charity which, without effort can unite itself to Jesus and become in His hands a sweet-sounding instrument of prayer, upon which His Divine Spirit will cause to resound those ineffable groanings which are always heard by the Celestial Father. In order to place herself in these dispositions, as much as possible, she should endeavor, before the commencement of the Office, and during the interval prescribed by the Rule, after the first sound of the bell, to purify herself from her faults by an act of contrition, and unite herself to Jesus Christ by a Spiritual Communion. She could renew these acts each time the Hebdomadary invokes the Divine Aid, by saying: "Deus in adjutorium," and likewise at the "Gloria Patri" of each Psalm unite her voice to that of the Divine Mediator in rendering homage to the Blessed Trinity.

It is evident that the Religious soul should make use of great precautions, in order to ward off all distractions, all thoughts which could trouble her and prevent the accomplishment of a duty so holy, and whatever might distract the attention of the other Religious. She has the obligation, first, of acquiring a perfect knowledge of the different parts of the Divine Office, of the Rubrics, of the Ceremonial — that is to say, the different prostrations, inflections of the voice, etc.; second, to study or mark in advance the Office of each day, the proper Antiphons, Psalms, Lessons from Scripture, Commemorations, etc. But that which is particularly essential is to understand the spirit of each part of the Office, in order to replenish and maintain not only her attention, but also her devotion. The "Little Hours," especially Prime, may be regarded as our morning prayer. It contains the most touching expressions of the Prophet, protesting his fidelity and his tender love for the law of the Lord; expressions and protestations which the Religious soul ought to apply in a special manner to the holy rules of her state; and after which follow prayers in which the Church begs God's grace for her children to pass the day in silence, recollection, and exemption from sin. Vespers are an evening sacrifice, in which the praises of the Lord are chanted. Compline is the prayer which terminates the day, and in which the Religious soul, after having acknowledged her faults by an humble "Confiteor," represents to herself the tender care of Divine Providence, and abandons herself with confidence into its Arms, for the night which is coming on.

Matins and Lauds are the prayer of the night. St. Teresa has assigned this hour for Matins, in honor of our Lord's agonizing in the Garden of Olives, and she wishes us to unite ourselves to the dispositions of His Heart in this mystery of sorrow and of resignation. This part of the Office is intended to make some reparation to our Lord for profanations and crimes which the darkness of the night envelops. The Religious should pay particular and respectful attention to the Canticles of the New Law; these are the "Magnificat" at Vespers, the "Nunc Dimittis" at Compline, and the "Benedictus" at Lauds. In the first, she should be penetrated with those sentiments of humility, thanksgiving, and annihilation with which the soul of Mary was filled. The same thoughts should occupy her in reciting the Canticle of the holy old Simeon, and while repeating the words of Zachary she will bless God for the ineffable benefit of the Redemption.

Examen Upon the Lecture

Have I understood the rigor, and the sanctity of my obligation of reciting daily the Divine Office? Have I applied myself to acquire the knowledge which would enable me to understand it, and aid me in acquitting myself well of this duty? Have I taken care, before going to choir, to read attentively the Ordo and mark carefully the Antiphons, Lessons, etc., looking over with attention those which I have been appointed to read, in order not to be distracted during this holy exercise, or to give distraction to others? Have I recollected myself before entering choir, and united myself interiorly to Jesus Christ, in order to acquit myself of this sacred act of Religion, in union with His Divine Spirit? Have I renewed the intention frequently during the Office?

Sixth Day

First Meditation - The Circumcision of Our Lord, Jesus Christ

"And after eight days were accomplished that the child should be circumcised; his name was called Jesus, which was called by the angel, before he was conceived in the womb.' — St. Luke, II, 21.

I adore Thee, O Divine Infant Jesus, shedding under the knife of the Circumcision the first drops of Thy Precious Blood, which upon the Cross Thou wilt shed with so much profusion. The name of Jesus, which is now given to Thee, is the only reward which Thou wilt receive today from this first Sacrifice. Ah! what sorrows it presages for Thee; what torments hast Thou embraced in accepting it! How precious should this Name be to me since it cost Thee so dear! Give me, Lord, a knowledge of this Mystery; teach me the relation which exists between the name of Saviour and of suffering, between the mortification of my disorderly affections (signified by the word circumcision) and the salvation which Thou comest to bring upon earth. Grant me grace to understand, that I can have no part in Thy Redemption unless I do violence to my natural inclinations.

FIRST POINT - Necessity of Mortification

God, in calling Abraham to His service, imposed circumcision as a mark of alliance. His children were to bear upon their flesh this bloody sign, used in consecrating them to God, and to separate them from the people living in idolatry. This operation, at once painful and humiliating, marked also the dependence in which this nation ought to live in relation to God, because of their origin from a prevaricating father. It was the mark of a double slavery, of nature and of sin. It should not then have been made upon the innocent flesh of the Infant God — a law made for sinners should not have been extended to Him. Ah! but the Son of God was made man precisely to substitute Himself for sinners. Thus, He has willed to receive in His Divine Flesh the marks of sinners, to subject Himself to the law of sinners, and by receiving circumcision to engage Himself to accomplish this law, leaving us by this conduct an admirable example of humility and of fidelity in fulfilling all the divine prescriptions.

But by submitting to this painful and humiliating law, He abolished it. He came, in order that to this ancient people, gross and carnal, attached to its exterior observances, a new and spiritual people might succeed, of whom He Himself would be the Father, and for whom the law would no longer be printed upon the tables of stone, but engraved by the Spirit of God in the depths of the heart. He came to substitute for this material circumcision of the body the true circumcision of the heart, to replace this painful cutting away of the flesh by an operation altogether spiritual, which, without being bloody, would be more painful, but also more glorious and more meritorious: the extirpation of vice and the mortification of the passions.

St. Paul speaks in his epistle of this circumcision of the heart instituted by our Lord Jesus Christ as of a law to which all Christians are obliged to submit. "The real circumcision," says the grand Apostle, "is that of the heart, in the spirit, not in the letter; whose praise is not of men but of God." He established this obligation in the most expressive manner. "If you live according to the flesh, you shall die; but if you mortify the deeds of the flesh by the spirit, you will live." Thus this circumcision of the heart — that is to say, this mortification of the senses and the degraded appetites — is for every Christian, and with greater reason for Religious, a rigorous law, and it is the principal fruit which we should draw from this Mystery.

To understand well this principle and the necessity of this spiritual circumcision, we should recall the source of the depravity of our nature. When Adam came forth from the hand of God, his flesh was entirely submissive to the spirit, and the spirit to God. But sinful man, reversing this primitive order, has caused the most frightful disorders to succeed to that beautiful harmony which the charity of God had made to reign in his soul.

As to the exterior, creatures no longer, except by force, submit to his empire; and as to the interior, he finds his soul fallen under the empire of the senses, and from being their master is become their slave. It was this sad reversion which St. Paul deplores in these memorable words: "I feel in my members a law which wars against the spirit, captivating me in the law of sin, which is in my members. Unhappy man that I am, who will deliver me from the body of this death?" And he hastens to indicate to us the Author of

90

our deliverance: "It is the grace of God which comes to us through Jesus Christ."

In effect, this new Adam gives us in Baptism His own spirit, the spirit which regulated in Him all the powers of His soul and body, and thus re-establishes us in the primitive order, or at least gives us the strength to overcome our flesh, with its evil inclinations; and in order better to excite in us that holy hatred of self, which He requires of His disciples, He arms Himself against His Flesh, so pure and so submissive; subjects it to the rudest treatment, and His pains become for us a source of particular grace, to combat courageously our evil inclinations. It was for this end that He submitted to the law of circumcision, that He embraced poverty with all the privations which accompany it, that He bore the fatigues and persecutions of His Public Life, which was terminated in so much suffering by the cruel pains of the flagellation, the crowning with thorns, and the crucifixion.

I understand now, Divine Infant, the harmony which exists between the sweet Name of Jesus and the Blood which I now see Thee shed, between the salvation which Thou bringest to us and the pains which Thou endurest.

If I wish to be saved by Thee, it is necessary that I suffer also — because I must combat — that I wage a continual war against my flesh, and against my soul insomuch as it follows the inclinations of my flesh. Ah! Lord, how is this! Thou, Whose Divine Interior was so well regulated, Who could not experience in Thy senses any revolt or even the least resistance, hast willed for love of me to endure in Thy Innocent Flesh, the most cruel dolors; and I, for love of Thee and my own salvation, am not willing to enter generously into the combat against myself, to which is attached the assurance of so glorious a victory? Thou hast said: "The Kingdom of Heaven suffereth violence and only the violent can bear it away." Ah, if until now, I have been so cowardly, so tender towards myself, enlightened by Thy Divine Light and fortified by Thy Divine example, I shall find in Thee the strength necessary to conquer my perverse nature, and to obey the requirements of Thy love.

SECOND POINT - Advantages and Practice of Mortification

It is certain that mortification is the essence of virtue. This word virtue signifies nothing else but strength, victory; and according to the doctrine of the saints, we should judge of our advancement in perfection by our progress in mortification. We need no longer be astonished that the holy rules of Carmel, whose end is to conduct the souls who embrace them to the summit of the holy Mountain, that is to say to the perfection of charity, require of them an entire mortification; a mortification generous, universal, constant, which subjects the interior as well as the exterior to its rigorous laws.

In the measure to which a soul closes the door of her senses to all exterior objects, and banishes creatures from her mind and her heart, the Divine Light will enter to enlighten the darkness formed by the forgetfulness of all created things; and the will strengthened a hundred-fold by this privation of creatures, will embrace its Creator with a vigor which will make her cry out with the Spouse in the Canticles: "I have found Him Whom my soul loveth, I will hold Him and I will not let Him go."

Have we not said elsewhere that it was by prayer that the holy Rule of Carmel proposed to conduct souls even to the Divine Union? Well, in order to acquire the spirit of prayer, it is absolutely necessary to practice a real and generous mortification. How, in effect, can a soul be capable of Divine communications, how pretend to converse reverently and familiarly with the great God, if she appears before Him with unmortified senses, a mind filled with frivolous images, and a heart occupied with sensible attachments? "Where our treasure is, there is our heart." She will be where her affections place her, where her thoughts carry her — her body alone will remain at prayer.

I now understand the indispensable necessity and the precious advantages of perfect mortification, in order to reach my sublime end. Ah, Lord, this is not the work of a day, nor child's play! Alas! if Thou didst command me to combat an exterior enemy, even one most terrible, perhaps I would find in myself enough resolution to attack, and to vanquish him. But Thou hast taught me that this enemy is not far from me, not outside, but within me — that it is myself. What then is this new kind of warfare where one is at once the aggressor and the attacked; the conquered and the conqueror? What is this new courage which consists in plotting against one's self? This new kind of victory for which it is necessary to be stronger than self? Where shall I seek the vigor necessary for such an enterprise! It is impossible to find it in myself. Whence then, O Lord, cometh this strength which Thou demandest of Me?

O Religious soul, you have just meditated upon the circumcision of your Divine Master, the true symbol of that mortification which He requires of you; you have seen His Precious Blood flowing, and did not your ear catch the Name which has come down from Heaven? Ah! then listen again and be filled with hope, for it is this holy Name which gives strength and victory. This Name is not like unto the names of other men, a name of earth; it was sent from Heaven. It is the Name above all other names, and there is no other name by which we may be saved. It is a substantial Name which gives life; it is a nourishment which fortifies, a light which enlightens, an armour of defense with which to attack our enemies. It is a delightful harmony which charms the heart. This name is "JESUS" By pronouncing it with reverence, according to Saint Paul, by calling "JESUS," your Master, you call for His Spirit, and with it the impression of His virtues. Ah; pronounce often this blessed Name of "JESUS" Repeat a thousand times "JESUS," "JESUS," for in the measure that you read it and pronounce it, it will pass from the eyes and the lips into the depth of the heart; there to repose, to inflame and transform it. When overcome with sadness, say "JESUS," and soon joy will return. Art thou in trouble? Call "JESUS." He is thy peace. Dost thou feel overcome in the struggles of thy warfare? Arm thyself with this strong Name, repeat it with fervor, and thou wilt regain strength. Does a sudden passion take possession of you? An emotion, a word about to escape you "JESUS," "JESUS," and the waves are appeased. Is there question of a generous sacrifice; is it necessary to submit to a humiliation, or to bear a sudden sorrow or disappointment? Call "JESUS," because Jesus is in your heart to give you humility and strength. Finally, behold Satan advances: you are surrounded by his shafts, enveloped by temptation as by a thick cloud, you are about to perish — fear not, seize thy weapon — call "JESUS" It is a cry of victory and already thy enemy takes flight. O my Divine Saviour, what treasures I discover in studying Thee, in approaching Thee! Today, I take Thy Name as a shield which gives strength, which contains a marvelous power. O admirable Name, O new Name promised to the ancient people as their only hope! Ah! I have hitherto left unused and neglected a weapon so powerful, an instrument so full of melody, a food so sweet. The saints have penetrated this Mystery of Thy Name; they had it always on their lips, and I have made no use of it to conquer my passions, to triumph over nature, and to call forth Thy Life in me. O sweet Name of JESUS, henceforth Thou shalt be my strength, my virtue, my light, as Thou art the pledge of my eternal happiness. Amen.

Second Meditation - Flight into Egypt

"After the Magi had departed, behold an Angel appeared to Joseph in sleep, saying; Arise, take the child and his mother, and fly into Egypt: and be there until I shall tell thee. For it will come to pass that Herod will seek the child to destroy him. Who arose, took the child and his mother, by night, and retired into Egypt, and he was there until the death of Herod."— St. Matthew, II, 13-14.

I adore Thee, O my Divine Savior, in the arms of Mary and under the protection of St. Joseph, escaping by flight the cruel jealousy of Herod. Scarcely born into our world, Thou art pursued by those who seek to destroy Thee Who hast come to save them. Far from opposing Thy strength to their strength, or Thy power to their power, Thou dost fly precipitately, as if Thy divine wisdom had no other means of protecting Thee from the fury of Thy enemies. But thus was it ordained by Thy Eternal Father; and Thou dost abandon Thyself blindly to the guidance of His Divine Providence, so well represented in Thy holy parents. I supplicate Thee, O my God, to make me understand and feel the force of the admirable lessons contained in this memorable circumstance of Thy Divine Life.

Faith in the Providence of God

It was during the night that St. Joseph received from God, through the ministry of an Angel, the order to fly into Egypt. It is pressing, it will allow of no delay. Arise, but what! can he not prepare things most necessary for the

93

journey, take leave of his friends, at least await the dawn of day? No, arise — this very instant thou must flee. But where? Is it into another part of Judea, or perhaps into the country of the Holy Magi? There at least the Holy Family will find an assured asylum, and powerful protection. No, but into Egypt, a strange and distant land, of which they do not know the language nor the customs, and where they are to be exposed during a long period to all the rigors of indigence. Is there, then, no other means to confound the cruelty of Herod, to turn against himself his impiety and perfidy? Such are the ways of Divine Providence: it would wish that the means employed to save the Infant Saviour from the first snares of His enemies be as simple as they are natural; He must escape by flight, and He will not return into His own country until after the death of His persecutor, which will not be for many years. The exile of Jesus in Egypt enters into the Eternal designs, and God, to accomplish them, made use of the cruel order of Herod, as He had the enrollment ordered by Augustus, that the oracles of the prophets should be accomplished and His Son should be born in Bethlehem.

Thus our false wisdom with our pride and our eagerness are confounded. We would much prefer to read in this place in the holy Gospel that Herod was precipitated from his throne when about to consummate his fatal projects, or that some extraordinary event had hidden the Holy Family from his cruelty, and that they tranquilly returned to their peaceful dwelling. We forget that if Divine Wisdom arrives at its ends in an infallible manner, it prepares the ways by means full of sweetness, so that the delays, the obstacles, even the persecutions by which creatures strive to prevent them, serve only to assure their success, in perfecting, by tribulations, the instruments which He destines for their accomplishment.

It was because Mary and Joseph were filled with faith and with confidence in Divine Providence that, without delay, without reflection, they accomplished the order of heaven, complaining not of the malice of Herod, or of the blindness of the Jews, or of the long trial of labors and of sufferings to which they were obliged to submit.

Here, then, is an essential point, which I should endeavor to fix firmly in my mind in this meditation, ii is that all exterior events, vicissitudes, trials of the interior life, all contradictions, all the sufferings which I may have to endure, whether they come from the malice of the demon, or from my own depraved nature, or from creatures as my superiors, my companions, my relatives, or persons of the world, they always come to me by the will of God. I should, then, not regard those who try me, even should they be influenced by guilty motives or deceived by false and malignant reports — it matters not. God, without doubt, cannot will sin; but those actions which are the effect or the cause of sin, enter, nevertheless, in an admirable manner, into the designs of His Providence, and in the accomplishment of His views in relation to myself, and I should say in all events: "It is Thou, O Lord, Who ordainest this, and ordainest it for my greater good and for Thy greater glory." Penetrated with this truth of faith, I will conform my conduct to it, instead of making useless reflections and complaints, murmuring and showing resentments.

Ah, Lord, how far I find myself withdrawn from this lively faith and generous confidence in Thy Divine Providence. In all that happens to me, I 3top at natural causes, I attribute sickness to the inclemency of the seasons or my own temperament, cures to the remedies used, the success of an affair to the wisdom or the efforts of those who conduct it. I attribute the displeasure of my Superior at my bad conduct to dispositions unfavorable to me, and the coldness of my companions to caprice or malice, instead of raising my thoughts higher and recognizing in all these contrarieties the dispensation of Thy Adorable Providence, by which Thou desirest me to expiate my sins, to correct my secret vices, and sanctify myself by these different trials. Grant me, then, O my God, sentiments more worthy of Thy love, more worthy of the profession I have made, since I am clothed with the holy Habit of Carmel, and have promised to walk in Thy footsteps and conform myself in all things to Thee.

SECOND POINT - Abandonment to Divine Providence

I will consider, in the second place, the admirable dispositions of the Infant Jesus reposing in the arms of His Holy Mother, while being carried precipitately into exile. I will penetrate the sentiments of His Adorable Heart in this circumstance, and there find peace, a profound repose in the midst of the exterior agitation by which He is surrounded. He obeys or rather He abandons Himself into the arms of His Holy Mother, as into those of the Divine Providence of God, His Father, of which she is to Him the image. He resigns to her the care of His Person; He is disturbed by nothing, He wishes for nothing, He reposes peacefully under the Almighty power and wisdom of Him Who, as Master, disposes of all events, and Who causes to concur to His Eternal decrees the diverse and often opposed wills of men. The Divine Saviour disregards all that He could know as God of the motive for and the duration of His cruel exile, in order to see only one thing— —the will of His Heavenly Father. He wishes to ignore, and does ignore in a certain manner, all else, repeating already in the depth of His Heart the words which later on in His Public Life He will openly pronounce: "My meat is to do the will of Him that sent Me." "I do always that which is pleasing to His eyes."

O my Jesus, what canst Thou find so amiable in this humiliating flight, in this exile, in this being forgotten by Thy own creatures, if not that it is the will of Thy Heavenly Father? What dost Thou wish to teach me by this abandonment to Thy Blessed Mother and Saint Joseph, if not the abandonment of myself without reserve, without inquietude, to the dispensations of Divine Providence, by placing all my interests in Thy hands, blessing God in all the states in which I might find myself, either of soul or body; above all when assailed by temptations, aridity, pains of mind and conscience, distractions in prayer, when the demon tries to raise in my soul excessive fears, inquietude concerning my salvation, thoughts of despair or other suggestions capable of throwing me into discouragement, even into profound darkness of soul, when I no longer know where I am nor what to do. O my Saviour, Thou peacefully allowest Thyself to be conducted in this obscurity, because Thou art innocent and the worthy object of Thy Eternal Father's complacency. But I, who draw upon myself these trials by my sins and infidelities without number, where can I find any ground for confidence? It shall be in Thy mercy, which abounds where sin has abounded; for is it not true to say that all trials, if they are chastisements for my infidelities, are also the remedies for them, and consequently the effects of the loving will of my God, and I should always submit with peace and resignation.

This abandonment, far from preventing the soul, as some believe, from correcting her faults and advancing in perfection, on the contrary supports and causes it to advance by overcoming discouragement and sadness — sources of new sins — and by producing humility which, to be sincere, must necessarily be accompanied with confidence. I will then cry out with the Prophet: "Lord, my lot is in Thy hands," and again, "In Thee, O Lord, have I hoped, let me never be confounded." With Jesus on the Cross, I exclaim: "Father, into Thy hands I commend my spirit." May I often recall the exhortation of the Apostle, St. Peter: "Cast all thy care upon God, for He hast care of thee."

O Mary, O Joseph, with what punctuality, with what exactitude did you not execute the orders of heaven, however rigorous and extraordinary they appeared! It is necessary to start at once, and during the darkness of the night, for the land of exile, and you go without inquietude, without regret. It is true that Jesus is with you, that He holds for you the place of all things — parents, friends and country. And I, if I would only understand it, am I not in one sense more blessed than you? In quitting the world, my family, my goods, in breaking all earthly ties to enter this solitude, have I not found Jesus? Do I not dwell with Him? Can I not converse with Him every hour of the day, and carry Him always in my heart; if not so holily as you did, at least in a manner equally as real? And notwithstanding this I do not know, I do not appreciate my happiness. What inquietude, what troubles agitate my soul! What useless desires, what deceiving remembrances of the past, what secret returns upon persons and things which I have left for God, what solicitude for the future, what discouragement! Ah, it is because I will not, as you did, keep closely united to Jesus, by invoking Him at every hour of the day, abandoning myself to His love, and placing in Him all my hope.

O holy abandonment! O losing of myself, O remitting of all my interests to Jesus through the hands of Mary and Joseph, be ye henceforth my refuge, my defense, my life! This holy abandonment does not exclude vigilance over my faults, nor efforts to be delivered from them, it aids me to rise more promptly from my falls, and to strive more generously to attain perfection. O Mary! O Joseph! obtain for me from Jesus a share in that holy abandonment which you practised in so admirable a manner in this mystery, the Flight into Egypt. Amen.

NOTE — Here the Religious soul should turn on herself, to consider that her troubles and anxieties come only from her self-love, from her want of union with God, and from her little confidence. She will then take the resolution to labor to deliver herself from them by the preceding considerations. This ought to be one of the principal fruits of her Retreat.

Third Meditation - Return to Nazareth

"And Jesus went down with Mary and Joseph and came to Nazareth; and was subject to them."— St. Luke, II, 51.

Sweet Jesus, Model of the most perfect and the most generous obedience, I prostrate myself at Thy feet, I adore Thee, I thank Thee. What right has not Thy obedience to my admiration, my thanksgiving and my love, since by it I have been delivered from the most cruel slavery — that of sin and the devil. By it, I have entered into the liberty of the children of God, having the happiness of living under the maternal authority of the Church. In fine, it is to Thy divine obedience that I owe the happiness of bearing the sweet yoke of the Religious life, which assures me such precious advantages, if I am faithful to my holy obligations, renouncing my own will to accomplish Thine until the last day of my life. O Jesus! amiable Jesus! Jesus obedient for my sake even to the death of the Cross! I implore Thee by the merits of Thy obedience to teach me to appreciate Thy divine lessons, and to understand the value and the advantages of Religious obedience, in order to fulfill my obligations more faithfully than I have hitherto done.

FIRST POINT - Necessity of Obedience

The obedience to which my Divine Saviour devoted Himself during His whole life is a subject well worthy of my serious reflection and astonishment. I see Him born in Bethlehem in a poor stable, not only to conform to the Will of His Eternal Father, but to obey the order of a Roman Emperor, an obedience with which He had inspired His holy parents before His birth; and from that time to His last sigh on the Cross, He seemed to live and to breathe only to obey, making Himself the servant of all. Thus, at Nazareth until His thirtieth year, the Gospel says nothing of Him but that He was subject to Mary and Joseph. I see this Divine Child, from His first years, rendering to His holy parents the constant testimony of an obedience full of respect and love. First to His Holy Mother, according to His age and the measure of His strength, He rendered all the duties and all the services which could relieve her of the cares of her family and her house. Later on, He aided Saint Joseph in his hard labors; and when He had attained His full strength, He condescended to devote Himself, but always under His foster father's orders, entirely to the exercise of His trade, and allowed the hardest work to fall upon Himself. It was then that He subjected Himself to all the servitude of His profession, going generously to the city or to the country like an ordinary workman to execute the orders which had been given Him, and always in the same spirit of submission and of dependence. But it was, above all, in the exercise of His Public Life that Jesus Christ continued to verify this truth: "I came not to be served but to serve." For from that time, He was no longer content with obeying Mary and Joseph and the inhabitants of Nazareth; but went through Judea, obeying all who claimed His services, going where He was called, and replying to all who interrogated Him, never seeking to hide Himself even from His enemies, who surrounded Him with snares, submitting to His iniquitous judges, and abandoning Himself as a tender lamb to the fury of those who were putting Him to death.

O my Divine Saviour, teach me the secret of this Mystery; make me understand how the work of our Redemption is the Masterpiece of Thy Obedience. The Apostle Saint Paul teaches it in these remarkable words: "As sin and death entered the world by the disobedience of one man," Adam, "so salvation and life have entered by the obedience of one Man" — Jesus Christ, the new Adam.

In effect, what have we seen in the garden of Paradise? We have seen there the first man, innocent and happy by obedience. He obeys God, and his body with all his senses obeys him. But, seduced by the spirit of lies and of revolt, he lost this primitive rectitude by a crime ineffable in its baseness; he disobeyed, and thus became his own idol; he loved himself, no longer with that perfect love which made him seek his happiness in God and for God, but with a disorderly and miserable love which drew him from God — self-love, which is the source of all evil, as divine love is the source of all good. From self-love flows self-will, the accursed principle of all the crimes, and all the errors which inundate the world. Man thus degraded cannot be restored except through obedience. But who can give him strength enough to submit his will, to renounce self-love? Ah, it is Jesus Christ, Who has descended from heaven in order to practise and to teach this perfect obedience — this renunciation of one's own will, to do always the Will of God, manifested by the Commandments, and by the will of those whom He has placed over us. Thus is destroyed our disorderly self-love to give place to divine love, for Jesus Christ Himself has said: "If you love Me, keep My Commandments."

If we cannot be saved unless we love God, then we cannot be saved without obeying. Remember always that it is from self-will, that is to say, from the will that does not agree with that of God and of our Superiors, that come and ever will come all evils, and that by forcing it to die within us, we extinguish the flames of hell which it alone enkindles. Obedience is then the science of salvation. Yes, this admirable science is contained in the single word — obey. When Jesus Christ was about to leave this earth, He said to the Church: "Teach, govern My children"; and to the faithful: "Obey the Church" — "He who will not hear the Church, let him be to thee as the heathen and publican."

O self-will! O self-love! It is you who have caused the ruin of the human race, you who have covered God's fair earth with crimes and disorders, you who have caused all the schisms and all the heresies which have desolated the Church, and precipitated so many souls into hell. O obedience of my Jesus! I love you because without you I should now be the slave of my degraded senses. No longer, O my Divine Saviour, am I astonished to hear Thee exclaim: "I came not to be served, but to serve." By this admirable submission, make me understand the necessity of obedience. May I fear nothing so much as my own will, and may I renounce it from this moment, not only in some of my actions, but always and in all things, in order that by thus dying to myself, I may live only in Thee and for Thee, by doing at every moment the will of God, manifested to me by Thy Divine Commandments and those of the Church, by my Rule and through my Superiors. Alas! I have until now sought but myself in all my actions, even when I obeyed exteriorly. Touched by Thy divine example, I wish to be obedient to all creatures for love of Thee, as Thou hast obeyed for love of me.

SECOND POINT - Advantages and practice of Religious Obedience

The Vow of Obedience is so excellent that it ranks above the Vow of Poverty, by which we sacrifice to God all our exterior goods. It is greater than the Vow of Chastity, by which we renounce those satisfactions which right reason teaches us to despise, and which we have in common with vile animals. By Obedience, we give ourselves really and entirely, since it is freewill which makes a man, and when we sacrifice this upon the Altar of God, we truly immolate ourselves. Chastity and poverty offer to God the flesh and the fleece of the victim. Obedience burns in His honor, the entrails, the marrow and the heart. This truth is confirmed by the Holy Scriptures, which tell us that obedience is better than sacrifice; we can even say that without obedience there is no sacrifice, or at least no sacrifice agreeable to God. Self-will debases our best actions, and renders them disagreeable to the Divine Majesty. Saint Bernard says: "Your fasts, your vigils, your prayers, your austerities, your retreats, your silence, cease to please God from the moment that they are practised through your own will; He will even reproach you with the sufferings which you endure without any fruit, considering them not only useless, but even as injurious to His honor." "Your fasts are displeasing to Me," said our Saviour, one day to the Jewish people, "because they are inspired by your own will." This is, however, the delusion of many souls who, deceived by a secret pride, give themselves up to extraordinary practices, and who embrace indiscreet austerities, without the advice of their Superiors, and who merit by this conduct, so opposite to obedience, the reproaches addressed by Samuel to the unfortunate Saul, for having offered to God a sacrifice which He had not demanded of him. But if self-will corrupts our best actions, obedience, on the contrary, gives value to the most indifferent and the least, it shelters us from all dangers, and makes us practise virtues the most necessary and the most sublime. Behold the great advantage of Religious Obedience! In some Religious Orders, instead of making all the vows, the professed content themselves with one — Obedience, because in promising obedience to the rule and to the superiors, they engage themselves to observe not only Poverty and Chastity, but even all the pious customs and all the virtues of the Order in which they make their profession.

Christians who live in the world can, without doubt, by observing faithfully the Law of God, secure their salvation, but to what dangers does not self-will expose them? How many, in effect, lose their souls because they have too much liberty in the choice of a multitude of actions, in their reading, their recreation, their conversations, the occupations which compose their lives, and in which sometimes their state engages them. Insensibly they are led by self-love into dangerous ways, and thrown into proximate occasion of sin; while in the Religious life, the Rule extends its authority over all our actions in general and over each one in particular, even our thoughts, words and affections, withdrawing the soul from the dangers of self-will and self-love, and preserving it from an infinity of evils.

In effect, obedience, by determining the employment of our time, of our faculties, of our strength, fixes our indifference, takes us from ourselves, and from a thousand projects formed one day and abandoned the next. For, alas! left to ourselves, that which happens to so many souls in the world, who are perhaps better than we, might happen to us. After practising piety for a short time, we might abandon prayer, penance and the most essential duties, having had only a devotion of fancy, without solidity or consistency; while being obliged to follow the Rule of the Community, notwithstanding our natural weakness, we persist in practising all the means necessary to secure our perseverance. From this come calm and peace; for we are assured of doing the will of God, of being in the place which He has marked out for us, while we can say at every hour: "I am where God wishes me to be, I am doing what pleases Him." What a source of joy, of peace and of happiness!

From these considerations, we must conclude that obedience is a way the shortest, the surest and at the same time the most meritorious. However, it is not rare to see persons who believe that they merit more by doing things outside the Rule than by practising works prescribed by obedience. The truth is, however, that obedience augments the value of our virtuous acts, such as prayers, meditations, and gives merit to our commonest actions, such as work, recreations, repasts, etc., when we seek in them the accomplishment of the will of God. We may also add that the practice of obedience contains in itself the most perfect acts of all the virtues, and that it will receive the same reward. It is an act of humility, since it obliges us in the sight of God to submit to the creature; an act of mortification the most heroic, since it is the immolation of our free-will to that of another. It is an act of generous and sublime faith, which makes us respect the authority of God in His creature; in fine, it is an act of hope, since it is practised in view of obtaining eternal goods. And if it is true that love is nothing else than the union of our will with the will of God, the life of perfect obedience is then a continual exercise of love. O precious Obedience! O life of the soul! O love of transformation! O death to self, to live by the will of God! How is it that I have not loved Thee more, esteemed Thee more? How little have I appreciated Thy worth?

Ah! Lord, henceforth, with Thy grace, I wish to be perfectly obedient, to be penetrated with this truth taught in the Holy Gospel, that in hearing my Superiors, I hear Thee, and in resisting them, I resist Thee.

Yes, Lord, with this ray of faith, I will henceforth regard my Superiors. I will no longer consider them with human eyes as simple creatures. I will not stop at the imperfections of nature, I will love them, I will accomplish their will as being Thine; I will honor them for Thy sake, I will obey them promptly, joyously, simply, without reasoning, without delay; I will submit not only my will, but my judgment. O Obedient Jesus, grant me grace to accomplish faithfully all these sacred promises! Fortify my resolution, aid my weakness, in order that, having been subjected to others on earth, I may merit to reign eternally with Thee in heaven. Amen.

LECTURE - The Holy Sacrifice of the Mass

One of the most important duties, a duty which is also the sweetest to be performed by the solitary of Carmel, is the daily assistance at the Holy Sacrifice of the Mass. We must add that if it is accomplished with the faith and piety which it demands, the most precious and abundant fruit is drawn from it. But, alas! it happens, as a consequence of that unhappy facility of our mind and heart to lose imperceptibly the taste, the respect and the love of things which we practise daily, that habit familiarizes us with the most holy actions, and we perform them in a spirit of routine, which makes us lose all their advantages. The spirit of faith alone can remedy this evil and prevent the sad effects of our levity and natural inconstancy. Let us consider what this great act of Religion is, which we so simply call the Mass, and let us recall what the Church teaches us about this adorable Mystery. It is the great Sacrifice of the New Law, of which the sacrifices of the ancient alliance were but gross and imperfect figures. They, with all the blood of their victims, could not efface the least stain of sin, while one single drop of the Precious Blood of the Lamb without spot, immolated upon Calvary, suffices to wash away, and superabundantly, all the sins of the world. Now, the Sacrifice of the Altar is a continuation and a renewal of the Sacrifice of the Cross, of which the fruits and the merits are and will be applied until the end of the world, to all souls who form a part of the Church; in such a manner, however, that these souls participate in these fruits, and these merits, in proportion to their dispositions, their preparation and their union with the Lamb immolated.

It is certain, according to the words of the sacred liturgy, that not only the Mystery of the Cross is continued, renewed and applied to our souls in the Holy Sacrifice of the Altar; but that the Mysteries of the Incarnation, Birth, Life, Glorious Resurrection and Triumphant Ascension of Our Lord Jesus

101

Christ are represented equally, and their different fruits applied to our souls. There is, then, in this act of religion by excellence, a vast field for the attentive and loving occupation of a faithful soul.

If all Christians who assist at the Holy Sacrifice are obliged to unite their intentions with that of the Priest, as co-operators in that Royal Priesthood of which Saint Peter speaks, and to bring to the Holy Mysteries a lively faith, profound veneration, ardent love and gratitude; with what sentiments should not the spouses of Jesus Christ, the daughters of Mary, be animated? Will an ordinary attention to the great act which is being accomplished upon the Altar suffice to make them enter into the true spirit of their obligations? Seeing near the Cross their Queen and their Mother participating so intimately, so generously in the Sacrifice of Jesus Christ, immolating herself completely with Him for the glory of God and the salvation of souls, should they not strive as far as possible to enter into her admirable dispositions? The true solitary of Carmel, worthy child of Mary, will then bring to the great Sacrifice a spirit of zeal for the interests of God and her neighbor, a spirit of immolation of her entire self, and of union, absolute and without reserve, with the great Victim Who is being offered.

To this general disposition, she will add the intentions which refer to the four ends of the Sacrifice, intentions concerning which she should be perfectly instructed. In effect, the Eucharistic Sacrifice is offered first, to glorify God and in recognition of His Sovereign dominion over all creatures; secondly, in thanksgiving for all the benefits which His divine munificence ceases not to pour upon us in the temporal and spiritual order; thirdly, to offer to His justice a Victim, sufficient and even more than sufficient for our sins; fourthly, to obtain from His bounty in virtue of the merits of His Son, all the graces necessary for our salvation, and in general for all the helps we need. A soul enlightened by faith, which discovers to her the Value of the Blood of the Divine Lamb and the superabundant merits of His Sacrifice, clothed with them, presents herself with unbounded confidence before the Throne of God, knowing that she can offer worthy homage to His Infinite Greatness, thanksgiving proportionate to His benefits, and that she will be heard, whether she beg for new favors or for the pardon of sin. For the voice of His Blood, more powerful than the voice of her sins and miseries, will rise and ascend even to the Heart of God, to call down His benefits and His pardon.

As the Communion is the completion of the Holy Sacrifice, since it applies to the soul all the merits of the Life and Death of Jesus Christ, all the fruits of His Divine Passion; when we have not the happiness of communicating sacramentally, we should not fail to make a Spiritual Communion. At the moment that the Priest consumes the Sacred Host, the fervent Religious will form the most ardent desires of communal eating with him, and opening the door of her heart, she will beg her Divine Spouse to enter and dwell there, not only for a few moments, but during the whole day and the night which is to follow, to be the interior guide of all her steps and the motive of all her thoughts, words, actions and affections.

As to the method of assisting at the Holy Sacrifice, since there are many, one may choose the one most proper to nourish devotion, or most suitable to the state in which she finds herself. This diversity in the manner of hearing Mass is founded upon what has been said of the Holy Sacrifice being a renewal of all the Mysteries of the Life and Death of Jesus Christ, and of applying their graces to our soul. This application and this attention may vary, according to the times and the solemnities of the Church, such as Advent and Lent, Christmas, Easter, or Pentecost.

But as the Mysteries of the Passion are represented at the Holy Mass in a more lively manner than the other mysteries, we may return more habitually to the consideration of our Saviour's sufferings. When the Priest is at the foot of the Altar, we may consider Jesus appearing before His Father in the Garden of Olives, charged with the sins of all men. When he ascends the Altar, while he passes from one side to the other, until the **Sanctus**, we may recall His appearance before the tribunals of the high priests, of Pilate and of Herod. From the **Sanctus** to the **Agnus Dei**, we may meditate on His leaving Jerusalem and His Crucifixion. Finally, at the **Communion**, we place ourselves, in spirit, at the foot of the Cross, to receive in our souls the Precious Blood of this Holy Victim and to unite ourselves entirely to Him. Or we may content ourselves with a single feature of the Passion, or even with some one of the words of Jesus on the Cross. Thus each one may follow her attractions and use that method which will profit her most, and give more devotion.

Examen

Have I acquired a sufficient knowledge of the dogma of the Mass? Have I had for this Adorable Sacrifice a faith, a confidence, a veneration and a love proportionate to its sanctity, its sublimity, its marvelous efficacy? Have I assisted at it with respectful attention and tender piety? Have I offered it with the Priest, according to the four ends for which it has been instituted — Adoration, Thanksgiving, Expiation, Propitiation?

Seventh Day

First Meditation - Hidden Life of Jesus at Nazareth

"He went down with them and came to Nazareth."— St. Luke, II, 51.

I adore Thee, O my Lord, Jesus Christ, in the mystery of Thy hidden life. I contemplate Thee with an admiration mingled with astonishment, in this House of Nazareth, where Thou didst dwell unknown for thirty years. At the sight of this profound retreat, this forgetfulness of creatures, and the care which Thou didst take to hide Thyself from the eyes of all, Thou Who art the True Light, I am confounded and I exclaim with the Prophet: "Truly Thou art a hidden God!" But all hidden as Thou art, Thou dost willingly and graciously reveal Thyself to souls who seek Thee in this obscurity, and Thou discoverest to them admirable secrets. I will no longer ask, Lord, what dost Thou do in Thy solitude and why dost Thou appear to lose Thy time, which, according to human ideas, would be better employed in causing the light of Thy divine wisdom to shine before the world and in teaching men Thy sublime lessons; because this obscurity and silent life is itself the most admirable lesson. Thou hast led it during so many years to make me understand the merit and the advantage of retirement, the value of an obscure and ignored state; and to extinguish in my heart that love of being known, loved and esteemed by creatures, and of seeing them occupied with me, of occupying myself with them, and with a multitude of exterior cares that serve only to absorb my attention, which should be occupied with Thee alone.

FIRST POINT - A Hidden Life and at the Same Time a Common Life

As Jesus Christ was to be the Model for all men, He willed to lead a common life, a family life. He did not hide in the desert, far from the commerce of men, but left this extraordinary life to His Holy Precursor; yet He hid Himself more securely in the obscure labors of a vulgar trade. He lived with Mary and Joseph in a little town of Galilee, Nazareth, of which it was customary for the Jews to say: "Can any good come out of Nazareth?" It was in this despised place that He passed the greater part of His life upon earth. The world ignored Him, and the Jews themselves, notwithstanding the testimonies of the Prophets so precise and so numerous, are far from supposing that in this corner of Galilee, under the humble care of a poor workman, resides the Redeemer, expected from the commencement of the world, and promised to their fathers. There nothing shows a trace of His heavenly origin; He allows not to escape one ray of that celestial light, which will one day enlighten the whole world. The inhabitants of Nazareth regard Him with indifference, they do not penetrate into the interior of the Holy Family, which on their side remain strangers to worldly affairs and interests. Thus Jesus, Mary and Joseph live, ignored, forgotten and almost unknown to their fellow-citizens, but known to God, Who regards them with complacency, while He turns with indignation from a corrupt and corrupting world, given up to the demon and to sin, in which all is lies and nothingness, and which despises true goods for those which are deceitful.

O Life of Jesus hidden with Mary and Joseph! Perfect model of the life of Carmel; happy life where the soul doubly hidden from the world and herself, lives only for God, occupies herself only in pleasing Him, without any anxiety for the esteem of the world which she has abandoned. Ah, who will give me to understand the inestimable treasure which it contains! What security, what advantages in living unknown to the world, and without knowing it! If the world knew me, it would blame or it would praise me, and perhaps it would do both at the same time, but to the ruin of my soul; for if it praised me, it would be for pretended virtue, which existed only according to its mistaken judgments, and this would nourish in me the secret esteem which I have for myself; if it blamed me, it would be precisely on the occasion of my practising humility or penance, which form all my strength, and would disgust me with them. If I knew the world, I would, perhaps, love what it loves and esteem what it esteems, and thus fall into its snares.

Ah, it is much better for me to forget it and to be forgotten by it, for Saint Paul says: "If I please the world and the world pleases me, I am no friend of Jesus Christ." I am most happy in being not only hidden from the world, but even from myself, in the common life. In effect, in living the holy life composed of salutary practises which others share with me, I avoid singularity and escape vain glory; and, moreover, the exercises of the common life, far from losing their merit by being shared, add to their value that of obedience and the edification of the neighbor. Thus all souls enlightened by the Spirit of God have in general, a particular attraction for the common life, and avoid with care all singularity. This, O Jesus! is the fruit of Thy hidden Life, that precious grace by which the soul takes pleasure in the practices of the common life, which hides her from the esteem of creatures and her own esteem. However, she advances each day toward perfection, by an intention ever more upright and an affection ever more pure, with which she observes her Rule; but this interior progress escapes the view of man and even that of herself, and is known and appreciated by God alone.

But, alas! O my God, must I still find in myself so much opposition to this happy life, where all is hidden! What! do I still find it painful to consent to be forgotten by creatures! Do I not find it hard not to speak of them, not to hear of them, not to ask news of any person or anything? And when an occasion of breaking this silence presents itself, do I not seize it with eagerness? Does not my cell sometimes appear tedious to me, and the parlor perhaps agreeable? Do I not become fatigued with edifying conversations, because they do not satisfy my curiosity or nourish my vanity? O confusion! O sorrow! if in Carmel such inclinations do not die, if I occupy myself with attractions so opposed to the hidden life, which I should lead here!

SECOND POINT - A Life of Labor

What a touching picture! What a spectacle worthy the admiration of Angels and our most profound contemplation, is that labor which Jesus embraced from His earliest youth, and which He continues until His thirtieth year. All are occupied with the labor of their hands in the Holy Family. Mary attends to the cares of the house, Joseph supports Jesus and Mary and himself by a poor and laborious trade, and Jesus aids His foster father; and as He grows older the heaviest of the work falls upon Him. I see Him, Who has created the heavens and the earth, take in His divine hands the saw and the hammer, and forge the iron destined for the implements of labor for, according to an ancient tradition, this was the principal occupation of Jesus and Joseph, and in the first centuries, they showed with respect, some ploughs which came from this divine workshop. It was by the sweat of His brow that Jesus wished to teach us to submit ourselves to work, as to a penance imposed by divine justice, and to sanctify it by love and respect for the will of our Heavenly Father.

In the designs of God, work is something more than a penance. It is also a salutary remedy which engages the activity of our minds, and withdraws the imagination from vain and dangerous thoughts, consuming thus a part of the natural life of this body of sin, of which the ardors and the dangerous impetuosities pouring themselves out upon criminal objects, drag the poor soul far from the path of virtue. Let us, then, thank the goodness and the wisdom of God which has ordained that we should labor, and let us sanctify it by uniting ours with that of Jesus. What noble and sublime intentions animated His labor, so holy! What mysterious silence! What ardent aspirations to the throne of His Father! What inflamed desires for His glory! If sometimes the work of the Holy Family was accompanied by words or interrupted by intervals of rare conversation, how holy and useful were such discourses? How well-seasoned by the salt of wisdom and animated by charity? But they spoke little in the house of Nazareth, because where hearts are united to God, and lost in the contemplation of truth, words cannot express the sentiments with which they are filled.

The Rule of Carmel has wisely ordained that the time not consecrated to prayer should be entirely employed in manual labor, and that this work be nourished with holy thoughts; or when at the time of recreation, it is accompanied by conversation, this should always be edifying and foreign to the spirit of the world, which the soul should endeavor to forget. In a word, the interior of the monastery should resemble the interior of Nazareth. But, alas! O my God, Thy example serves to discover to me a multitude of faults which I show in the accomplishment of the work which is given to me, and in the discharge of the offices confided to my care. What eagerness, what natural activity in my occupations? With how many useless words are they accompanied! What little care to keep myself recollected, to unite myself to Thee by frequent aspirations! How often I endeavor to do my work quickly rather than to do it well, less to please Thee than to gain the approbation of creatures. But in general, what neglect, what forgetfulness, what inexactitude, in acquitting myself of it as it has been prescribed by holy obedience. Have I not followed my own will in preference to the Rule, the Holy Customs of the Order and to the will of my Superiors? Thus it has happened that nature, self-love, and levity have caused me to lose the advantages of labor, which I could have rendered so meritorious and so salutary by conforming to Thee, O my Divine Model!

I have worked all the day and I have done nothing for heaven!

O my Divine Jesus, grant that in this Retreat I may learn, after Thy example, to sanctify all my occupations, to render my labors worthy of my state, worthy of Thee, to the end that nothing may be given to creatures, nothing to self-love, but that all may be for Thy glory and Thy love. Amen.

Second Meditation - The Baptism of Jesus

"Then Jesus cometh from Galilee, unto John on the banks of the Jordan, to be baptized by him."— St. Matthew, III, 13.

After having lived in a most profound retreat for thirty years, Jesus Christ goes forth to manifest Himself to the world, of which He is the light and the salvation.

And behold, the first steps He takes are toward the banks of the Jordan, where John the Baptist is preaching penance and baptizing a multitude of sinners, who eagerly run to him. This baptism of John was only a preparation for that more excellent Baptism, which should be instituted by the Saviour. He advances, confounding Himself with the crowd of people, publicans and soldiers loudly confessing their sins, and presents Himself for baptism, but John knew Him, and was already pointing at Him and crying out: "Behold the Lamb of God, behold Him Who taketh away the sins of the world." John could not suffer himself to see Jesus thus humbled, and in the attitude of a sinner: "It is I," said he, filled with confusion, "who ought to be baptized by Thee; and comest Thou to me!" But Jesus answered him: "Suffer it to be so; that thus I may fulfill all justice." In the holy contest, the humility of our Saviour triumphed, and John, through respect to His wishes, yielded and baptized his Divine Master.

O my Saviour, always adorable, always admirable, what a new subject for astonishment and of contemplation does Thy Baptism offer me, but Thou art even more amiable, if possible, when Thou abasest Thy dignity before one who is Thy servant, sent before Thy face to prepare the way. Ah! Lord, a conduct so astonishing must contain some great instruction. Grant me the grace to penetrate it and to be docile to its teachings.

FIRST POINT

The first sense of these words of Jesus Christ: "Suffer it to be so that I might fulfill all justice," marks the intention which He had to confirm by this step the mission of Saint John the Baptist. He wished to honor the ministry which God had confided to him, in charging him to make known to man, the Messiah, and of opening to them, through penance, the way which should conduct them to His love. By this example, the Saviour teaches us to render on all occasions to those who are clothed with His divine authority for the government of the Church, or for the care of souls, the testimony of respect, and all the duties of Religion and of that submission which, as His representatives, they have a right to expect from us. Because **all authority**, especially that of the spiritual order, **comes from God**, and those who resist it, resist God Himself. Our Holy Father the Pope, Bishops in general, all ecclesiastical superiors, confessors, and for me in particular, the Superiors of the Monastery, especially the Mother Prioress, are living representatives of God, depositaries of His power and charged by Him to govern me and to instruct me in my duties.

If Jesus willed to honor in His Precursor, the Envoy of God, and to submit with prodigious humility to his ministry, which has been established only for sinners, how can I, dust and ashes, disregard that respect which I owe to those who are clothed with an authority, all divine, for the guidance of souls? Have I understood that I am obliged to show them all deference, submission, and love, acting in their regard, with a spirit of faith, seeing in them not the creature, but Jesus Christ, Whom they represent.

It is to establish and preserve this spirit that our holy Constitutions impose upon us in regard to our Superiors, above all to the Mother Prioress, the duties of the most profound respect, and of a submission, the most humble and entire. With a little reflection on what they prescribe to me in her regard, as to the manner of speaking and listening to her, and of receiving her advice and corrections, it will be seen that such testimonies are becoming only to Jesus Christ, and that by this, my Rule reminds me unceasingly that she is for me the most lively image of Him in the Monastery. But if these exterior demonstrations are not accompanied by a profound spirit of faith and piety, it is evident that I render myself culpable of a kind of hypocrisy, and lose at the same time, the precious fruit of these acts of Religion.

But, O my God, how far withdrawn am I from this spirit of faith! How little have I profited by these means so numerous, which have been offered to me to increase in virtue by imitating Thee! But I wish henceforth to walk in Thy footsteps, and to say with Thee, in regard to my Superiors: "Suffer it to be so that I might fulfill all justice."

SECOND POINT

But if Jesus Christ, by this solemn act, recognized and honored the ministry of His Holy Precursor, did He not destroy His own? By mingling with sinners to ask baptism from John, did He not expose Himself to pass as a sinner, and thus destroy in the minds of all men a belief in the truth that He was the source of all the graces necessary for penitent? And, in effect, what a prodigious abasement! I am not surprised at Saint John's repugnance to consent to the desires of His Divine Master to be baptized as a sinner. But Jesus troubles Himself not about the judgments which the multitude will pass upon Him. He cares not — He is the representative of sinners, He comes to pay the penalty of their sins, and with this title, He humbles and annihilates Himself, and honors in Saint John the ministry of public penance, and it is in this sense that we should understand these words: "Suffer it to be so."

He regards not what refers to His Divine Person, it is the affair of His Father; His own is to glorify His Father and to abase Himself. And the Eternal Father chooses this circumstance to show forth the Divinity and the Glory of the Saviour: "Jesus after His baptism, being come out of the water, behold the heavens were opened above His head, and the Spirit of God descended upon Him in the form of a dove; at the same time a voice from heaven was heard saying, 'This is My Beloved Son in Whom I am well pleased.'"

It is thus that God is pleased to pour down His cherished favors, and to mark with the seal of His Spirit those who forget their own interests to occupy them with the interests of His glory, who seek after humiliations, or at least fear not to abase themselves before those who bear the mark of His authority. In effect, it suffices not, if we wish to enter into the Spirit of Jesus Christ, that we treat superiors with faith and respect. It is necessary besides not to fear to abase ourselves, to humble ourselves before them in presence of all, that is in presence of the Community; to render to them the most humble duties, to receive their orders with submission, to accept their advice and corrections with a good heart without opposing any excuse interiorly or exteriorly, without testifying any discontent; on the contrary, the humble posture of our body and the expression of our countenance should testify that we recognize ourselves worthy of these reproaches and of others more severe, and that we receive with gratitude their admonitions, having a sincere intention of profiting by them.

But, O my sweet and humble Jesus, how Thy example covers me with confusion! How different my conduct from Thine! How little have I practised this submission of mind and heart to the advice and correction of my Superiors! How little have I observed with an interior spirit that point of my Rule which obliges me to humble myself before them! I content myself with a vain ceremony, and I accomplish it without sentiments of confusion, of deference, of acquiescence, in which consists all its value. O my most amiable Redeemer, perfect Model of all virtues, and particularly of humility and obedience, grant me during this Retreat the grace to be penetrated with their importance and their value. May I henceforth practise them more faithfully, that by imitating Thee I may learn to love Thee on earth and possess Thee in heaven. Amen.

Third Meditation - Jesus in the Desert

"Jesus being full of the Holy Ghost, returned from the Jordan and was led by the Spirit into the desert. For the space of forty days; and was tempted by the devil. And having eaten nothing during those days when they were ended, He was hungry." — S. Luke IV, 1-2.

I adore Thee, O Divine Solitary, in a spirit of admiration and gratitude, because of the marvelous example which Thou dost give us of the eremitical

109

life. Thou didst deliver Thy Innocent Body to rude austerities in the Desert, and didst submit Thyself to a most humiliating trial for my instruction, that of being tempted by Satan. It is true that this temptation was only exterior, for Satan had not the least power over Thy Divine Person, and that he found in Thee no matter of temptation — all there being holy and perfectly regulated, and nothing in Thy sacred flesh or holy mind capable of being troubled without Thy express will. But Thou hast willed to teach us by Thy example how we should conduct ourselves in our combats with the enemy; and hast furnished us by the grace which flows from this Mystery, with the arms necessary for overcoming him. Be Thou always blessed for it!

FIRST POINT - Jesus in the Desert, the Model of the Solitary Life

The Solitary Life is an extraordinary life which cannot be followed except by a small number, and which should, consequently, not be chosen except by a particular attraction of the Spirit of God.

It was for this that it is related in the Gospel that Jesus Christ was led by the Spirit into the De3ert; and in living there forty days, He has merited for His Church those abundant graces, whose marvelous effects have peopled the desert with a multitude of Solitaries who have followed Him, and who have astonished the world by their detachment, penance, and the practice of all virtues. Our Saviour, in the Desert, had no other companions than wild beasts, no other shelter than the rocks, no other bed than the earth, and He consecrated all His time to prayer, accompanied by an uninterrupted fast.

The Solitary Life, when the soul is called to it by God, is most fruitful in spiritual benefits of all kinds. In this happy life, the soul withdrawn from all communion with creatures, finds herself near to God, and disposed for His Divine communications. The noise of the world, the impression of its joys, its affairs, its affections, and its concerns, reach her not, and she understands that God is all and takes the place of all things. Insensibly, she begins to taste His sweetness and to repose in Him above all creatures, above all that is not God; and the more she enjoys the Sovereign Good, the better she will understand the utter nothingness of all that is not God. She ends by forgetting the world and herself, to repose in Him Who is her life. O happy life, source of the purest joy, of an abundance of holy tears, and of an astonishing familiarity with God!

But, as nature, the flesh, and self-love are always living there — because the Solitary soul, not being able, alas! to separate entirely from them, has brought them with her into the desert — this soul, led by the Spirit of God, must be continually accompanied by prayer and penance. Without these precautions, the solitary life will be for her only an illusion full of perils. This Jesus teaches us — He went into the Desert only when He was led by the Spirit of God, and while there He lived in continual prayer and austerity. Now the soul who wishes to imitate Him with security in her solitude, must remain there with a spirit of docility, of obedience, of prayer, and a hatred of

110

self which she must never abandon.

While the life of Carmel is a community life, it is, nevertheless, pre-eminently a solitary life. The spirit which reigns there is an eremitical spirit; a Carmelite is e hermit of the holy Mountain of Carmel; she ought to be as perfect a solitary as if her cell were built in the midst of a desert, placed at a distance from the others of the community. The spirit of solitude, which is the spirit of her vocation, ought to effect in her this holy disposition, and she will be a perfect solitary if she maintains herself in a state of abnegation and of death, indifferent not only to the interests and affairs of the world, but even to those of her own Monastery, that is to the work, to the affairs, to the employment of her companions, in a word: to all that does not refer to her own particular duties. If she is faithful to the holy law of renouncement taught in her Constitutions, and so strictly followed by all the holy Religious of her Order, she will avoid looking around, raising her eyes to consider the countenance of any one, or to occupy herself with what is going on, giving her opinion or asking news. If a careful observer of the holy laws of modesty and of silence, she will speak only when necessary or very useful, and then in a moderate tone of voice, avoiding all boisterous mirth, or those exterior manifestations which would make her lose that spirit of habitual recollection in which she ought to live. She will be a perfect solitary if, besides exterior silence, she observes that interior silence of the spirit which forbids all use-less thoughts and remembrances, that silence of the heart which renounces all attachment, all affections for creatures — parents, friends and all objects which could occupy her contrary to the spirit of her state. In fine, she will be a perfect solitary, if she is fervent in filling her mind and heart, thus emptied of creatures, with images and affections drawn from the life and death of our Saviour; if she nourish herself with His Divine Word and with the frequent aspirations which His love will inspire. O holy solitude of Carmel! O sole be-atitude, which has conducted so many of its holy inhabitants to the highest perfection of love; why have I until now profited so little by advantages so precious? Ah! I understand it now: it is because in the midst of solitude I have been little solitary; I have found there an occasion of sin rather than a means of perfection, a martyrdom rather than a consolation; and because I did not possess its spirit, I failed to gather its precious fruits. In occupying myself with what was going on around me, and wishing to see and hear eve-rything, I have lost the spirit of recollection, and consequently those holy thoughts, those inflamed desires which are the life of a solitary soul, and thus I have closed the entrance of my heart to the visits of the Holy Spirit, and to the inspirations of His grace.

O Jesus, Divine Solitary, grant me in this Retreat, the spirit of solitude which is the soul of the life of Carmel, and for this end, grant me the grace to overcome the sallies of an unmortified nature, which bears me so violently toward exterior objects, drawing me away from the sanctuary of my heart, where Thou so much desirest to stay, if Thou couldst find me there and alone.

SECOND POINT - Jesus Is Tempted by the Devil to Teach Us by What Means We May Overcome Him

But the more important solitude is for drawing the soul to God and causing it to produce fruits of the most precious virtue, the more Satan, jealous of these advantages, seeks to disturb and turn away souls who embrace it, from an enterprise which can procure so much glory for God, and is so powerful an aid to Holy Church. Thus, while he attacks lightly, persons engaged in the world where the are so many occasions of falling and so many subjects of scandal, he redoubles his efforts against solitary souls, and endeavors to lay snares under their feet. But by an admirable dispensation of the Providence of God, for Whom they have left all, such deceits of Satan serve only to purify these generous souls, and afford them new means of sanctification. At the same time, their victory over the cruel enemy turns to his confusion, glorifies God Who is the author of it, and prepares for them brilliant crowns.

It was for this end that Jesus, as the Model of solitary souls, descended first into the arena, conducted by the Spirit, and defied to the combat, the proud enemy, in order to give us by His victory, an illustrious example of the conduct we should follow in the solitary life which is a perpetual warfare. The temptations to which He condescended to submit, are those which ordinarily assail solitary souls. The first is a temptation to sensuality, under the pretext of necessity: "Command these stones to be changed into bread"; but Jesus in replying to the tempter, "Man liveth not by bread alone, but by every word which proceedeth out of the mouth of God," teaches the solitary soul when tempted to relax the holy rigors of mortification, that we must seek relief in our sufferings and our wants, only according to the Rule and the advice of our Superiors, in order to avoid falling into the snares of nature — always eager to satisfy itself.

The second temptation is a foolish presumption, under the pretext of showing forth the power of God: "Cast Thyself down from the pinnacle of this temple, if Thou be the Son of God; for it is written, He has given His Angels charge over Thee." But Jesus replied: "It is written, thou shalt not tempt the Lord, thy God," warning the solitary soul of an illusion very dangerous, and nevertheless very common, into which the devil draws certain persons. Under pretext of the glory of God, and greater perfection, they aspire to extraordinary states of prayer. Deceived by the enemy, they produce by the imagination, or receive really through the power of the devil, pretended visions and revelations, which serve only to nourish self-love.

The third attack of the devil upon our Lord was to present Him with a fantastic image of the false glory and the vain grandeur of the world, which he promised upon condition that He prostrate and adore him. It is thus that Satan strives to relax the fervor of the solitary in her search after perfection, by recalling to her memory the vain pleasures and goods of the world, which he wishes to make her regret, and perhaps may succeed in engaging her to return to their enjoyment. Jesus Christ teaches her here to arm herself against this temptation by the remembrance and the love of her Sovereign Good, in saying: "The Lord, thy God, alone shouldst thou adore, and Him only shouldst thou serve." God alone is my beginning and my end; God alone can give me joy and happiness: I have chosen Him for my portion, I shall never quit so good a Master to become the slave of Satan and the world.

But the Religious soul should never forget that, according to the example of her Divine Saviour, she must oppose to temptation fasting, that is to say, a constant mortification of the senses, and a prayer accompanied by continual recollection. And in the same way that our Lord had humble recourse to the Word of God, in replying to the devil, so should she, in all temptations, have recourse to her Superior, who is the sacred oracle where she may find her replies, the spiritual arsenal where she will obtain arms to attack the enemy. Without this simplicity, without this humble communication to those charged with guiding her, she will remain exposed to the attacks of Satan and will soon be overcome, while very often the simple avowal of a temptation will serve to banish it, and to put the tempter to flight.

Oh! how true it is, my God, that those who enter Thy service must prepare their souls for temptation. How dangerous are the temptations of the enemy against those who have left all to follow Thee! What violence, what ruses, to attack each one in the weakest point! Then often the Angel of Darkness transforms himself into an Angel of Light, in order to draw us into illusions, discouragements, or a foolish presumption. O my God, how can we escape so many dangers, if we are not aided by Thy example and assisted by Thy grace? With this double help, I hope to triumph over him. It must then be by prayer, by mortification, by recollection, and an humble opening of my heart to the guide of my soul, that I can gain the victory. O my Divine Saviour, I beg of Thee this grace, through the victory Thou didst gain over him in the desert. Amen.

LECTURE - The Solitude Proper to Carmel

In the same way that in the Religious life in general, they are poor only by vow and in spirit, since in reality nothing is wanting, not only of what is necessary, but even useful for the support and well-being of life; thus in Carmel, where all are obliged to an eremitical state of life, they can be solitary only by affection and in spirit. In reality and materially, they live in society, that is, in constant contact with the other members of the community. But as the poverty which is practised in Religion is real and full of merit when one has its true spirit; so the solitude of Carmel is real and marvelously fruitful, when one possesses the grace for it. But here is the difficulty, and it must even be admitted that few persons attain perfection in the eremitical spirit, because there are few souls generous enough to persevere in the constant efforts which it is necessary to make in denying themselves all useless intercourse with creatures.

Now by creatures, we understand here persons, even those nearest to us, and by intercourse, we understand the relations which we keep up with them by the senses. For we communicate with our neighbor by the eyes, the mouth, the ears, even by the imagination and the heart. When once a soul succeeds in imposing silence on all her senses by closing the door through which she pours herself out upon creatures, and becomes in the midst of her companions as solitary as in the desert; when she loves her cell, cherishes retirement; when she is a stranger to all care, to all curiosity, to all desire to know or to speak, then she begins to find a charm all divine in her solitude, and soon tastes the sweetness of God to such a degree, that all which does not recall to her His holy presence or remind her of His love and benefits, is insipid. It is in this precious solitude that is found the source of those tears which purify the soul, day and night, and enables her to attain an astonishing familiarity with God. Because from the moment that we speak no longer with creatures, and remember them only so far as charity and our duty to God require, our intercourse with the Creator becomes more easy and more frequent, and the soul thus prepared by her habitual intercourse with our Lord, has no difficulty I will not say in recollecting herself in her prayers, since she is recollected even in the midst of her exterior occupations, but in raising herself to God, and uniting herself to Him by this intimate communication.

By what steps may we arrive at this spirit of solitude of which the fruits are so precious? The first step is silence. Silence is, in effect, one of the most admirable means which the Holy Spirit has suggested to Religious of all times and in all lands, to arrest the source of a multitude of irregularities and sins, of which the tongue is the principle, the occasion, or the instrument. Not only is the tongue an instrument at the service of all the passions, but it even awakens and excites them when they are dormant, and apparently extinct; and in consequence of the intemperance of the tongue, the wise are often taken in great straits; while, on the contrary, as the Scripture tells us, a fool may pass for a wise man, if he will but keep silence.

To these advantages, which we may call negative, we can add many of a positive nature, which it procures us. By silence we learn to become master of ourselves, according to the Word of God: "He who holds his tongue, keepeth his soul," and, consequently, it makes us practise the most excellent of mortifications. It obliges us to enter into ourselves, to speak to God, or to listen to His Holy inspirations, in order to obey them immediately. By silence, we imitate the holy inhabitants of the desert, who live withdrawn from all converse with creatures, in order to contemplate more easily heavenly things. We understand, then, that silence is an indispensable condition for attaining the spirit of solitude. It is unnecessary to add that this exterior silence will have no value, at least will produce only a small part of the happy effects of which we have just spoken, if unaccompanied by interior silence; that is, that attentive care to banish from the mind all dangerous and even useless remembrances, from the heart, all affections and sensible attachments which could disturb it.

The second means is the spirit of abnegation and of death to all that is not God, and an entire indifference to all that relates not to His glory, His service, and the accomplishment of His holy will. It is here that the difficulties augment and combats will multiply. It is no longer the mouth only which must be closed to all useless converse; the ears must be shut to the noise that attracts our attention and excites our curiosity. The eyes must be closed, first to those with whom we treat, then to their occupation and their work; to all places through which we pass, and the objects which we meet. Then we must control our walk, avoid precipitation; apply ourselves to become modest and guarded, in order that the soul may not be tarnished by levity and indiscretion. The mind, so prompt in fixing upon all that presents itself, must be restrained from making reflections, and prevented from giving advice for which we have not been asked. In a word, we must resemble a dead person, who has eyes and sees not, ears and hears not, a mouth and speaks not.

But as there is in the heart of man an intense craving, and in his mind an extreme activity, solitude will become insupportable, even impossible, if with the deprivation of all converse with creatures he does not force himself to converse habitually with God. This is at once the means and the end of the solitary life, which at first sight seems contradictory, but which, nevertheless, is well founded upon reason. In the beginning, without doubt, solitude will appear tiresome and conversing with God difficult; however, in the measure that we, on one side, withdraw our hearts from creatures and, on the other, turn to God by short and fervent prayers and loving aspirations, the weariness of retreat will diminish, and the sweetness of this intercourse with God will soon make itself felt. Thus we soon reap the first fruits of our efforts. This is the place to make known the importance, the necessity even, of frequent aspirations and of ejaculatory prayers, called by masters of the spiritual life loving movements or elevations of the soul toward heaven. In vain should we pretend to arrive at real prayer, and much less at contemplation, if we do not accustom ourselves to these familiar conversations with God, to these frequent aspirations. Without doubt, and it is an admitted fact, this habit is difficult to contract, and we cannot succeed in it without a special grace from God. But when a Religious soul perseveres in this design, which she profits by all occasions to offer to God her labors, and to express to Him her desires, her love or her regret, according to the circumstances or dispositions in which she may be; if she determines beforehand the number of times during the day that she will raise her heart to God, as at each hour the clock strikes, the beginning and end of each occupation; if she apply herself to formulate in advance a certain number of aspirations of love, of faith, of confidence, of humility, confusion, mortification; and if she study to employ them according to her needs and her attractions, making use of certain means which will recall this holy practice, she will certainly attract to her the benevolent regard of her Creator, Who will not fail to recompense her perseverance by the precious gift of a habitual remembrance of His holy presence, a gift which will be infallibly followed by that of prayer. Few persons are courageous and persevering enough alas! never to abandon this holy resolution, when once taken; and behold why so few are true solitaries, why so few attain to contemplation.

As to myself, I am a Carmelite and, consequently, I am called in a special manner to unite myself to God by prayer. I should then never neglect the most efficacious and indispensable means of corresponding to my vocation, and this means is to exert myself to become a solitary and a contemplative. I will remember the lessons and the examples of our Holy Mother, Saint Teresa, who teaches me to enter within that "little heaven of my soul and to regard nothing outside of it, in order to find there the One who created it." "Those who have entered upon this way should know," says she, "that they walk in an excellent way, and that in a short time they will drink of the fountain of Living Water." "This habit of recollection," again says the Holy Mother, "is one that depends on us. It is acquired by striving, little by little, to render ourselves masters of ourselves, and recalling our senses within, retrenching their exterior uses, to make them serve for our interior recollection. So that, if we speak, we try to remember that we are to converse with One within our own soul; if we listen, we should remember that we are about to hear One Who speaks most intimately to us, and if we wish, we may never be separated from this Divine Companion. Let the soul, if she can," continues our Holy Foundress, "practice this often in the course of the day, or at least sometimes; by accustoming ourselves to this, we shall, sooner or later, derive great advantage from it. God will no sooner have granted this grace to a soul, than she would not wish to exchange it for all the treasures of earth. In the name of God, since nothing is acquired without trouble, do not complain of the time and application which you employ in this; and I assure you that, with the assistance of Our Lord, you will succeed at the end of one year, or perhaps in half that time."

Oh! how well adapted are these words to encourage and animate me to this holy labor. Whence is it, Lord, that, after so many years in Religion, I find myself so far from this holy custom? "Ah! my Lord," exclaims our Holy Mother, St. Teresa, in answer, "all the evil comes from our not understanding the truth that Thou art so near to us. We act as if Thou wert far away. Ah! great indeed would be the distance were it necessary for us to go to heaven to find Thee. I would wish, at present," she adds, "to make them understand that to accustom ourselves to fix our mind, in order that it may know what it says, and to whom it speaks, it is necessary to recollect our interior senses, and give them something to occupy them, having no doubt that heaven is found within us, since the Creator of heaven dwells there. I confess never having known what it was to pray with satisfaction until He taught me this method, and as. I have derived so much profit from thus recollecting myself, this is why I have insisted so long on this subject."

Examen.

Am I well persuaded that a solitary spirit is essential to the holy Order to which I have the honor of belonging, and that, without it, I do not merit the name of Carmelite? Do I understand the inestimable value and multiplied advantages of solitude? Have I the spirit of solitude? To know whether I possess it, I have only to examine whether I love the retreat of the cell; whether I find my delight in silence and recollection; whether I have a horror of the parlor and of useless conversations, of worldly news, of dissipation and noise. Have I not, on the contrary, a desire, a kind of need to converse with creatures and to know what is going on? Have I not readily seized the occasion of leaving our cell, or the place of my ordinary occupations?

If I have so little of the eremitical spirit, should I not attribute it to my little care to keep silence, which I break without scruple and for the most frivolous reasons, thus depriving myself of its precious fruits? It is not also because of my little zeal for the mortification of the senses, for the practice of abnegation and of the spirit of death, that I am so little solitary and, consequently, so little recollected during the day and that I have so little fervor in my prayers? Have I not my ears open to every word and every sound; my eyes attentive to or distracted by all that excites my curiosity; my mind awakened by a crowd of objects which ought to be strangers to it, and my mouth always ready to express the sentiments which they excite?

To attain and to nourish this spirit of solitude, have I made use of frequent ejaculatory prayers? Have I not neglected this practice because it required care, attention, and perseverance, despising thus one of the most frequent recommendations of our Holy Mother, Saint Teresa?

Eighth Day

First Meditation - The Public Life of Jesus

"He went about doing good."— Acts of Apostles X, 38.

I will contemplate Thee to-day, O, My Divine Master, in Thy Public Life. What subjects of admiration present themselves! Each one of Thy steps is marked by miracles; words full of grace fall from Thy lips for our instruction; brilliant testimony is rendered to Thy Divinity by men, by Angels and by God Himself, Who several times declares that Thou art His Beloved Son. But my Saviour, that which strikes me above all in these marvels is Thy ineffable charity to man, that love so pure, so disinterested, so patient, so generous, so strong, so constant, so magnanimous to those whom Thou tenderly callest Thy brethren, and whom Thou lovest even so far as to forget Thyself, sacrificing to their interests the most pressing necessities, the legitimate care of Thy sacred Person, its consolations the most holy, its repose, its sleep and even

Thy conversations with Thy Eternal Father. Admirable charity which belongs only to Thee, and which has made Thee abandon the care of Thy reputation and even of Thy life. Thus Thy great Apostle, St. Paul assures us that Thou didst never seek Thy own satisfaction and wast occupied with one thing only — to save men and to do good to all, at Thy own expense.

O ineffable charity of Jesus! May I in this meditation be so penetrated with Thy sweetness, that my heart inflamed by Thy divine ardors, may no longer be touched by anything but the interests of Thy Glory and the salvation of souls.

FIRST POINT - The Charity of Jesus Conversing with Men

The Holy Gospel, properly speaking, is nothing but a history of the charity of Jesus Christ. Nothing is more admirable, nothing more touching than the picture which it offers us on each page, of the Saviour conversing with men. I open at hazard this Sacred Book, and everywhere I find Him instructing the ignorant, consoling the poor and the afflicted, and curing the sick, without giving Himself either repose or relaxation. He went on foot through the cities, the villages, and the country places of Judea, surrounded and pressed by a multitude of persons, for whose wants He provided, at one time nourishing them with material bread which His charity multiplied at another, dispensing to them the more precious bread of His Word. He cured their infirmities and supported their importunities without ever testifying the least weariness. They stop Him in His discourses and He listens; they interrupt His repasts and He abandons them; they call Him from His prayer and He follows; they press round Him with requests and He satisfies them; they present Him with insidious questions and He replies with wisdom and sweetness. He supports without complaint the grossness of His disciples, the injuries of His persecutors, and the calumnies of His enemies; showering upon all new benefits, and calling upon all without exception, to come and seek in His Divine Heart, relief in their labors and rest for their souls, and to prove by a happy experience the sweetness and humility of this Divine Heart. It was thus that Jesus showed Himself during the three years of His Public Life; making no account of Himself, seeking Himself in nothing, immolating Himself each instant in His most pure satisfactions in His tastes so holy, and in His most imperious needs. And if, with the light of faith, we penetrate the mind and the Heart of our Divine Model, we will find there only one thought, one desire, which presses and consumes Him, it is to sacrifice Himself entirely for those for whom, in His immense love, He has descended from Heaven; which made the Apostle say: "Jesus Christ did not please Himself in anything."

O Jesus! teach me the source whence Thou hast drawn this sacred fire which Thou earnest to cast on earth, and dost so ardently desire to see inflaming all men. Ah! this love so generous, so pure, so disinterested, which I admire in Thee, Thou hast drawn from Thy love for Thy Eternal Father, in Thy zeal so perfect, for His glory and His interests. Thou teachest me also that the precept of the love of my neighbor is the same as the precept of the love of God, because it is essentially contained in it. In degenerate man, Thy divine eyes have discovered the effaced image of God, and by taking human nature, Thou hast accepted the work of repairing it. "Scarcely," says the Apostle, "can we find one who is willing to die for a just man," but that which shows forth Thy infinite charity is that Thou wast willing to die for us, who were sinners, and Thy enemies. Thou hast no need at all of us, and it is entirely gratuitous that Thou dost love us with so much ardor and support us with so much patience, await us with so much longanimity, and save us with so many sorrows and ignominies. O love, love so pure, so generous, so tender, so compassionate, mayst thou prevail over my insensibility, my hardness of heart in the accomplishment of the precept of charity!

In effect, whence comes it that I find in myself so much egotism, that I seek myself in all things, that I am so touched by what refers to myself, and so little by what concerns others? Ah! it is the sad heritage of my first father Adam; that self-love which is the fatal source of all evils, and from which flow in a direct line faults against the love of our brother — hatred, jealousies, suspicions, calumnies, contempt, and that cruel insensibility for the suffering and misfortune of others. Ah! my God, if I loved Thee truly, I would also love my neighbor, since he is Thy image and Thou wishest that I regard him as Thyself. If I truly loved Thee, O my God, I would love myself less, or rather I would love myself better by loving myself for Thee, and in Thee. I would find my happiness in sacrificing, after the example of Thy Divine Son, my own personal interests and satisfaction for the requirements of my neighbor, and thus I would advance more and more in Thy love. Oh! who will give me to draw water from the fountains of the Saviour, sacred source of charity where is extirpated the root of that cursed tree, self-love, which produces only the bitter fruit of sin.

SECOND POINT - The Character of True Charity

In order to know whether I really have in my heart that charity for my neighbor, of which Jesus Christ has left us so admirable an example, it is necessary that I examine well in this Retreat, its characteristics as they have been traced for us by St. Paul:

1st. — Charity is patient; it supports with a good heart, the weakness, the humors, and the imperfections of its neighbor.

2nd. — Charity is sweet and kind; it never allows harsh or proud words to escape; and when it sees that the persons to whom it speaks have little virtue, it offends them not easily, it treats them with caution, never using stern words or reproving them with anger, or commanding them with arrogance.

3rd. — It envieth not. Far from envying the happiness of its neighbor or being afflicted at his progress in virtue, it rejoices as if it were its own gain, and wishes for him what it desires for itself.

4th. It acts not through caprice or humor. It knows not how to feign, dissemble or flatter, it is not light, inconstant or bold.

119

5th. It is not proud. It makes each one have a greater esteem for his neighbor than for himself, showing deference to one another, honoring one another, according to this precept of the Apostle.

6th. — It is not ambitious; that is to say, it has no desire to domineer over others.

7th. — It seeks not its own: it is ever ready to sacrifice for the good of the community, its own interests, its ease, its tastes, and on certain occasions, even its spiritual advantages when God requires this, abandoning to Him the care of compensating it by more abundant graces.

8th. — It is not easily provoked to anger. It is never irritated against any one, but feels towards all sentiments of kindness.

9th. — It thinketh no evil: it is not suspicious. It never suspects actions or attributes them to bad motives, and far from reflecting upon the evil which may have been done to it, it excuses, pardons, and forgets all.

10th. — It rejoices not in iniquity; on the contrary, it rejoices to see good accomplished, to see the good qualities and virtues of its neighbor; and far from secretly triumphing over his falls, his defects, and his imperfections, or over the confusion of those publicly corrected, the charitable soul is grieved and reflects that she herself is capable of even greater disorders.

11th. — It suffers all things; that is, it accommodates itself to different characters, to the imperfections, to the requirements of its neighbor, without appearing to notice them, knowing that this patience with the faults of others is a sacrifice most agreeable to God.

12th. It believeth all things. It believes all the good it can of its neighbor, and willingly admits that his intentions must be good.

13th. — It hopeth all things; that is to say, although it sees imperfections in others, it hopes, nevertheless, that they will amend, because it never loses the good opinion it has that they will listen to grace with a good will.

14th. — It beareth all things, and its constancy in serving its neighbor is so great that it cannot be shaken by contempt, or suffering, or any temptations.

In this admirable picture of charity, traced by St. Paul, it is easy to recognize it as Queen of all the Virtues, and although it be not itself patience, humility, meekness, modesty, endurance and fortitude, it makes the soul practise these virtues while they without it have no value, or at least merit no reward. The same Apostle says: "If I have faith enough to move mountains, give all my goods to the poor and my body to be burned, and have not charity, it profiteth me nothing, for without charity, I am as sounding brass and a tinkling cymbal." Alas! my God, when I compare my sentiments and my life to this divine image of charity, have I not cause to fear that I have done nothing and that all the practices of the Rule, all the austerities of the Religious life in which I am engaged, are useless, because I have not charity? If in effect, I turn seriously upon myself, how far I find that I am withdrawn from the practice of this most necessary virtue. Have I that sweetness and patience with others? Am I not often surprised by feelings of jealousy, of secret joy at their faults and mistakes? Am I not impatient with them, little inclined to comply with their desires and to assist them in their little wants? Have I not nourished interiorly, aversions toward them, and expressed openly my disapprobation of their actions? When it became necessary to render them some service, have I not shown displeasure, have I not sometimes refused? Have I not been irritated by their words said often without intention of offending me? Have I not kept secret resentments? Have I not complained of their humors, of their character?

O my God, a child of Carmel should be all charity. The most tender love should unite all hearts, even so far that each should be ready to give her life for the others. Without this disposition I dishonor the title of spouse of Jesus Christ, and do not even merit that of disciple.

O my Jesus, by the ineffable charity of Thy Divine Heart, by that love which Thou didst have for all men, I supplicate Thee to grant me in this Retreat, the gift of true fraternal charity, without which I bear in vain the name of Carmelite. Grant me the grace to love all men with a true charity, and above all my sisters with whom I live. May I have with them but one heart, one soul, one sentiment, in order that being united with them on earth by the bonds of most tender charity, I may not be separated from them in a happy eternity. Amen.

Second Meditation - Jesus Washing the Feet of His Apostles

"Before the festival day of the pasch, Jesus knowing that the hour was come that he should pass out of this world to His Father; having loved his own who were in the world, he loved them unto the end. And when supper was done, knowing that his Father had given all things into his hands, and that he came from God and goeth to God. He riseth from supper, layeth aside his garments, and having girded himself with a towel, he putteth water in a basin, and began to wash the feet of His disciples, and to wipe them with the towel with which he was girded. Until coming to Peter, who at first forbade him, then on the menace of Jesus to have no part with him he consented, like the others."— St. John XIII.

O my Divine Master, what prodigy is this, which infinitely surpasses all human intelligence! I see Thee at the feet of Thy disciples to fulfill in their regard a most abject office! Thou didst reply to the chief of Thy Apostles who was confounded at Thy humility: "What I do thou knowest not now; but thou shalt know hereafter." Grant me then this knowledge, Lord! Even more than Thy Apostles do I need it. Teach me why Thou, the King of heaven and earth, into whose hands the Eternal Father has committed all things, didst abase Thy Divine Majesty so low.

FIRST POINT - The Practice of Abjection

The Evangelist, in order to make us better understand how admirable and stupendous was this action of Our Saviour, and what a testimony of charity it contained, prefaces his recital by these solemn words: "Jesus having loved his own who were in the world, loved them even unto the end." Admirable contrast of the sublimity of the Person with the baseness of the action. To show more clearly the greatness of this humility of Jesus, we must remark that the Apostles were all rough men belonging to the lowest of the people, and above all that Judas, the perfidious traitor, was among them; and many of the holy Fathers think that Our Blessed Lord commenced with the traitor, in order that an action so touching might soften his heart. But that which fills us to overflowing with admiration, and is for our instruction, is the manner full of care and diligence with which our Saviour accomplishes this duty.

He rises promptly from table, lays aside His garments, girds Himself with a towel, without the aid of any one, He takes a basin, pours into it the amount of water necessary, and immediately kneels at the feet of His disciples and begins to wash them, taking thus in their regard not only the form but the humble functions of a servant. By this divine ex-. ample, He teaches us the exact care with which we should perform all that we do, even things the most lowly and most humiliating. What must have been the feeling of the disciples when they saw the Divine Master dragging Himself on His knees, so to say, to render them so humiliating a service! What must they have thought and felt when He washed their feet and kissed them with love! Ah! the Gospel speaks only of Peter, but without doubt the others mute and immovable from aston-ishment, could only express by tears their sentiments at the sight of this strange abasement of the Son of God.

Jesus after having washed the feet of His Apostles, replaced His garments, while they still stupefied, awaited in silence the explanation of this mystery of humility and love. Then He said: "Know you what I have just done to you? You call me Lord and Master; and you say well, for so I am. If then I, being your Lord and Master, have washed your feet; you also ought to wash the feet of one another; For I have given you example, that you may do that which you have seen me do."

This act of abjection on the part of Jesus Christ took place on the very eve of His death, and at the moment of instituting the Adorable Eucharist — the Master-piece of His love, the Divine Seal of the New Alliance. This admirable act of humility is then like the preface, or rather like the first article of His Testament, and the most precious heritage He has left us, after that of the ineffable gift of His own Body and Blood. It is then of the greatest importance that I treasure it up by forcing myself to enter into a study of this Mystery, and apply it to myself by a constant and faithful practice of the lessons it teaches me.

In effect, it suffices not that I believe humility to be the root of all virtues, the guardian of all graces, a safe-guard in temptations; that without it the place, the habit, the profession will be but inefficacious guarantees against the perils of life; it suffices not even to have an esteem, a desire of humility, if I do not join to this a true and constant practice of it. For it often happens that we seek to delude others and deceive ourselves, by dispensing ourselves from reducing this virtue to practice; we adopt what does not cost us much; its language, its air, its manners, even to a certain point, its sentiments. Thus, by a hypocrisy more common than we imagine, we exteriorly humble ourselves by our words, or by receiving with apparent submission, corrections and reproofs; while interiorly we excuse and justify ourselves, preserving an esteem for ourselves, and making up for the bad opinion of others, by attributing to ourselves qualities and virtues which we suppose are unknown to them; thus nourishing thoughts most dangerous to humility.

Learn then, O Religious soul, after the example of your Divine Master, that true humility consists in a love of abjection; that the soul which is really humble or at least endeavoring to become so, recognizes her faults, her defects, her daily failings, and makes continual efforts to correct them; while she loves the abjection attached to them, that is to say; the confusion they cause her before God, before others, and in her own eyes. In regard to God and herself, far from letting this confusion cast her down and discourage her, she takes occasion from it to reanimate her confidence. She puts all her trust in grace, is happy to lose all reliance on herself, and regards with a kind of joy her extreme misery, because she hopes that this great weakness will attract to her the mercy of God. In regard to others, that is in presence of the community, she is very happy to be despised, and in the accusations which she makes of her failings, she represents them in a manner the most humble and sincere, seeking to make them known and to suffer the confusion they deserve.

True humility, far from seeking extraordinary gifts in prayer, loves, or at least receives and bears with profit for its spiritual advancement, the prayer which humbles, the trial which mortifies, the afflictions which detach, the temptations which show our own corruption, our own weakness, and what we would be without grace; while in these same circumstances false humility would cause sadness, complaints, and discouragements.

O my Divine Master, to what illusions would we be exposed in regard to humility, if Thou hadst not taught us by Thy own example, that there is no humility without the love of abjection, without a sincere contempt of self? My God, grant me a love for abjection, teach me to take pleasure in what causes me confusion before men, to be glad on the occasion, that my want of virtue be recognized and my imperfections and defects appear. May I rejoice at having few talents, little ability, little education, little intelligence, little address; and far from seeking to avoid the humiliations which come to me from this, may I find my happiness in being nothing, because I will thus be more hidden from the snares of self-love, which is so great an obstacle to Thy grace. Then, Lord, I will expose my misery and my weakness to Thee with more confidence, I will run to Thee as to the source of all good; and Thou wilt supply for my insufficiency by the abundance of Thy grace, Thou who abasest Thyself for the little, and! fillest with Thy favors those who acknowledge their own indigence.

Jesus Christ added: "If you know these things, you shall be blessed if you do them."

By these words, Jesus Christ recommended to us the practice of self-abjection. St. Bernard teaches that the most efficacious means of attaining humility is humiliation. But the occasions of humiliation are rare enough in a community where charity reigns in the hearts of all, and tempers in the heart of the Superior that which in the most just correction might be too sensible for self-love. The soul which has drawn from the teaching and the example of her Divine Master a knowledge of the precious advantages attached to acts of self-abasement, will eagerly seize every occasion of practising them, making use even of expedients and holy ruses, to procure these humiliations which she values so much. As to the rest, the Rule comes before all her desires. Among the excellencies of the Rule of Carmel which distinguishes this Order from all others, we must remark that the practices of humility are very multiplied, and that they hold the first rank in the duties of the Order. The accusation of one's faults publicly, receiving reprimands and penances, never to open the mouth to excuse one's negligence, or to justify innocent actions when misrepresented, to embrace humiliating practices, to impose upon one's self the penances in use before the Sisters assembled in refectory or other places, this is what the Rule commands, permits, and authorizes, and by multiplying these practices of abjection, we enter into its spirit.

But to draw all the advantages from these practices and the many others with which God inspires souls who are truly humble, or filled with a desire to become so, it is necessary to join a true contempt of self to the interior sentiments which correspond to the exterior acts which we are performing. It is necessary then, that the religious soul should believe herself the least among her companions, that she should esteem herself the poorest and most deficient in the community, and far from desiring charges and offices which would bring her into prominence, she wishes for the lowest place, and embraces by preference the humblest employments in the community.

But, O Divine Jesus, are there in Thy House, any employments which can be called little or low? Are there any which cannot be called great and estimable, and if some are more preferable than others, are they not those which draw us nearer to Thee, and make us participate more abundantly in Thy spirit? Ah! unhappy me, if I can for one minute permit in my heart a desire for offices which give me authority over others, or which give me prominence in the community. Unhappy me, if I find any employments little or contemptible among Thy spouses, if I feel any repugnance in fulfilling them, forgetting what Thou, my Divine Master, didst teach me: "He who would be the first among you, let him be the last, and esteem himself the servant of all."

In effect, it is for this reason that superiors, who are obliged by their office to direct the community, and command others, should after the example of Jesus Christ, constitute themselves the servants of all, and in this spirit regard themselves as obeying them, when providing for their spiritual and temporal wants.

But, O Divine Jesus, in order to preserve these sentiments, we have great need of grace to triumph over our inborn pride, and to dissipate all the subterfuges of this hidden enemy, which sometimes persuades us that we will be more useful to Thy service and glory in those employments which attract the attention of others, for without Thee, Lord, we are blind and soon seduced by vanity.

O Heart of Jesus! Heart so humble! be my refuge, grant me to be always ready to suffer with joy, to be abandoned by all creatures and counted as nothing, in order that I may possess within myself a solid peace, receive they grace, and become perfectly united to Thee for time and for eternity. Amen.

Third Meditation - Institution of the Most Holy Eucharist

"After having washed the feet of his disciples; and whilst they were at supper, Jesus took bread, and blessed, and broke, and gave it to his disciples saying: 'Take and eat; This is my body.' And taking the chalice he gave thanks; and gave it to them saying: 'Drink ye all of this. For this is my blood of the new testament, which shall be shed for many unto remission of sins.'" - St. Matthew XXVI, 26-28.

What marvels, O my Divine Redeemer! What riches, what grandeurs, what love in these few words! The Holy Eucharist which Thou didst institute upon the eve of Thy death exhausted, so to speak, Thy power and Thy goodness. For Thou art not able to do anything greater or more excellent for man; never could he have had such a thought himself; and if, which is impossible, it could have presented itself to his mind, never could he have dared to ask its execution. This Mystery is truly an abridgment, a memorial of all Thou hast done for Thy people, the reality of all the figures contained in the holy Books, the accomplishment of all Thy promises, the seal of the new and veritable Alliance. This is the real and true sacrifice of which the gross victims of the Jewish law were but dark shadows. It is the Tree of Life planted in the field of the Church to give us immortality. It is the mirror of all virtue, the inexhaustible source of all grace, the bread of the traveler. In a word, it is our entire religion, the only religion worthy of God; for there are united in Thy Divine Person, my Jesus, the Temple and the Altar, the Priest and the Victim, the oblation and the prayer: all that forms the essence of religion. How then shall I be able to enter into the contemplation of so high a Mystery, if Thou dost not aid me and elevate my mind above my own weakness and misery? But as my profession makes it my duty to consecrate myself to love and honor this Master-piece of Thy charity, I confidently hope Thou wilt not refuse me the succor I humbly beg.

FIRST POINT - The Eucharist is the Abridgment, the Center and the Reality of all Religion

Adam placed in that perfect state of innocence and felicity which we have so often considered and admired, possessed in the Tree of Life a precious fruit which secured for his body immortality; and in the ineffable grace which united him to God by charity, the assurance of a life still more precious. This double life the first man should have transmitted to us, but alas! he lost it, and has instead transmitted with his sin, the two-fold death of soul and body. Irremediable loss, fault ineffable in its greatness, and absolutely irreparable since it outraged God Himself!

But Jesus Christ has become through love the Repairer of humanity, thus fallen; not only did He immolate Himself to the justice of an offended God, but He has willed to fulfill to the very end the mission He had accepted, that of replacing man in the happy state from which he had fallen. Upon the Cross He paid, superabuntantly, all our debts, and fully satisfied God by a sacrifice of infinite value; and this sacrifice He perpetuates in the adorable Eucharist, in order to apply to our souls until the end of ages, its precious fruits — fruits much more excellent than those of the Tree of Life; for these only assured us of the life of the body while the Body and Blood of Jesus Christ deposits in our flesh, a germ of immortality, which ought to make it one day rise gloriously from the tomb, and restores to our soul the true life which it had lost. Thus are accomplished the admirable promise of Jesus Christ: "He that eateth my flesh and drinketh my blood, hath everlasting life: and I will raise him up on the last day," and the terrible menace not less formal: "Except you eat the flesh of the son of man, and drink his blood, you shall not have life in you." It is therefore in the Divine Eucharist that we find the true Life which was destroyed by Adam's sin. It is also the perpetual sacrifice where Jesus Christ is at once the Priest and the Victim; since it was this Divine Saviour Who was offered upon the Cross, upon the Altar of His Heart and in the only temple worthy of God, which as He Himself declares, is the temple of His Body, "with supplications and prayers which are heard by God on account of His reverence."

The Eucharist which contains and renews so many marvels, resumes and contains all Religion. It is to this great act of Religion that all our ceremonies refer, with all the functions in the Church. If there are bishops, priests, deacons, sub-deacons, acolytes, lectors, exorcists and porters in the holy Hierarchy, it is to offer the great Sacrifice of the New Law in the Name of Jesus Christ the only and Sovereign Priest, or to serve at the Sacrifice, and to dispose all things for its oblation. When then I partake of this great and ineffable Mystery by receiving Holy Communion, I apply to my soul the Blood of the New Alliance, the Seal of my Redemption, and the pledge of my reinstatement in the rights of my celestial inheritance.

O Ineffable Mystery! O Marvel of Wisdom, Power and Divine Love! Adorable Sacrifice where the Princes of the Heavenly Court assist invisibly, where the Seraphin and Cherubin annihilate themselves, veiling their faces with their wings; incomparable prodigy, which astonishes all Heaven! Why is it then that the earth remains so insensible? How can man assist at it with so much indifference? Why have I my self until now, so little comprehended this supreme act of Religion? Why have I taken so little care to bring to it proper dispositions? Now it is necessary that these dispositions be the same as those of Jesus Christ, to Whom I should particularly at this solemn moment unite myself entirely. I should immolate myself with Him to the glory of God, for the accomplishment of all His designs in me, by making to Him the obla- tion of my body, my soul, and all my desires, my affections, my entire self. Ah! if this great and adorable Sacrifice were offered only once a year by the Sov- ereign Pontiff, in the chief city of the Catholic World, and that only once in my life I had the happiness of assisting at it, would I not preserve its memory with veneration, gratitude, and love! But because all priests have the power to offer the Holy Sacrifice, and because each day I have the signal honor of being present at this Holy Oblation, should I be less touched, less grateful? Ah! am I not more ungrateful, more indifferent to this gift of God because He has so multiplied it, and rendered a participation in it more frequent and easy? O hardness of my heart! O deplorable consequence of our familiarity with holy things!

O abuse of graces the most precious, by reason of their very abundance! Preserve me, O my God, from such a misfortune! Grant that my fervor and my love increase in proportion to the facility with which Thou dost admit me to a participation in this Divine Mystery.

SECOND POINT - By this Mystery, Jesus Christ Prolongs among His Children the Life Which He led on Earth

This consideration is as true as it is consoling; but it is little understood and appreciated. Jesus Christ on ascending to heaven quitted not this earth; He still lives and converses among His own, and it is the Holy Eucharist which renders Him present in the midst of us. We can see Him, speak to Him and listen to His divine responses. He leads in this Adorable Sacrament a most admirable life, He there practises virtues the most sublime, and the most worthy of our imitation.

Yet we pay no attention to them, we do not comprehend them. If we were well penetrated with this Presence, as real as it is admirable, of Jesus in this Adorable Sacrament of our Altar, we would not envy the happiness of the disciples who lived in the company of our Beloved Saviour, who each day witnessed the examples of virtue which He gave them, and who gathered the words of grace and truth which fell from His divine lips.

Say not that their happiness was greater than ours, because they could see Him with their eyes, hear Him with their ears, and touch Him with their hands; while it is not given us to see Him, hear Him, or touch Him except by faith, as if they could have enjoyed these inestimable advantages otherwise than by a supernatural light. In effect, to follow Him and to listen to Him in a profitable manner, His disciples were obliged to elevate themselves above the senses, in order to recognize in His Sacred Humanity the Son of God, the Mediator promised to their fathers. It was this Faith which Jesus Christ praised and recompensed in St. Peter when that Apostle confessed loudly, that He was the Christ, the Son of the Living God; the Divine Master added that He had spoken thus by a particular inspiration from His Heavenly Father. The priests and the Pharisees who persecuted Jesus saw Him with the eyes of the flesh, and perceiving in Him only a man, they hardened themselves. Thus, as the Word was then hidden under the veil of our humanity, and was profitable only to those who saw and heard Him, according to faith, so now Jesus Christ still hides Himself under the Eucharist species, but His Life there is as real, as profitable, and as full of marvels as when He was among His disciples, and the souls who apply themselves to the contemplation of Him, in this state, discover there ever new subjects for imitation and love.

Jesus in the Adorable Sacrament is in a continual state of Victim and of Priest. From the tabernacle of love which He has placed upon our altars, He raises His Sacred Voice without interruption toward the throne of God, offering the labors, the sufferings, the humiliations, the merits of His life and death, to draw down upon us the blessings of God, and to arrest the divine anger, ready to strike sinners. What poverty in so many sanctuaries, despoiled of all ornament, and in tabernacles so miserable, which serve as His dwelling! What obedience for eighteen hundred years to the voice of so many priests, whatever be the disposition of their souls, alas! so often imperfect! What abnegation, what solitude, what silence, what patience in awaiting the sinner, what charity, what devotedness, what prodigality of Himself!

Ah! when He instituted this Adorable Mystery, He foresaw all: the places, the times, the profanations, and the abandonment in which He would be left in so many deserted sanctuaries, where no one would come to pay Him homage, or even speak to Him. What bounty He there shows to a faithful soul, what sweet words He makes her hear? "His conversation has no bitterness."

O! my Divine Master, what confusion, what regrets, should I not feel for having so little known, so little loved Thy Eucharistic Life. And this, notwithstanding that I live under the very same roof with Thee; for we, children of Carmel, more happy far than the ancient Israelites, who had in their midst only a figurative tabernacle, possess day and night in our monasteries, Thy true Tabernacle; and from Thy glory, Sweetly veiled, rays dart forth to all parts of this holy house; and Thy amiable Presence makes itself felt in the cells, even those most distant from where Thou dwellest. I am continually with Thee, I can speak to Thee, and listen to Thee; I can come to the foot of Thy holy Altar to learn of Thee the spirit of immolation and of sacrifice, the spirit of obedience and of poverty, the love of silence and of solitude, of abnegation and of self-contempt.

And until now I have seen nothing, understood nothing of this adorable Mystery, so grand and so significant; but to-day, awakening, like Jacob, after the vision of the mysterious ladder, I would cry out: "The Lord is in this place and I knew it not!" that is to say, I did not think of it, I did not occupy myself with it. But henceforth, O Jesus, my Adorable Master, I wish to attach myself to Thy Eucharistic throne, and to repeat without ceasing with Thy Prophet: "Thy Tabernacles, O Lord God of Hosts, are dear to me. Blessed are they who dwell in Thy House. The sparrow has found herself a house, and the turtle dove a nest, but Thy Altars, O my God, are the only asylum I seek. One day spent in Thy Court is better than a thousand in the rich dwelling of sinners."

THIRD POINT - This Life of Jesus in the Holy Sacrament Is Given to Us by Holy Communion

If the advantages of this Divine Sacrament were limited to what has just been considered, they would be most worthy of my admiration and of my eternal gratitude. But the love of Jesus Christ for men does not stop here. This admirable Life which He leads in the Holy Eucharist is the same which He led upon earth, with all its marvels and acts of heroic virtue; the precious fruits of His Birth, His Passion and Death are communicated to us by the participation of His Body and Blood.

If the Oblation of this Adorable Victim and the consummation of this Sacrifice is the living and efficacious representation of the Life and Death of our Saviour, and this is undoubted, the participation in this Mystery, by Communion, applies them to the soul so that she may live the life of her Divine Redeemer, that she may be penetrated with His sentiments and filled with His virtues; that, in a word, she may become transformed in Him. Holy Communion is the principal means of this formation in our souls of the New Man — Jesus Christ. It is true that this transformation of ourselves according to the interior man is accomplished only by successive degrees, and this is why the adorable Eucharist has been established under the form of our daily nourishment. But this progress, although slow and sometimes insensible on account of the imperfection of our dispositions, is no less real, in proportion to the faith and the love that we bring to Holy Communion. As the manna in the desert, figure of the Eucharist, had all kinds of tastes and took the flavor of the most delicious meats, according to the desires of those who partook of it, while it was tasteless and insipid to the murmuring Israelites, thus this true manna will have for us, according to our intention and desire when receiving it, the taste, the divine unction of someone of the graces, the virtues, and the lights attached to the Mystery of the life or the death of the Saviour, which we wish to apply to ourselves; and losing, little by little, this natural and gross life our miserable selflove, and of the senses, we will succeed by partaking of this Sacred Food, in living the very Life of Jesus Christ.

It is by frequently approaching the Adorable Sacrament that the Religious of Carmel receive the grace and the strength necessary to overcome their passions, correct their natural defects, detach themselves from creatures and from self; practise abnegation and mortification of the body; and by humility, solitude and silence, attain to the divine union which consumes them by charity. It is true that prayer is for them the source of abundant graces, and that by contemplation of the Mysteries of the Life and Death of Jesus Christ they communicate with His Divine Interior; but the graces and the lights of prayer being subject to many illusions, and the demon and our own natural inconstancy rendering success in this holy exercise doubtful, or at least imperfect, even its best and most precious fruits are ripened and perfected in the soul only by the seal of this Sacrament. It is true that this Sacrament can no more dispense with prayer, than prayer can with the Sacrament: that is to say, if the Religious soul be not habitually disposed for Holy Communion by solid and fervent prayer, she will draw from it little or no fruit; but it is always to be regarded as incontestable that this Sacrament consummates the union of a soul with Jesus Christ, and that the virtue which it will acquire by receiving the Holy Eucharist is assured to it in a manner much more excellent, more noble, and more inalienable than by prayer or even by fidelity to heavenly inspirations. In Holy Communion, it is Jesus Christ Himself Who encompasses the soul and transforms it into Himself, becoming its purity, its charity, its patience, its humility, its fidelity and its constancy. The soul which understands the greatness of the grace she here receives will strengthen herself more and more in humility; knowing that it is Jesus Christ Who acts in her, she will attribute to Him all the good she accomplishes, and reproach herself for the imperfections and faults which may mingle with it, easily distinguishing the sallies of nature from the inspirations of grace.

Blessed, a thousand times blessed, O my Divine Spouse, is the Religious soul who understands all the treasures which she possesses in the Sacrament of Thy Love, and who endeavors with great care to unite herself to Thee, and to cause Thee to increase in her. But, alas! what cause have I to humble myself and to weep in Thy Presence, for the little I have profited by the precious advantages I possess in this Adorable Sacrament. I press my lips so often to this divine source of Life and Love, and I am not refreshed; I approach this sacred Fire and I remain cold, when I ought to find there strength, fervor and life.

Our Mother, Saint Teresa, teaches that one Communion well-made suffices to sanctify a soul and to change it entirely. And I, after all my Communions, am so tepid and so imperfect! Ah, I understand, my God, that I should attribute my tepidity and imperfections to my negligence in disposing myself to approach Thee, because I have not understood that these dispositions consist in making my whole life a preparation, by prayer, and consequently by a spirit of recollection, mortification and abnegation. And in effect, how canst Thou fill with Thy grace a soul occupied already with the multitude of foreign objects, bound by a thousand unworthy attachments, and full of immortification and tepidity? If Thou couldst find there a sincere desire to break these ties, Thou wouldst lend Thy aid and strength. But, alas! Thou findst there only tepidity, indifference and laxity. It is done, O sweetness of my soul, O my only Treasure, O my Light, O my Love! I wish henceforth to die to all, to live by Thee, and for Thee alone. It is as yet but a desire, but a resolution: Thou wilt strengthen it, Thou wilt render it efficacious, and wilt lead me to that blessed state which Thou hast promised, saying: "He who eats of this bread shall live forever." Amen.

LECTURE - The Spirit of the Rule of Carmel

We have already seen that the Religious Orders, beside their common end, which is perfection and the practice of the evangelical counsels, have also a particular end, and that it was by their different Rules and Constitutions that each could attain this end of its Institute. We conclude from this, that it is not a matter of indifference to follow or to neglect these observances, and that although the Rule does not oblige under pain of sin, properly speaking, it is very difficult to offend against it, apart even from contempt, without rendering ourselves guilty of a grave fault; because ordinarily these infractions come from tepidity, laxity, and the abuse of grace.

It is necessary, then, to observe all points of the Rule and Constitutions, the customs and Religious traditions with great exactitude and a sustained fervor since, having been written or established by holy souls who were inspired by God, and approved and proposed by the Church, they are for us the faithful expression of the divine will, and the most efficacious means by which we may attain the perfection of our holy state.

The Order of Carmel can claim the greatest antiquity. From the first centuries we find Solitaries dwelling upon Carmel, heirs of the zeal of the Prophets, and given up to contemplation in order, like Moses, to call upon the Christian people combatting upon the plain the necessary succor to conquer their many enemies. Their life consecrated to poverty, obedience, profound retreat and habitual silence, they divided between the recitation of the Psalter, and almost continual prayer, with fasting and other rude practices of penance.

Their clothing, their nourishment, their customs, their language show this eremitical spirit. The reform of Saint Teresa had for its first object the reestablishment or maintainance of the antique and venerable customs of the Order of Carmel, and to preserve in its Religious, its particular character of solitude, of penance, and elevation above the things of this earth. She wished to form and did form, in effect, a congregation of Solitaries who, considering themselves as strangers and pilgrims on earth, would disregard its customs and regard only those of the home toward which they were traveling, living by faith, preserving in their occupations, and even in their most natural habits, such as eating, sleeping and dressing, something of the supernatural, the holy, and the sacred, which they draw from the element in which they live, and with which they are clothed as with a vestment.

It is this which strikes with admiration or at. least with astonishment, those who enter one of our monasteries to share in the occupations and the saintly life led there. The Religious occupy separate cells, ranged in the upper part of the house, around the Holy of Holies, elevated in His Tabernacle, as upon the heights of Carmel. Their beds are hard and poor, their sleep brief, the first watches of the night are consecrated to the chanting or the grave recitation of sacred hymns. The day is divided between the Divine Office, assisting at the Holy Sacrifice, prayer, and manual labor. The solitude is profound, the silence almost continual, and the time accorded, more by indulgence than by the Rule, to innocent or pious conversation, to holy relaxations — which they call recreation — is not stolen from mortification and solitude, because of the spirit of abnegation and of death which are there prescribed, these if they are faithfully followed, scarcely give any other liberty to the soul than that of charity, and to the mind than that of piety. The true Carmelite is able to leave this exercise more recollected, more mortified, more fervent, and more generous than when she began it.

The same may be said of Refectory, where they assemble only on leaving choir, after having obtained at the feet of Jesus Christ in the Blessed Sacrament, the dispositions of mortification and purity of heart for the accomplishment of a function so carnal, and where a Religious soul should have no other intention than to support her body, in order to Consecrate all her strength to the service of God.

It is with the recitation of prayers that the Religious go to the Refectory. The repast is preceded and terminated with prayer; before giving to nature an indispensable satisfaction, Grace is said, for, according to the words of Jesus Christ, when replying to the tempter, "Man lives not by bread alone, but by every word which proceeds from the mouth of God." It is only at the signal of the one who presides, that the Religious, after having made an inclination to mark the dependence which nature has upon grace, kiss their bread in a spirit of submission and of gratitude, after having renounced all natural eagerness. The manner of taking their food, of drinking and of eating, the modesty, silence, and attention to the reading by which the soul is nourished as well as the body, the practices of penance in use during meals, all, in fine, in this exercise is capable of elevating the soul to God, of ennobling it and of separating it from the gross satisfaction of the senses and of itself.

The other practices in use in this holy Order, especially the public acknowledgment of faults; the prostrations — in presence of the Blessed Sacrament on entering the choir, during the Holy Sacrifice, when they acknowledge their faults, and when they are reproved; those marks of extraordinary respect toward the Mother Prioress, when they speak to her or receive her directions; all these holy prescriptions have a character especially adapted to the end of the Order, and to the excellent virtues which one is obliged to practise in it.

But the more extraordinary these observances and the more rigorous this discipline, the more necessary it is that they be accompanied by the true spirit which established them. If destitute of this spirit they become not only useless, but impracticable.

There are here two opposite abuses to be noted, and it is not rare to encounter them among the Religious of Carmel. One is to forget the reproaches of Our Lord to the Pharisees of neglecting the laws of God, particularly that of charity, to attach themselves to human traditions, and observing the exterior practices of the law without taking pains to animate them with an interior spirit, attaching themselves to the letter which kills, and putting aside the spirit which vivifies. Therefore, while we must carefully practise these, we must not neglect the other. Such souls show themselves very zealous for the practices, customs, and observances of the Order, crying out when, for legitimate reasons, Superiors believe it their duty to interpret them otherwise, or to accord a momentary dispensation. Nor do they take care to profit by these occasions of practising humility, renewing their faith, their reverence and love for the Most Holy Sacrament, and the Blessed Virgin, respect for Superiors who are the representatives of Almighty God, and love and zeal for religious obedience.

The second abuse is a certain wrongly-conceived idea oi the perfection and the virtues proper to the Order, and in consequence of which these souls persuade themselves that it suffices to belong to it, in order to be in possession of the highest virtues, and to aspire to gifts of the most sublime grace. Such souls have ever on their lips only terms of the highest spirituality, and they can name the different degrees of prayer taught by mystic writers; they speak only of the heights of Carmel and of the sublime functions of the redemptrix and victim, which a Carmelite should fulfill on earth, and of the delights of the garden of the Spouse. They enumerate the virtues and the duties which the Carmelite should practise, but they omit all that regards the elements of perfection, and remembrance of the four ends of man — degrees through which all Christians should pass, even in Carmel, before arriving at divine union. We find even in books which contain excellent practices, this defect, which thus strengthens the illusions, too common, of taking the sentiments and the definitions of the virtues proper to Carmel, for the virtues themselves.

The spirit of Carmel is, above all, one of universal crucifixion of nature; and it is only by this generous and continual mortification of the senses, interior as well as exterior, joined to a spirit of recollection, solitude, and separation from creatures, that the true Carmelite, after having purified herself by penance from her past sins, and from her evil inclinations by abnegation, becomes capable of entering into the divine union by prayer. And very far from it being necessary that she aspire to sublime states of prayer, she will be more capable of attaining these, the less she thinks about them.

Without doubt, nothing is more sublime than the perfection of Carmel; but at the same time it is very simple, since there is only question of loving God and hating self; and the whole Rule of Carmel, when it is observed in the spirit proper to it, will infallibly result in conducting to this perfection the souls who embrace it. A Carmelite is then necessarily called to the divine union, but she must understand and remember that it is only on the Cross that this union can be formed and consummated.

Examen Upon the Lecture

Forgetting what Saint Paul teaches, that the letter killeth, and the spirit vivifieth, am I not too much attached to the letter of the Constitutions, drawing perhaps vanity from a certain exterior regularity with which I follow them, while I neglect to animate them with a spirit of faith and purity of intention, which alone constitutes their value? Have I understood well that the merit and value of the observance of the Rules of Carmel consist principally in the spirit of humility, abnegation and solitude, which should constantly accompany them? In consequence of my neglect to nourish myself with this spirit, have I not lost innumerable occasions of practising virtue, in the actions which form my daily life? Thus have I not performed acts of Religion such as adoration, prostrations, inclinations, chanting or reciting the Divine Office, etc., without increasing in reverence for the Adorable Sacrament? Have I not shown demonstrations of respect, obedience and submission to my Superiors without producing these acts interiorly? Have I not performed acts of humility without humility, of penance without the spirit of mortification?

Have I not kept our cell without love for solitude and exterior recollection, without the interior spirit? In fine, have I not fallen into the delusion of thinking that the virtues of a Carmelite consist in a knowledge of the degrees of prayer and a certain sentimentality, without taking pains to go to the depths of things, and lay the foundation by a profound contempt of self, and true mortification?

NOTE - Preliminary Advice for the Ninth Day

This day is very important, because upon its being well employed depends the fruit which we will draw from the Retreat. In effect, there is question not so much of taking resolutions, (which is done always) resolutions very soon forgotten, but of establishing in ourselves a will of amending our lives and of advancing in the ways of perfection, so firm that nothing will be capable of making us change it, whatever be the difficulty of the undertaking. Now, according to the sentiments and the experience of the Saints, nothing is more proper to give to the will that decisive impulse, that strength which will enable it to triumph over all the obstacles raised by Satan and our own weakness, than consideration of the sufferings and the death of Jesus Christ. In effect, a soul who has formed the generous design of giving herself to God, must expect to be proved by rude combats, either on the part of hell, or from her own self-love, and the victory will always be uncertain, or at least incomplete, until she embraces courageously sufferings and humiliations. But where will she be able to obtain strength sufficient to practise things so contrary to nature, and to practise them generously and constantly? It will be in assiduous meditations upon the Passion of her Divine Master.

It is for this reason that the Ninth Day is entirely consecrated to the contemplation of the Sorrowful Mysteries, in order that, at the sight of all that her Divine Saviour has endured of torments and opprobrium for her salvation, the soul inflamed by divine love will burn to testify her gratitude and her love by the practise of things the most painful and difficult. To give more efficacy to the meditations of this day, it will be necessary: First — to withdraw the mind from all other thoughts save those of the sufferings of Jesus Christ, and especially from thoughts which afford joy to the soul. Second— - to keep herself more recollected than usual by seeking places the most retired and hidden, representing to herself during her repasts the gall and vinegar given to our Saviour upon the Cross, and using on this day some particular austerities. Third — to try to obtain, by a deep consideration of the opprobrium and the torments of her Saviour, that generous disposition which, if the choice were given her of a life full of spiritual consolation with the approbation and affection of creatures, or a career full of humiliations, suffering and contradictions she would choose the latter way, as the more sure and the more conformable to that which Jesus led — even when by the other way, God would be equally glorified. This disposition to suffer after the example of our Divine Saviour, is indispensable for the Religious soul who wishes to ascend the heights of Carmel. In fine, in order to be profoundly touched by these meditations, it is necessary to represent to ourselves the circumstances of the Passion in a manner so lively, that we seem to be present at the sorrowful scenes, see Jesus attached to the column, crowned with thorns, raised on the Cross; that we be witnesses of the cruel treatment which He endured at the hands of His murderers, hear the blows of the hammer, the insults of the soldiers; and in this state contemplate Him, speak to Him just as though we could see His sorrowful looks fixed upon us, assuring us that it was really for us and for the expiation of our sins, that He endured all these evils.

Ninth Day

First Meditation - Jesus in the Garden of Olives

"At that time Jesus went forth with the disciples over the brook Cedron, where there was a garden into which He and His disciples entered. And He said to the disciples: Sit you here till I go yonder and pray. And taking with him Peter and the two sons of Zebedee, He began to grow sorrowful and to be sad. Then He saith to them: ... My soul is sorrowful even unto death; stay you here and watch with Me, and going a little further, He fell upon His face praying and saying: My Father, if it is possible, let this chalice pass from Me. Nevertheless not as I will but as thou wilt. And He cometh to His disciples and findeth them asleep, and He saith to Peter: What? Couldst you not watch one hour with Me? Watch ye and pray that ye enter not into temptation. The spirit indeed is willing but the flesh is weak. Again He went the second time and prayed, saying: My Father, if this chalice may not pass away, but I must drink it, Thy will be done. And He cometh again and findeth them sleeping, for their eyes were heavy. And He went again; and He prayed the third time saying the self-same word. And being in an agony, He prayed the longer. And His sweat became as drops of blood trickling down upon the ground."— St. Matthew, St. Luke and St. John.

How mysterious, how astonishing is this first scene of Thy Passion, O my Divine Master! I enter with Thy suite into this bloody career, I prostrate myself before Thee, and I supplicate Thee to admit me into Thy company during the course of Thy Passion, and to initiate me into the secrets of Thy sorrows, and into the holy dispositions of Thy Sacred Heart, abyssed in a torrent of bitter woes. May I learn after Thy example, how to suffer, to pray, to be silent, to immolate myself for the glory of God and the salvation of souls. I will commence by that fear, that sadness, with which Thou art seized at Thy entrance into the garden, the first theatre of Thy sufferings, and I conjure Thee to grant me a share in Thy anguish, and to permit me to approach so near to Thee, that I may be able to hear and to treasure up some of the words which Thou didst address to Thy Eternal Father, and to receive into my soul, so weak and so languishing, some drops of the precious sweat with which Thy Sacred Person was inundated. Ah! Precious Blood, inundate me! Precious Sweat of the agony of Jesus, purify me! Divine soul of Jesus, sanctify me!

FIRST POINT - Jesus a Voluntary Victim

What can be the cause of the change just now operated in the soul of Jesus? Only a few moments ago He was conversing tranquilly with His disciples. He was speaking to them of His sufferings and of His approaching death, as of an hour ardently desired, impatiently awaited; of a bloody baptism in which He desired to be plunged, because it would put a seal to the glory of His Heavenly Father, and satisfy His immense love. And now that this hour has come, He fears, He is troubled in spirit, He is overcome with a sadness so profound that, according to His own testimony, it is enough to cause His death. He, Who is to be the strength of the martyrs in raising them by His grace above the fear and the terrors of death, appears to me at this moment weak, trembling, and almost discouraged. "My Father, My Father," He cries, "if it is possible, let this chalice pass from Me."

What a profound mystery! Who can penetrate it? Ah! I may do so by entering into the garden which is about to become a place of reconciliation and of salvation, as another garden had been, in the first days of the creation, a place of perdition. The Man-God will here present Himself to His Father, and renew the obligation which He had made of Himself at the first moment of His Incarnation. Behold. I hear Him say, the Victim, substituted for all the ancient victims which were not agreeable to Thee, see as gathered upon my Head, all the iniquities of the world, see nothing in Me but the guilty human race. Strike only Me, allow to fall upon My Person all the blows which should fall upon sinners: Behold Me! This time the Eternal Father accepts the exchange. He wills to see no longer in Jesus Christ His co-equal Son, but only a victim destined to pay the death penalty, and even when He has drained the chalice of opprobrium and suffering which His justice has prepared for Him, He will still look upon Him with anger. It is to conform Himself to this decree which He accepts, and which He had Himself ardently solicited, that Jesus at this moment abandons His holy Soul to sadness and fear. These sentiments are not in Him as in other men, because of the passions which prevent the will, and carry them to great excesses which they can no longer master. This sadness and this fear are as admirable in their principle, as they are noble in their effects, because it is He Himself who has called them forth, and they are to become a fecund source of consolation and of the most precious grace to souls, and they stop at the point and the moment which He wills. Thus, far from being scandalized by this apparent weakness of my Saviour, I find in it a great proof of His power and infinite mercy.

If there are here sadness and fear, they are the sadness and the fear of a God; if the prayer which they force from Him expresses terror and seems to bear the impress of trouble and discouragement, it is because He prays as a Mediator, and this prayer, joined to His admirable acquiescence to the divine will, is to furnish a memorable example of the conditions with which we must pray, if we wish to be heard, and it has obtained for us most powerful helps to attain perfection.

O my Saviour and my God! Behold then the principle of Thy sadness and Thy fear. Without doubt they are occasioned by the sight of the frightful torments prepared for Thee, and the torrent of all the iniquities of the earth, which are become Thine own, and submerging Thy innocent soul, throw Thee into such a state of confusion, that Thou art not able to bear the look of Thy irritated Father. But, Lord, I need seek no other cause for Thy sorrowful feelings, because it is none other than Thy love for poor sinners of whom, alas! I am the greatest. For it is because Thou hast charged Thyself with all my sins and assumed the consequences of such a responsibility, that I see Thee almost succumbing under the weight of such a burden. Ah! if notwithstanding my sins, or rather because of them, I could, after Thy example, offer myself to Thy justice as a victim for my brethren, it seems to me Lord, that I would be disposed to do it in order to pay Thee, as far as in me lies, my immense debt of gratitude.

SECOND POINT - Jesus Agonizing

To these first motives of the fear and sadness of Jesus, others were added which reduced His soul to extremity, and enveloped it as with the shadows of death. In effect, it would have been little for His love to accept the chalice of opprobrium and of suffering which had been offered Him, if at the same time, He could have foreseen the reward of such an immolation, that is to say, the confirmation of the ancient Alliance which God had made with His people, and the salvation of all men. But He must listen to the ferocious cries of that decidal people demanding His death, and die by the hands of those whom He had come to save. He must see the reprobation of the Synagogue with the dispersion of the holy Nation, and that desolation of desolation even unto the end of time presents itself before Him, notwithstanding His sacrifice. If again, the nations, which are to be given the heritage lost by His chosen people, would only respond perfectly to the grace of their vocation to the faith — but alas! of the many nations which received successively the precious light of the Gospel, how many allowed it to become extinct after having been enlightened by it! And among the Churches the most flourishing, how much cockle mingled with the good grain! What heresies, what schisms! How many souls among the most fervent Christians, in Religious Orders the most holy, miserably perish notwithstanding the inestimable price which has been paid for them!

It was then the sorrowful knowledge of the inutility of His Blood for so great a number of souls for whom it was shed, that filled His soul with mortal agony. Behold the subject of that prayer, so fervent and so often repeated! Behold the cause of the seeming struggle with the eternal decrees of His Heavenly Father, a mysterious struggle, prefigured by that which Jacob had with the Lord Himself, in the person of an angel; and by his prayer begging that his cherished spouse might at least escape the fury of his brother Esau. So did Jesus long to save His unfaithful Synagogue; and behold the sense of these words: "If it is possible," spare me the reprobation of my people. "If it is possible." give me all the souls for whom I am going to die. It was then, exhausted by this struggle of which the sorrow and the agony had covered His Face and entire Body with a bloody sweat, that He fell with His Face to the ground, feeling as at the approach of death, convulsions, tremblings, and the oppression of a cruel agony, without abandoning for a single instant the exercise of prayer, but on the contrary redoubling the fervor of His prayers to obtain what He so ardently desired. At this moment an angel descended from heaven bringing for His suffering, the only solace of which it was susceptible. He doubtless represented to Him the return of the Jews at the end of time, the great number of faithful and generous souls who would tread in His footsteps, and imitate His example; he doubtless showed Him the Apostles with a multitude of the faithful accompanying them, the victorious band of the martyrs, the solitaries who would people the desert, and the pure and faithful virgin souls who would follow Him in His career of suffering even to the Cross, associating themselves by their love and their crucifixion of the flesh, to His sufferings: the Bridgets, the Catherines, the Teresas, etc.

And Lord, I also hope to join these holy souls and to bring my share of alleviation to the sorrows which oppress Thee, in that ocean of bitterness in which Thou art plunged by Thy mysterious agony. I wish to separate no longer my cause from Thy cause; I wish to walk in Thy bloody footprints, embracing for love of Thee and with Thee, sorrows, contempt, and crucifixion; rendering myself present by assiduous contemplation of the Mysteries of Thy Passion, and applying to my soul their precious fruits. I wish above all to have part in that ever memorable prayer which Thou didst address to Thy Eternal Father with so much fervor, in the midst of Thy sorrows, of which the meaning is so deep and the effects so marvelous. In asking that this chalice might pass away, Thou didst wish to prevent the damnation of so many souls; and by adding, "Thy will be done," Thou didst merit a multitude of victorious graces which would bring forth the elect. This FIAT, more admirable than the one by which Thou didst draw forth light from the bosom of darkness, brought forth the supernatural light, which enlightens the Church and makes saints. It is this FIAT which gives charity to the Apostles, strength to the martyrs, science to the doctors, and purity to the virgins. Ah! and Thou didst also ask for me the virtues which form solitaries — victims of Thy love. I reply with Thee a thousand times, FIAT, FIAT! May Thy will which desires that I be sanctified in this Retreat, be accomplished. FIAT, FIAT!

THIRD POINT - Jesus Bound and Led Away Captive

Now the hour is come when Jesus is to be delivered into the hands of sinners. Judas advances at the head of a band of Roman soldiers and servants, the one armed with swords and sticks, and the other with lanterns. He is followed by the unworthy pontiffs themselves who have not blushed to join the ministers of their vengeance. This confused mob approaches the garden of Gethsemane. Jesus is still abyssed in the horrors of His desolation and painful agony. But He knows how to dissipate the sadness and the terror with the mortal agonies which are their effects. Sovereign Master of Himself, He will show His enemies that He is able to exterminate them with a breath, and that if He is delivered to them, it is because He so wills it.

In effect, He rises full strength and assurance, He goes to His sleeping disciples, and after sweetly reproaching them for the little part they have taken in His sorrows, and their want of vigilance, He announces to them the approach of the traitor, and goes Himself in advance to meet His enemies, deceiving thus their cruel hopes of surprising Him. "Whom seek ye?" He said to them. They, struck with blindness, visible punishment of their malice, instead of casting upon Him the reproaches and charging Him with the crimes they had prepared^ recognized neither His voice nor His features, nor His vestment, nor anything which distinguished Him from others. Judas himself, although His disciple and familiar friend, and precisely because of this, more blind than the rest, did not know His Adorable Master; and they all replied, "We seek Jesus of Nazareth," "I am He." said Jesus. At these words, by an effect of the almighty power of the One who pronounced them, as prompt as it was unexpected, the numerous band fell as one man, prostrate in the dust. Jesus however, instead of profiting by the state of confusion inseparable from their sad fall, satisfied with what He had done, because His hour had not come, suffered all of them to rise, and He repeated the question: "Whom seek ye?" and they, more hardened and more blind, again responded: "Jesus of Nazareth." "I have said it, I am He," replied our Saviour, and immediately giving a brilliant mark of that empire which He had exercised over Himself and over others, and which surpasses all the strength of human nature, He regulated the conditions of His; captivity; for before giving Himself up, He provided for all that concerned the glory of God, the security, and even the edification of His disciples. He occupied Himself even with the traitor Apostle and with His enemies, offering them a last means of instruction and of salvation: "If ye seek Me let these go away," said He, speaking of His disciples. Then turning to Peter, who had already taken his sword and struck off the ear of one of His transgressors, He taught him that it was not with such arms that His cause should be defended; indignant with this Apostle who had wished to prevent Him from drinking of the chalice prepared by His Father.

After this reprimand, freeing Himself with dignity from those who had already commenced to surround Him, He approached the wounded servant and cured him. But our Saviour saw another wound, much deeper than the one which He had just healed: it was that of the ulcerated heart of Judas. Twice He endeavored, but in vain, to apply the remedy of His charity: "My friend, wherefore art thou come?" "Ah Judas! it is with a kiss that thou betrayest the Son of Man?" Then He addressed Himself to the multitude, and especially to the priests and the pharisees, making a last effort to enable them to recognize their malice: "You are come to Me," He said with sweetness, "armed with swords and clubs, as to a robber; while I was daily with you in the temple, teaching, you laid not hands upon Me; but now is your hour and the power of darkness:" giving them to understand by these words, that if He was faithfully accomplishing the will of His Heavenly Father, they were only ministers of hell, and instruments of its malice. After these last words, having regulated all things, and said to each one what He wished to make known, He presents His adorable hands which are immediately loaded with chains, and the cruel wolves throw themselves upon this Immaculate Lamb, ill-treating Him and striking Him, while they push Him before them, toward that unfaithful Jerusalem, which is to be the theatre of the greatest of all crimes. They conduct Him to the palace of the High Priest where His enemies were already assembled, hiding under the sacred robes of judges, the hatred of accusers and the rage of cruel murderers.

O Jesus! Thou Who hast just cast to the ground by a single word, the whole cohort of Roman soldiers, Thou Who hast just confounded Thy enemies by Thy wisdom, and astounded them by Thy goodness, Thou couldst with the same facility have exterminated them, or have sent them away disarmed and confounded. These chains would have given way at the first touch of Thy sacred hands, more easily than the cords with which the Philistines had bound Samson. But there is a power more formidable which retains Thee captive, it is Thy love. It is Thy ineffable love which makes Thee forget Thyself. It is love which chains Thee and delivers Thee up to Thy enemies, love for me in particular; yes, I can say with Thy Apostle: "He has loved me, and delivered Himself up for me."

What can I do to acknowledge so much love? Ah! I can give myself up a captive for Thee, as Thou hast done for me. I am so already, enclosed by these walls which separate me from the world; I am so by the sacred ties which bind me to Thy service, by the holy Rules which restrain my liberty, and which permit not my corrupt nature to pass the limits of Thy holy Law. But I have not cherished these holy chains, this glorious captivity ,1 have not borne them with love, because there was no charity in my heart, or at least it was very languishing. This is finished; Thy love has triumphed over my tepidity, and, after the example of one of Thy Apostles, in seeing Thee deliver Thyself to death, I will say: "Let me go and die with him." Yes, may I die to all things of this world, that I may live with Thee in eternity. Amen.

Second Meditation - Opprobriums of Jesus During His Passion

"He shall be filled with reproaches."— Jeremias III, 30.

I prostrate myself before Thee, O my humbled Jesus, I adore Thee, steeped in opprobrium, soiled with spittle, wounded with blows, and covered with a veil of ignominy. "We have seen Him," cries out the Prophet, "and we have not known Him." But ah! Lord, I recognize Thee, I love Thee thus disfigured, as my Spouse and my King, and the more changed I find Thee by sorrow and the contempt of men, the more dear and venerable Thou art to me, for it is Thy innocence and sanctity which excite the fury of hell and the malice of Thy enemies. Ah! discover to me the secret of Thy opprobrium, give me to understand all that Thou didst endure during Thy bitter Passion, both interiorly and exteriorly, in the darkness of night and in the light of the sun, before the face of Thy judges and out of their sight, on the part of Thy enemies, Thy friends, and from strangers, from Jews, from Gentiles, from magistrates, from soldiers, from the servants, and from all the people who insulted Thee, envied Thee, and loaded Thee with injuries. Teach me above all, the graces, the lights, and the blessings hidden under humiliations and contempt, since Thou hast endured such bitter woes for our salvation, in order that I might, after Thy example, love and embrace them and draw the precious fruit which Thou hast attach to them.

FIRST POINT

The first outrage which Jesus received is a brutal blow from a menial officer who struck His August Face saying: "Answerest Thou thus the High Priest." From that moment Jesus gave up His Adorable Face to insult and sorrow, wishing to present to the eyes of all, an expressive and touching sign of the ignominious state to which He allowed Himself to be reduced for love of us. This blow accompanied by an unjust reproach, gave occasion of the admirable response of Jesus to the High Priest, who was interrogating Him upon His Doctrine and His Disciples: "I have always taught in the Synagogue, and in the Temple, whither all the Jews resort, and in secret I have taught nothing. Why askest thou Me? Ask those who have heard Me." A necessary reply, since it established even in the presence of this iniquitous tribunal, and for all ages, that His Gospel was not announced in darkness but in public, that it had been most conformable to all rules of justice.

For this reply so wise and measured, Thou receivest, O my Divine Jesus, the most bloody outrages. How comes it that Thy Holy Angels, witnessing the insults offered to their King, did not exterminate that barbarian; why did not the heavens launch forth at him a thunder bolt, or the earth swollow him up? But O my Divine Master, Thou didst prefer to give us by Thy patience in suffering this insult, a striking example of Thy sweetness and humility. And so instead of keeping silence, Thou sayest to this barbarian, with a moderation all divine: "If I have spoken evil, give testimony of the evil, if well, why strikest thou Me?" It is that Thou mightest not remain to the eyes of all future ages guilty of this contemptible accusation.

Witnesses are at last brought in, witnesses, who being bribed, accuse Him falsely. Then Jesus, interrogated in the Name of the Living God, renders testimony to the truth, and declares Himself the only Son of God. It was then that the High Priest rent his garments as a sign of horror, and condemned Him to death as a blasphemer and an impostor. Immediately they abandon Jesus to a crowd of cruel servants and soldiers who, seconding the hatred of their masters, take a barbarous pleasure in striking and insulting Him. It is not only one buffet which He receives on His Adorable Face, but a shower of blows which bruise and disfigure it. They soil it with vile spittle, and cover it with an ignominious veil, as if they had not already veiled its Majesty and beauty by the insults with which it was loaded, and they defy their Saviour with cruel irony, to prophesy who had struck Him. They redouble their blows and insults, and thus they pass a great part of the night. Ah, Jesus! is this not enough to satisfy Thy love? Alas, it is only the commencement of Thy sorrows and Thy torments! And yet the Gospel spares us the details of these sad scenes. But Thou, dearest Lord, deignest to reveal to souls who know how to watch with Thee, Mysteries still more astonishing, enveloped in the darkness of that night.

At the first sign of day, the priests and scribes hasten again to seize their Victim to conduct Him to the Roman Magistrate, who must confirm their parricidal sentence. Jesus is then dragged to the Tribunal of Pilate, in the sight of a multitude, which the tumult and cries of His enemies had gathered. Here the unworthy priests abandon the accusation of blasphemy, which does not appear to them of sufficient influence with a pagan judge, and call Him a seducer, a rebel, and an enemy of the Roman Empire. Pilate, it is true, had little difficulty in recognizing the innocence of Jesus, and attributing His capture to the jealousy of the priests; but sacrificing justice to policy, instead of granting Him His liberty, he profited by an opening which was made to send Him away to Herod, hoping thus to cast upon another, the discharge of an affair which He had not the courage to settle by his own authority.

Jesus then appears for the second time in the streets of Jerusalem, more despised and insulted by the populace. For the vulgar judge only by appearance; and seeing Jesus treated with contempt and insulted by those whom they were accustomed to respect, they conclude that He is guilty. But Herod, will he at least, not be able to recognize in Jesus that Divine Wisdom which shines above all His ignominy? Will he perhaps understand that the One who keeps so silent and preserves His patience in the midst of so many insults, is more than man? But no, Herod is one of those vain princes, who seek only new means of enjoyment and of satisfaction for their curiosity. He rejoices to see Jesus appear in His presence, thinking that he is going to see Him operate some great miracle. But Jesus is silent, and in keeping silence, performs a miracle far more admirable than that which had been expected — a prodigy of patience, of strength, and of wisdom. But this insensate King, is he capable of understanding it? No, he despises Jesus, he and his court with him, and he clothes Him with the livery of a fool. And thus Jesus returns to Pilate followed by the insults, the derision, and the bitter irony which is more easily understood than explained. Oh, who can teach me the secret of Thy divine silence, my Adorable Master, if I learn it not from Thyself when contemplating Thee in this Mystery!

Jesus finds Himself a second time in the presence of Pilate whose vile weakness prepares for Him new outrages more cruel than any He had yet endured. "Which one do you wish that I deliver unto you?" demanded the cowardly magistrate, of the crowd surrounding his tribunal, whose ferocious instincts had been excited by the priests, the Pharisees, and the demons themselves. "Which will ye that I deliver up, Jesus or Barabbas?" And in this unworthy parallel between good and evil, sanctity and sin, to the eternal shame of the Jews, of the world, of sinners and consequently, of myself, alas! Barabbas the impious, the criminal, is preferred; and Jesus, the good, the meek, the amiable, the innocent Jesus is rejected and condemned! Ah! what bitterness, what anguish His Sacred Heart must have felt at this new outrage, this new ingratitude of His own people. O my Saviour, Thou hast not yet finished the chalice of humiliation which Thou wilt drain to the dregs. Pilate wishing to soften this barbarous people, implores only a little pity for Jesus, while his conscience and justice would oblige him to send Him away acquitted, in the presence of all His enemies. He imagines he will do this by having

Him flogged. They despoil Jesus of His garments, and in this state of nakedness so painful to His modesty, He is exposed to the gaze of the multitude, shamefully tied to a column, and whipped as a vile slave. To this barbarous punishment, this inhuman torture inspired by hell, they added insults and injuries. After this bloody scene, they plait a crown of cruel thorns and press it upon His adorable head; upon His wounded shoulders a purple rag is thrown; in His sacred hand, trembling through the excess of His sufferings, a reed is put for a scepter. Then some bend the knee before Him, while others strike His Adorable Face with His derisive scepter, and mockingly salute Him: "Hail King of the Jews!'. In this sad state, He is again presented by Pilate to the people, and again rejected with renewed fury.

After having re-clothed, so that all might recognize Him, and having loaded Him with the ignominious woods of the Cross, they conducted Him to Calvary in the midst of the vociferations of His murderers. When He falls through weakness they strike and insult Him. O my Saviour, O my Master, O my Spouse, permit me to follow Thee in company with St. Veronica who wiped Thy Adorable Face, with the compassionate and heroic women, and with Thy most Holy Mother, to share Thy sufferings and opprobrium!

O my Saviour, can I henceforth desire the esteem of the world, when Thou art thus abandoned, unknown, and betrayed! It has thus treated Eternal Wisdom and Infinite Charity; and can I wish for anything more precious, more honorable to the eyes of faith, than to receive the same treatmr.it as did my Master and my God?

SECOND POINT

To understand better the greatness of the humiliation of Jesus in His Passion, let us now consider Who He is that is thus outraged; who they are from whom He endures these outrages; and for whom and why He suffers.

He Who is outraged is the Eternal Son of God, the mirror of His wisdom, the delight of Heaven, in a word, God Himself. He is the most amiable, the most benevolent, the most beautiful among men; it is He Whom we have seen showering upon us His abundant charity, and Who merits the love, the adoration, and the gratitude of all men.

And by whom is He treated with so much ignominy? By contemptible men, by traitors, by priests unworthy of their sacred calling and given up to their most vile passions; by soldiers, by servants, by a populace made up of the most perverse men.

And how does Jesus, the Divine Jesus, suffer their insults and their outrages? With an admirable sweetness, unalterable patience, and invincible silence. He could have so easily enlightened His judges and confused His accusers and, according to our human views, it seems that He ought to have done so, as there was question of His Father's Glory, the reputation of His Holy Mother and His Disciples, and of His own honor of which He should have had regard, because of His Doctrine and those who professed it.

Yet, notwithstanding all the apparent reasons, He would not defend Himself, but kept silence and suffered in peace all these outrages, leaving to His Eternal Father the care of regulating all things which seemed irreconcilable, and abandoned Himself to the will of sinners whom He recognized as the executors of Divine Justice.

O patience of Jesus, O sacred silence which has given strength to the saints to be so reticent in their own defense, even so generous as to keep silence in union with their Divine Master, when one word from them could have cleared them of the most injurious calumnies.

O my God! how little have I profited by Thy divine lessons, I, whom all see so eager in defending myself from the least accusations and the slightest suspicions, whilst Thou didst keep silence under the weight of the greatest accusations accompanied by the most humiliating injuries and atrocious calumnies. Ah Lord, if I understood well the value of this silence, this humility, this tacit avowal of the faults for which I am reproached, even when I cannot believe myself guilty, with what humble confidence could I not present myself before Thee to beg mercy for guilty souls. What a source of consolation I would find in acting thus! What assurance I should feel at the hour of death!

But, alas! I lose all these precious advantages by my self-love and desire of the vain esteem of creatures. O Jesus! grant me the grace to appreciate the value of Thy humiliations, so that when Thou appearest in glory I may appear also with Thee.

THIRD POINT - Why Does Jesus Suffer These Humiliations?

Jesus endures these humiliations as a remedy for our pride. He has willed to espouse opprobrium and ignominy, to suffer the most bloody affronts, in order to render amiable in His Person that from which nature flies in such horror.

Although we cannot see how this opprobrium contains anything profitable to us, we ought still to love it, because it has been the portion of Jesus; yes, humiliation, opprobrium, contempt of creatures have become divinized; and the one who under the empire of Jesus loves them not, and seeks them not, has not entered far into His Heart. This is what grace, what profound meditation on the humiliations of Jesus should teach all Christians, and should even delight the Solitary of Carmel.

Jesus, my Divine Master, since Thou hast chosen humiliations for Thy portion, it ought to be evident to me that they are a hidden treasure. It should suffice to know that Thou hast espoused them for love of me, to cause me to espouse them for love of Thee. Grant me this grace, the greatest which Thou canst give me in this life; for if I die to the esteem of creatures, I will at once commence to live for Thee alone; blessed life not only for time but for eternity, Amen.

Third Meditation - What Jesus Suffered in His Body

"He was wounded for our iniquities. He was bruised for our sins." - Isaiah, LIII, 5.

I come now, O my Divine Redeemer, to contemplate the wounds which Thou didst receive in Thy sacred body, in order to heal those which sin has made in my soul. Alas! "from the sole of the foot even unto the head there is no soundness in Thee." Who would try to count these wounds, since they are innumerable?. Who could tell how many thorns have entered into Thy sacred head, and pierced Thy brow? Who can say how many stripes have fallen upon Thy sacred shoulders and torn the flesh in all parts of Thy divine body? Thy hands and Thy feet are pierced by the nails, Thy knees are all torn and bleeding from the falls occasioned by Thy weakness and the brutality of the soldiers.

Oh Lord, in seeing Thee thus, I understand what Thou hast said by the mouth of Thy Prophet: "I have thought Him become as it were a leper, and as one struck by God, and afflicted." The leprosy of sin must then be inveterate, since it can be cured only by such a remedy.

FIRST POINT - Jesus Scourged

To limit myself to the principal circumstances of the Passion of Jesus, I will first represent to my mind His cruel scourging. I will consider my Saviour bound by the hands to a column in such a way that His body, despoiled, is exposed to the strokes of the scourge. These instruments of torture were made, some of little chains armed with points, and others of the sinews of oxen or rings of green and thorny wood. The executioners of this bloody torture were sixty in number, according to the revelation made to St. Mary Magdalen de Pazzi, and they took turns, two by two. as their strength was exhausted. These cruel tormentors pressed around this tender lamb, like tigers thirsting for His blood; they are also animated by the fury of the demons, and secretly excited by the Jews, who fear that Pilate may succeed in snatching their victim from them. They strike Him violently and with redoubled strokes; His flesh is torn in shreds, His veins are broken, His blood flows and the earth is inundated therewith.

Jesus could not have sustained this horrible torture, exhausted as He was by the blood He had shed in His cruel agony and by all the torments He had so far endured, if His love, upheld by His omnipotence, had not prevented Him from succumbing. He wished to preserve Himself for other sufferings, and by new wounds to open to us new sources of grace. St. Bernard estimates the number of stroke? which our Saviour received in the cruel flagellation to exceed six thousand, and no doubt He would have received many more, had not His weakness at last robbed Him, so to say, from the rage of

His executioners. He falls at the foot of the column, exhausted by suffering and the loss of blood. They raise Him up and hastily replace His garments — the only dressing, alas! applied to His wounds.

O my Divine Saviour, who could have obliged Thee to suffer a torment so cruel and inflicted only on slaves? Ah! I understand: by this torture Thou didst wish to expiate in Thy body, the shameful and criminal pleasures which the children of Adam have allowed theirs; it was necessary that Thy horrible sufferings should be the remedy for their infamous pleasures; that Thy innocent flesh should be bruised and torn, in punishment for the delicate care they have given their sinful and criminal flesh. Thou didst wish by this, not only to teach us to master our rebellious flesh and to subject this body of sin — a slave always ready to revolt — but also to merit for us the grace to obtain a complete victory over ourselves; so that reducing our senses to servitude, we ought to treat our body as a dangerous enemy, which we should fear and hate, because it cares not if it lose us and itself too, provided it be satisfied. Infinite thanks to Thee, O my Divine Redeemer, for so great a benefit! Ah! I will come often to the foot of this column, to receive the salutary dew of Thy Precious Blood; here I will find strength to reanimate my courage, to triumph over my malicious nature, which always seeks to draw me into relaxation and softness; here I will receive the grace necessary to subject the flesh to the spirit.

SECOND POINT - Jesus Crowned with Thorns

What is this new torment which Thy enemies are preparing for Thee, O my Divine Redeemer? Torment unheard of and unknown in the annals of human cruelty — even invented for Thee. The wicked! are they not satisfied with all that they have made Thee suffer, and the painful death they have in reserve for Thee? I see them pressing around Thee, O sweet Victim! Again they tear off the garments with which they had covered Thy bleeding body, and replace them by a torn purple mantle. And after having made Thee sit on a seat of sorrow — a throne truly worthy of such a King — they placed on Thy Sacred Head, which alone their lashes have not wounded, a crown formed of thorny reeds, the long points of which penetrate deeply, being rudely pressed by these barbarians with clubs, and the reed that serves as a sceptre which they place in Thy hands after using it so cruelly. Thy sacred brow is pierced in every part. Oh! who could express the insupportable suffering which Thou didst endure at that moment, and which will increase until Thy last sigh? The blood flows over Thy eyelids covering Thy eyes with a thick cloud, and inundates Thy divine Face, mingling with the vile spittle with which it is again covered. Thus is accomplished the sorrowful ceremony of Thy Crowning, O my Divine Redeemer! Ah! permit me to turn my eyes away from this cruel spectacle, which they can no longer endure, and raising them toward Thy Heavenly Father, ask Him what His infinite wisdom and mercy have hidden in this sorrowful Mystery; for it is He who has ordained and regulated all the circumstances of it. Thy executioners think only of obeying their cruel instinct, and of seconding the hatred of Thy enemies; and they are without knowing it, the instruments of Him Who, by their hands, confers upon Thee to-day the investiture of the most beautiful, the most desirable, the most glorious of all royalties, and decorates Thee with the insignia which by right belongs to Thee alone. Precious insignia, the splendor of which infinitely surpasses the riches and the magnificence of the crown and the purple of kings! Yes, Thou art King, O Divine Saviour! Thou art Kings by right of birth — King from all eternity as only Son of the King of the universe, and King in time as heir of David. Thou hast become King by right of conquest; and this peaceful conquest Thou hast not accomplished in the manner of ordinary conquerors, by ravage, ruin, and the blood of nations, but by shedding Thy own Blood, and covering the earth with Thy blessings. That crown, that sceptre, that royal mantle, Thou hast not acquired by imposing taxes on Thy subjects — they are the price of Thy sufferings and ignominy. Thou hast willed to be shown in this state to Thy people and to all the peoples of the world, with these words which will be repeated to all future generations: "BEHOLD THE MAN," in order to teach us what guilty man merits, and the true value of the honors and authority to which he can pretend. O, Thou art in truth the grandest, the most amiable, the most powerful of kings: Thou art the most magnificent of conquerors! To-day, prostrating at Thy feet, to adore and glorify Thy royalty, I will say: "I salute Thee, O my King!" Thou art and Thou shalt always be the King of my heart; there never was, and there never will be another like Thee.

Not content with saving us by Thy sufferings, by these sufferings Thou dost also wish to instruct us. Thy head pierced with cruel thorns, teaches us what the honors and vain distinctions of the world should be for Thy friends. In seeing Thee thus, could I again seek that which flatters my vanity and nourishes in me vain glory? O Divine Teacher! Who has thus traced in Thy body, in characters of blood, the lessons so necessary for me, engrave them also in the depths of my heart that, after the example of St. Catherine of Sienna, and so many other of Thy faithful spouses, I may prefer Thy crown of thorns to any other ornament.

THIRD POINT - Jesus Crucified

The Jews, far from being touched at the sight of Jesus Whom Pilate leads out to them, His head crowned with thorns, His face livid and bleeding, His shoulders torn and bruised, and in a state capable of moving the hardest hearts, become only more furious. "Behold your King,' Pilate says in presenting Him to them, and they respond by demanding His death in loud cries. This weak magistrate, having tried in vain to speak to them by the touching spectacle of the sufferings of Jesus, endeavors to bend them by reminding them again of His quality of King, and of the recognized falsehood of all the accusations accumulated against Him. The people excited by the priests, cry out with renewed rage: "Let Him be crucified!"

Then by a judgment unique in the history of all ages, this prevaricating judge, at the same time that he condemns Jesus to death, proclaims His innocence in these ever memorable words: "I am innocent of the blood of this just man." To leave an eternal and characteristic memorial of this contradictory sentence, he has water brought to him and washes his hands in presence of the whole multitude. In this unique judgment visibly shines forth the just judgment, declared in heaven by the Eternal Father, and willingly submitted to on earth by His beloved Son. Yes, Jesus is innocent! He is the Just by excellence, He is Sanctity itself; but man whose place He has taken is guilty, guilty of the crime of revolt against the Divine Majesty — behold the mystery of the apparent contradiction between the declaration of Pilate who openly recognizes the innocence of Jesus, and the sentence by which he condemns Him to the last torture.

O! who can tell with what inexpressible joy Jesus hears this sentence of death, veritable sentence of life for the children of Adam? Who could express the eagerness with which He seizes the cross presented to Him and presses it to His Heart? This new Isaac lovingly taking on His shoulders the wood for His sacrifice, prepares to ascend the mountain on which He will immolate Himself for the salvation of the world. It is true that the exhausted strength of His body no longer responds to that of His love; He will fall several times under the weight of this burden, He will be forced to accept the aid of the Cyrenean; but this weakness and the relief which He receives will enter into the economy of our redemption. We shall there find new strength to rise from our falls, and ineffable consolation in all our trials and afflictions; for these sufferings, if I accept them with faith and love, are the very sufferings of Jesus which I share — they assure me then, a share in the graces which He has merited for us, and ample recompense for eternity.

At last, Jesus has arrived at the summit of the mount of sacrifice. His feet and His hands extended with effort, are cruelly pierced and nailed to that Cross which He has dragged so far with so much suffering and fatigue. Ah! it is not without a great design of mercy that He has chosen this frightful torment, and that He remains thus immovable, fastened by horrible wounds to this mysterious wood during long hours, without consolation, without relief, having only vinegar and gall to quench the thirst which devours Him, nothing whereon to rest His adorable head, and unable to make any movement without augmenting His insupportable sufferings. In this state He merits for us the grace to nail with Him to His Cross, our passions, our vices, and all the sallies of our rebellious flesh. He renders, finally, His last sigh with a loud cry, which attests at the same time His Divinity and the extreme anguish of His sacred Humanity. Ah! let me now contemplate for my salvation Him whom I have thus pierced.

Divine Redeemer! Not content with offering us the price of our ransom, Thou becamest Thyself this inestimable price. Our souls were wounded and sick and Thou, charitable Physician, offerest the remedy which must cure them, and this remedy is Thyself. This it is that absorbs, so to speak, all the attention of Thy spirit which cannot be cast down by so many sufferings. This is the great and one thought which occupies Thy holy soul during the whole course of Thy sorrowful Passion. This it is which maketh Thee to speak and to be silent. If Thou openest Thy mouth on ascending Calvary, and if Thou consolest the pious women who follow Thee, it is to turn their compassion from Thy sufferings to those which are to strike a people which denies Thee. If, from the height of the Cross, a few words fall from Thy dying lips, it is again to pardon, to console, and to instruct — praying for Thy executioners opening heaven to the good thief, leaving Thy holy Mother to the beloved Disciple, and to all men in his person; complaining of Thy abandonment in order to make known to us the desolation to which our sins have reduced Thy soul. Thou sayest: "I thirst," and thus discoverst to us Thy great desire for the salvation of souls. Finally, "in remitting Thy soul into the hands of Thy Father," after having solemnly declared that "all is consummated;" Thou givest a new and sublime example of Thy submission to the orders of Thy Father. Thou dost declare that Thou hast accomplished all that He had ordained for my salvation, and that Thou dost die by obedience.

O Jesus Crucified! Thou art a book open to all people, to all future generations, where each can contemplate and learn all the essential truths: the greatness of God, His infinite justice. His ineffable mercy, the value of our soul, the enormity of sin, the chastisement it merits, and finally the inexpressible love of our Redeemer. In contemplating this book, this divine image, each should and ought to say: "He has loved me and delivered Himself for me."

O my Saviour, how little have I read of this admirable book! How little have I applied myself to study and learn that which is so important for me to know! How slightly have I been touched by that excessive charity, carried even to the folly of the Cross! Alas, how weak has been my love in comparison with Thine, or rather is it not an insult to say that I love Thee, offering Thee sentiments so unworthy of Thy extreme tenderness? Should I not abyss myself in a sorrowful confusion, seeing that I do so little for Thee, my Creator and my Redeemer — I, Thy creature, covered with Thy blessings and redeemed by Thee at so high a price, since it is by the very Blood of the Son of God, Immaculate Lamb which has expiated the sins of the world!

"Ah! the charity of Jesus presseth me, considering that if one has died for all, all being dead, and if He has given His life in order that we may live, our life belongs no longer to us, but to Him who has died for us." Oh pressing consequence! I belong no longer to myself, O Jesus, my loving Redeemer, I am Thine! I am Thy conquest and I wish, cost what it may, to live only for Thee. Tear me from myself; take from me all my supports; disembarrass me from all those affections, from all those researches, from all those attachments to creatures and to myself, which envelop me as with a sad vesture; in order that despoiled, as Thou hast been, I may be attached through love to Thy Cross, remaining united to Thee on this bloody and sorrowful bed, and thus attain an eternal union with Thee in heaven, Amen.

As the life of Carmel is entirely consecrated to the exercise of holy love, the life of Jesus in the Most Blessed Sacrament, which is the most perfect model as well as the source of the most ardent charity, is therefore the object of the most particular devotion. It is there that the Religious of this holy Order should enkindle in her heart the flames of that perfect love with which she should be animated. Thus devotion to the Blessed Sacrament holds, in Carmel, the first rank.

The end proposed in this Institute is divine union. What means more sure, more prompt, more sweet of attaining this love, than receiving this Adorable Sacrament! Nor can we doubt this truth when we hear Jesus Christ addressing to His disciples these admirable and astonishing words: "As the living Father hath sent me, and I live by the Father, so he that eateth me the same also shall live by me!" We see indeed, that the Saviour compares the union which He contracts with the soul in the Holy Sacrament, to His union with His Heavenly Father, which is the closest and most noble that can be imagined. Thus as the Father is in the Son and the Son in the Father, the same, my analogy however, in Holy Communion our Lord is in us and we in Him, and by our union with His Humanity, we ascend to His Divinity. God the Father unites Himself to His Son in unity of essence by begetting Him eternally; the Son unites Himself to man in the Incarnation by unity of person, and then to all men by unity of the Sacrament; and by means of the union which He gives them with His Humanity, He unites them with His Divinity and through Himself to His Father. Behold the term of the Incarnation of the Word coming from the bosom of His Father to descend into the womb of Mary, to come to us; it is for this reason and with all justice and truth, that the reception of the Holy Eucharist is called the extension of the Incarnation.

But it is not enough to renew daily on the Altar, and continue until the end of time, the sacrifice which He offered on the Cross for the salvation of the world, and to apply to us the fruits of it in Holy Communion; He wishes to remain with us day and night in our Holy Tabernacles, a prisoner of love, to the end that we may be always sure of finding Him there and of receiving from Him all the blessings, all the assistance, all the consolation of which we have need in this valley of tears. Seated on His Throne of Mercy, He is always ready to welcome us, to listen to us, and to grant all the requests which we will come to make to Him for His glory and for our salvation. Who can number the holy souls who have found their delight in these loving conversations with Jesus in the Blessed Sacrament, who have passed days and nights contemplating the marvels therein enclosed, uniting their prayers and their immolations with His, praying for the conversion of sinners and their own sanctification.

More happy than the Israelites traveling in the desert toward the promised land where the tribes camped round the figurative tabernacle, while the cloud which covered them — darkness for the Egyptians — enlightened this chosen people, the Religious of Carmel ranged round the true Tabernacle of the new Alliance, traveling toward the true land of promise, through the desert of life, are enlightened by the rays of this true light, while the world remains plunged in the darkness of ignorance and incredulity. These divine rays not only shine over the place particularly consecrated to prayer, they penetrate all parts of the monastery and into each cell in particular, so that there is no place where this Divine Presence should not be felt, awakening in the soul sentiments of profound piety, and maintaining in it modesty and recollection. For this reason, the interior of the monastery ought to inspire silence, and it can never be troubled nor interrupted by useless conversation and untimely noise without detriment to the respect due to the holy presence of God.

After these considerations, it is easy to understand why devotion to the Most Blessed Sacrament is one of the Mother devotions of the holy Order of Mount Carmel, and what this devotion should be. It ought to be for the Carmelite an esteem and a love proportioned to the greatness of the benefits contained in this mystery, the master-piece of the love of God, the abridgment and the memorial of all His marvelous works. Now, the Eucharist being the Sacrament by excellence which exhausted, so to say, the divine omnipotence, since God could give us nothing better, nothing greater, nothing sweeter, nor in a more perfect manner; the faith of the Religious soul in this mystery, her love, her respect, her zeal should have no other limits than her power, always infinitely below the blessings contained in the Blessed Sacrament. Considering then that in the Tabernacle is hidden not only the greatest treasure which she has in the world, but her one, only, and sovereign good, her heart remains there, always enclosed with this great object of her love, according to these words of Jesus Christ: "Where thy treasure is, there is thy heart also." Therefore, without returning here to the dispositions which she should bring to the Holy Sacrifice, because this has been sufficiently treated of already, she should apply herself continually to reanimate her faith and veneration for this Adorable Sacrament, referring to it all her works, and finding in it the assistance and consolation of which she has need in the trials and temptations to which she is continually exposed. She should redouble her respect and affection every time she approaches the place where Jesus resides, or touches the objects that serve for His worship.

But it is above all in her preparation for Holy Communion, that she will display her zeal and her fervor. Being indeed obliged by her Rule to frequent Communion she cannot pay too much attention to the preparation, for inasmuch as this holy banquet is advantageous to a soul who brings to it holy dispositions, so it is dangerous and sometimes injurious to the one who approaches only with tepidity: for familiarity with holy things, when it passes into routine, produces a certain hardness of heart and blindness of spirit, the least result of which is the abuse of the most precious of graces.

To avoid this misfortune so common in communities, Carmelite Religious ought to recall the thought of their holy Mother, St. Teresa, who compares the soul to a castle where there are several dwellings of which the last, which is the most retired and the most beautiful, represents the sanctuary of the will, that is to say, that superior part of which God is so jealous, being very certain that when He enters there and reigns as Master and as Spouse, the soul is entirely His. Now that He may reach this secret apartment of the spouse, the Religious soul must open successively all the doors of the other apartments. Without this care, He is received only in the first, and sometimes is obliged to remain at the door. To open these doors is nothing else than to overthrow, by means of the mortification of the senses, of the mind, of the judgment, and of the will, the obstacles which our attachments, our lightness our sensuality, our curiosity, our vanity, in a word our self-love, place in the way of the graces which' Jesus Christ would wish to grant up. When He is received in Holy Communion by a tepid, negligent, and unmortified soul, His remains as it were at the entrance without penetrating intimately into the soul.

The first disposition of a Carmelite Religious for Holy Communion should be a generous and constant mortification, as well interior as exterior. She should never present herself at the holy Altar to receive the Adorable Victim, without first having performed some mortification to prepare for this great act.

To this disposition which may be called general, she should add a more particular preparation which will consist in proposing to herself each time she approaches the Holy Table, beside the ordinary intentions — sufficiently indicated by the rules and habits of piety — a particular end, which will always be a virtue to acquire, a defect to correct, a victory to gain over temptation or corrupt nature, or some other spiritual good of which she may feel the importance for her advancement in perfection. The moments immediately following Communion are very precious for offering these lively and reiterated petitions, because then the soul is united with Him whose prayer is always heard by the Heavenly Father. Unhappily, few persons know how to profit by so favorable an occasion for obtaining everything from their Divine Guest.

In fine, the Religious should not be less attentive to excite in herself, the evening before, the most holy desires for this Sacred Banquet by making fervent and ardent aspirations — above all when going to rest at night and in the morning on awakening — than to converse during the rest of the day with Him Whom she has received into her house. What means sweeter, and at the same time easier and more advantageous for keeping us in the holy presence of God, than to represent to ourselves Jesus Christ residing in the sanctuary of our soul, seated on a throne of love, always ready to listen to us and to reprove us, according to the solemn promise which He has made in these words: "He that eateth my flesh and drinketh my blood abideth in Me and I in him."

Oh! how deplorable to see so many Religious who, forgetting this intimate union which they have contracted in the morning with their Heavenly

Spouse, pass the entire day without thinking of it, without recollecting themselves to keep company with Him who has come to dwell within them, to fill them with every blessing.

Examen On the Lecture

Have I a true devotion to the Holy Sacrament of the Altar, being habitually filled and penetrated with faith, respect, and love for this ineffable mystery of the charity of Jesus Christ?

Is it in such sentiments that I enter the choir and remain in the presence of the Adorable Sacrament? Is it not only through custom, without sentiments of humility, veneration, and love that I prostrate on entering this holy place where He reposes, lowering my head to the dust and kissing the floor?

Have I not forgotten that the presence of Jesus Christ in the Blessed Sacrament should be felt all over the monastery, and that His divine eyes follow me wherever I go, in the office or the cell where I remain; and instead of making use of this thought to keep myself constantly modest and recollected, have I not given way to dissipation or to thoughts foreign to my holy vocation?

Have I understood how essential it is not to abuse frequent Communion, and how easy it is to fall into this misfortune, by neglecting to reanimate my faith, respect, and love for this great Sacrament with an ardent desire to receive it? Have I prepared for it by some act of mortification, by recollection, and by ardent and repeated aspirations?

On the eve of my Communion days, has the happiness of the morrow been my last thought at night, and the first in the morning on awakening? Have I always proposed some particular fruit to be drawn from my Holy Communions, in order to sustain my attention and devotion?

Finally, have I not neglected to profit by the precious moments which follow Holy Communion, by opening my heart to Jesus Christ, exposing to Him my needs, and making my petitions, not ceasing to pray until I have obtained all that I desire?

Note on The Last Day

This last day of the Retreat is consecrated to the exercises of the Unitive Life; not that the Religious soul can flatter herself that she has attained to it in so short a time, but she will go through an abridgment of the degrees of this happy life. She has already seen in the preceding days which refer to the Illuminative Life the means by which she can arrive at this.

Tenth Day

First Meditation - The Resurrection of Jesus

"The Pharisees and chief priests being assembled went to Pilate and said to him: Sir, we remember that this seducer said during his life: I will rise three days after my death. Order therefore that his tomb be guarded until the third day; lest perhaps His disciples take away His body, and say to the people, He is risen: and the last error shall be worse than the first. Pilate answered; you have a guard; go guard it as you know. They going, sealed the sepulchre and left soldiers to guard. However at the first gleam of the third day, there was a great earthquake. An Angel descended from heaven, approached the tomb, and rolling back the stone, sat upon it. The soldiers were seized with great fear, and remained as dead men. Some of them went and announced to the chief priests all that had taken place. And the Angel of the Lord said to the holy women who had come to embalm the body of Jesus: fear not, He whom you seek is risen."— St. John 19; St. Matthew 28; St. Luke 24; St. Mark 16.

I adore Thee, O Divine Victor over death. Thy enemies had thought to assure their triumph by obtaining from Pilate Roman soldiers to guard Thy tomb, and by placing the seals of the Empire thereon; but what could the vain precautions of human wisdom do against the designs of Thy divine wisdom? They have only assured their defeat and Thy triumph. The time of humiliations, sufferings, and persecutions is forever passed for Thee. Clothed with Thy body, for the future immortal, as with a glorious vesture, Thou art going to enjoy Thy victory in peace, and rest from Thy long labors and hard combats. But, what do I say, Lord? I forget that this is not the object of Thy triumph. If Thou didst die for me, it is also for me that Thou hast risen to-day. If Thou hast been nailed to the Cross to deliver us from our iniquities, by nailing to it also the handwriting of the condemnation we had merited, Thou hast come forth from the tomb to restore me to immortality. Thy Resurrection must be the model and pledge of mine. It is because Thou hast been resuscitated that I shall rise on the last day. And it is not enough to assure thus to my body an abundant participation in Thy glory to the end of ages; Thou dost wish, even now, that I reap in my soul fruits of Thy victory over death, by rising spiritually, that is to say, by entering, even during this mortal life, into a perfect state of detachment from earthly things, and of elevation toward heavenly things. Make me understand, Lord, the value of this grace and the conditions necessary for meriting it.

FIRST POINT

Nothing is more true or more consoling than this truth; in virtue of the

Resurrection of Jesus Christ, if I have the happiness of dying in His grace, not only shall I come forth one day from the tomb with all mankind, but I shall come forth clothed with a body, beautiful, glorious, and incorruptible — a body more brilliant than the sun, more indestructible than the diamond, more agile than the eagle in its rapid flight through the air. This glorious body will be given as companion to my soul, which had shared here below all the works of patience, of purity, of mortification, and of penance. The old Adam had caused me to lose immortality, the new Adam has restored it to me. It is by faith in His glorious Resurrection that I receive the first assurance of mine; but, above all, it is by uniting me in Holy Communion with His glorified Body, that I receive a more certain pledge of this happiness, and more efficacious means of acquiring it. Yes, the flesh of my Saviour is like a precious seed of the Resurrection sown in my corruptible flesh which, like a precious germ, will develop and transform my body fallen into dust, into a body resplendent with glory. Immortal graces have been given to Thee, O Divine Victor, and though far above what I could expect, deign to share Thy victory with me, a poor creature. It is then true, O my Divine Redeemer, that united one day with all the elect, "I shall see Thee, and my eyes shall behold, and not another." I shall contemplate Thee in the midst of the assembly of the Saints, I shall enjoy the sight of this magnificent spectacle with this glorious company, and my happiness shall be doubled because of the joy that shall be mine in sharing it with this nation of brothers, conquered by Thy victories; and all together, under Thy peaceful sceptre, we shall reign eternally with Thee. O dear hope, hide thyself, sink hidden into my heart, live and repose in my breast! Render me, therefore, more generous to combat this flesh, to subject this body a few days longer to the hard labor of mortification, and to the privations which the law of the Lord requires. It is thus that I shall be truly the friend of my body, because I shall prepare it for such great glory, for enjoyment so pure, beauty so perfect, e» vesture so glorious.

Ah! when I flattered it, when I allowed it its liberty, when I gave it a soft bed, when I clothed it richly, and gave it its ease, then I was its enemy. But today, O my Divine Saviour, I understand these words coming from Thy divine lips: "He who hates himself for eternal life loves himself truly." Grant me this holy hatred of my flesh, a horror of all that flatters the senses, in order I that may share more abundantly in the glory of Thy Resurrection.

SECOND POINT

The second fruit of the Resurrection of Jesus Christ is a grace which raises us above the weakness of nature, earthly attachments, affection for creatures, and establishes us in a continual intercourse with God. It is this grace which Saint Paul refers to in these words: "If you be risen with Jesus Christ, seek the things that are above where Jesus Christ sits at the right hand of God. Mind the things of heaven, not those that are upon earth."

We must not confound this happy state of spiritual resurrection of which we are speaking, with the state of grace, which is common to all souls exempt from mortal sin. It is much more elevated, more excellent. By its happy effects, it establishes the soul in a manner almost unalterably fixed in the love of her Divine Spouse.

The Apostle St. Paul describes the different characteristics of the spiritual resurrection. In considering them attentively, I shall be inflamed with a desire to attain them, and shall see how far I have succeeded in this during my Retreat, destined to operate this happy resurrection. These characteristics are drawn from the Resurrection of Our Lord Jesus Christ:

1. Jesus Christ is truly risen, *surrexit vere*. Is my resurrection true? Have I really risen from the tomb of my vices, of my immortifications, of my tepidity, of my attachment to self, from my self-love and self-will? Am I truly changed, and resolved to live for the future as a true Carmelite? Is my heart changed, does it now belong as much to God as it formerly did to creatures and to myself?

2. Jesus Christ is not only risen, but He shows Himself such to a great number of persons, and on many occasions they see Him, touch Him, hear Him speak, and see Him eat, act, etc. It is by my actions that it will be seen and that I myself will recognize whether I am truly risen: for my conduct marked by obedience, mortification, regularity, fidelity, charity, the reserve of my words, and even the expression of my face and modesty of my eyes should show and prove to all that I am truly risen. Thus I shall repair the disedification formerly given by my dissipation, my lightness, and the intemperance of my words.

3. In showing Himself to men, to His Apostles, and to the holy women, Jesus Christ appears only as long as is necessary for the glory of God, His Father, and the strengthening of their faith. After that He withdraws from their sight; not that He abandons His stay upon earth, but while remaining here, He is entirely occupied with His communications with His Heavenly Father — communications so intimate and ineffable that they surpass all the conceptions of celestial intelligences, and which no human tongue can describe. Behold the third characteristic of the happy spiritual resurrection on which I am meditating. The soul having reached this state can converse no longer with creatures, except for the glory of God, or to fulfill the precept of charity toward her neighbor. Conversations, occupations and relaxations in which she does not find the enjoyment of her God are insupportable to her. Alas, until now, how far I have been from this happy disposition!

4. Finally, "Jesus Christ risen from the dead dies no more," says Saint Paul. The soul, having arrived at this state of happiness, has so great a relish for the things of faith, and attains by this supernatural taste to such a contempt of all the goods and all the pleasures of earth, that it is, as it were, confirmed in grace and established in the love of its God, and therefore with a little fidelity, should no more die to the spiritual life. Ah, how precious is this privilege of the Resurrection, and to acquire it, how easy should every sacrifice and suffering appear!

Now the conditions by which I shall infallibly attain to it, are all included in the faithful fulfillment of my Rule, which is one of crucifixion, death, and of burial. If Jesus Christ passed through these different states before rising again, is it not necessary that I also pass through them before reaching the spiritual resurrection? I must be crucified with Him: for says the Apostle, Saint Paul, "they that are Christ's have crucified their flesh, with the vices and concupiscences." This explains the continual mortification prescribed by the Rule of Carmel. If the Religious soul enters generously and faithfully into this practice, she will be aided by the Holy Spirit, Who will teach her the science of that war which she must declare on her senses; and if she persevere therein, she will die at last that mystical death of Jesus on the Cross.

Happy state in which this soul, for the future a stranger and, as it were, dead to all that passes, to all that is said or done around her, remains indifferent to all except what concerns the glory of God, and touches the accomplishment of His most holy will. But the requirements of grace go still farther; Jesus Christ after His death was buried and placed in a tomb; and this burial of Our Lord has brought forth a grace of spiritual burial, by which the soul, already dead to all things, is yet more profoundly buried and hidden from creatures and from herself, to be known only to God alone; until Jesus Christ, seeing in her a spirit of life, raises her to that spiritual resurrection described by Saint Paul.

Yes, Carmel is a Calvary where the flesh is crucified; it is a tomb where the soul is buried, in order that, disengaged from its earthly bond, it may rise with Jesus to a new life, by perfect union with its Divine Spouse. Nature shudders at such a destruction; it Seeks to change the requirements of the divine union; it would wish to satisfy them by some acts of exterior mortification; but when it must come to that death to all things, and to descend into that tomb where she is no more occupied with creatures or they with her, she recoils affrighted: this is why so few souls, in this holy and perfect Order of Carmel, attain the perfection of their state.

Ah! when I consider that a solitary of Carmel, by the sole effect of the grace of her vocation and of the practices attached to it, can and should arrive at this spiritual resurrection, so as to have no more taste for anything of this earth, aspiring only to things above, conversing with the Angels in heaven far more than with men on earth; what confusion to see myself, after so many years, still so far from the term which I should have reached. How is it that I am still so natural, so attached to creatures and to myself? O Jesus, Divine Conqueror of death! Draw me after Thee, out of this tomb where I languish; give me the grace which Thou hast merited for me, to crucify my senses and to die to all, in order to live truly in Thee, for Thee, and with Thee alone. Amen.

Second Meditation - The Ascension of Jesus

"They saw Him raised up: and a cloud received Him out of their sight. And as they were beholding Him going up to heaven, two men in white garments stood by them and said: Ye men of Galilee, why stand you looking up to heaven? This Jesus who is taken up from you into heaven, shall so come as you have seen Him go into heaven." — Acts of the Apostles, 1—9, 10, 11.

What a ravishing spectacle for my faith, O my Jesus, is Thy glorious Ascension and return to Thy Father. Thou dost leave at last this earth which Thou hast sanctified by Thy presence, purified by Thy Blood, and enlightened by Thy teaching. Thou dost return to the bosom of Thy Father, from which Thou didst come forth, and in taking Thy seat at His right hand, Thou dost bring there the whole human race of which Thou art the head and representative. Thou goest to prepare a place for Thy elect, for, O my Saviour, in Thy triumphs as in Thy sufferings, it is still man that Thou hast in view. For me Thou wast immolated, for me Thou didst rise from the dead, and to-day, it is again for me that Thou goest to take possession of Thy kingdom. Ah! Lord, give me the grace to open my heart to this hope, so that for the future my thoughts may be entirely with Thee, and at the same time to render myself more worthy of that glory. I may live in the expectation of that great day when, as the Angels tell us, Thou shalt descend from heaven in the same manner in which Thou didst go up. Thus my heart, piously balanced between fear and hope, shall become more and more attentive and faithful to profit by the means of sanctification offered.

FIRST POINT

It is not without a design well marked by Divine Providence, that Jesus terminates in view of His disciples, His career of suffering and glory on earth, by His triumphant Ascension. In raising Himself to heaven before their eyes by His own power, as He had raised Himself from the dead, He places the finishing touch to the numerous testimonies of His divine mission, and at the same time, gives a last and important lesson on the end of their labors and the only object of their ambition and their efforts. In resuming thus, the road to His heavenly Kingdom, He dissipates the gross illusion of His disciples, who asked Him a few moments before whether He would re-establish the Kingdom of Israel: and He teaches not only His Apostles, but the faithful of all time, who are to enjoy by faith the magnificent spectacle 'of His Ascension, not to rest their desires and their hopes on things here below, but to raise toward the heavenly country all the thoughts of their minds, all the desires of their hearts, and to dwell there by faith; so that their conversations be no more with men on earth, but with Angels in heaven.

Such is the fruit of this glorious mystery — a lively faith or rather an anticipated possession of heaven, in the person of our Brother, our Spouse, and our Divine Saviour, so that our thoughts, our desires, be more in heaven than on earth. This grace, attached to the Mystery of the Ascension of our Lord Jesus Christ, is well expressed by these words of the Apostle: "You are dead; and your life is hid with Christ in God; when Christ shall appear, who is your life, then you also shall appear with Him in glory." Behold the fruit of this glorious Ascension, for the soul that is dead to all things on earth: to live with Jesus Christ in heaven, and finally to return with Him in glory and happiness, when He shall again appear on earth, to commence that reign which shall have no end, after having pronounced judgment on all men.

Our Holy Father Saint John of the Cross teaches that by this hope for the goods of the other life, the Religious soul dies more really and more completely to the things of earth, than by any other means. Thus, while, by continual mortification, she detaches herself and succeeds in dying to all earthly affections, soon rising to a new life she reaches a state more perfect still — that of the spiritual ascension, an eminent grace, raising her above all created things, enabling her to dwell in spirit in heaven, according to these words of Saint Paul: "Your life is hid with Christ in God." But, alas, how far am I from this state, how different my sentiments from what they should be! When, then, O my Divine Jesus, shall I possess this happy fruit which is a grace properly belonging to the holy Order of Carmel? When shall I think of Thee alone, and perfectly dead to all things around me, have no other desire or expectation than that of contemplating Thy glory in heaven? Oh, that I were, like the Prophet, inspired by the Holy Spirit with these sublime aspirations, which I desire to repeat with the same sentiments: "O Lord, how lovely are Thy tabernacles!" "Blessed are they that dwell in Thy house!" "As the thirsty stag pants after the fountains of living water, so do I sigh for Thee, O Lord." "When shall I contemplate Thy face?" "Oh, how my exile is prolonged!" "On the rivers of Babylon they have asked me to sing the canticle of Sion in a strange land?" Oh! yes, let us keep for our heavenly home, the canticles and hymns of joy and gladness; for me, in my solitude of Carmel, I will sigh night and day like the lone sparrow on the house-top, I will sigh like the dove, and I will weep at the remembrance of Sion.

SECOND POINT

While the Apostles, ravished with admiration, were seeking with their eyes, Him Whom the cloud had just hidden from view, the Angels descending from heaven completed the instructions of this great day. "Ye men of Galilee, why stand ye looking up to heaven? This Jesus, Who is taken up from you into heaven, shall so come as you have seen him going into heaven."

Not for the Apostles alone were these words solemnly pronounced, they are addressed to the rising Church and contain important instruction for the Church in all ages, placing it in a state of expectation of the second coming of

Jesus Christ. The Apostles, and particularly Saint Paul, by these words, "the Lord is nigh," warn the faithful to keep themselves in continual vigilance, accompanied by prayer and fear, in expectation of the second coming of Jesus Christ; as in the old law the just expected the first coming of the Redeemer, and prepared for it by the practice of all the virtues, so the faithful of the new law should live in expectation of the second coming, and prepare for it with all the more care, since this last coming of Jesus Christ must be one of terror and of justice. Thus the Divine Master continually warns us to watch and to pray without ceasing, because of the uncertainty of the day of His coming. Hence those numerous parables, where He recalls this obligation by the most striking comparisons: now it is the vigilant servant with loins girded and lamp in hand, awaiting the return of the Master; again it is the virgins, who watch in order to follow the Spouse when He shall arrive; but the same words always terminate these comparisons — "Watch and pray, for you know not the day nor the hour of the Son of Man; know only that He will arrive when you least expect Him: not to be surprised, you must watch always." "As the men in the time of Noah, while marrying, and building, and occupied with their ordinary affairs, were surprised by the deluge, and all it once buried in the waters; so will it happen to you if you do not watch unceasingly."

This, then, O my Jesus, should be the disposition of my soul: that of expectation — an expectation full of vigilance, of fear, and of love, but where love is greater than fear. Thou hast represented this expectation by the faithful servant who loves his master, and awaits his return to render an exact account of his services during his absence — it is that of the bride who awaits the return of her spouse. This expectation is loving, but it is vigilant and generous. Therefore, I should divide my life between mortification and prayer.

Why, indeed, have I left the world? Why have I renounced all occupation with the things of the earth? Why have I broken the ties of flesh and blood? Is it not to occupy myself with the service of God alone, and to have no other care than to please my Creator and Redeemer, awaiting His coming like a wise virgin, keeping the lamp of charity ever burning in my soul? This, certainly, is the principal spirit of my vocation. Behold the motive of those mortifications and those continual exercises which oblige me to watch over all my acts, all my thoughts, and to prepare myself for the coming of the Spouse.

But, alas! until now, I have had so little of this spirit! How far I am from that watchfulness over myself, from that care to mortify my senses and guard my heart, which constitute Christian vigilance; and yet I should be a faithful servant, with eyes always fixed on the movements of my Master — a faithful Spouse, preparing myself unceasingly for the return of Him Whom I have come here to seek. Moreover, I am a child of Elias — that great Prophet who, according to an ancient and respected tradition, supported by the formal texts of both the Old and the New Testament, is destined to come at the end of time, to reawaken men from their indifference and their mortal lethargy, and to prepare them for the last coming of Jesus Christ. It belongs, then, to the Solitaries of Carmel, inheritors of his spirit, to keep up by their vigilance, their profound recollection, and the practice of penance, this expectation of the Sovereign Judge of the living and the dead.

O my Lord Jesus Christ, I wish, by Thy grace, to enter into this spirit of expectation of Thy coming — into this disposition of fear, of desire, and of love. Grant that the mystery of Thy glorious Ascension may produce in my soul these happy fruits. Raise me above everything which is not Thee. Transform me into Thyself, and render this transformation such that I may never fall from this happy state. May my spirit, O Jesus, rise unceasingly by its desires and thoughts toward Thy eternal tabernacles, and dwell there in advance! May my heart, disengaged from all earthly affections, regard Thee as the only object of its hope and its love. May my soul, at last considering the earth only as a place of exile, hasten by its desires the moment when, leaving the prison which retains its captive, it can fly toward Thee, and take part in Thy eternal triumph. Amen.

Third Meditation - Descent of the Holy Spirit on the Apostles

"The disciples were altogether in one place: and suddenly there came a sound from heaven, as of a mighty wind coming, and it filled the whole house where they were sitting. And there appeared to them parted tongues as it were of fire, and it sat upon every one of them. And they were all filled with the Holy Ghost."— Acts of the Apostles, II, 1-5.

What, then, is this sacred fire which enlightens and inflames the Apostles without consuming them, which fills them with strength and wisdom; so that from men, timid, gross, pusillanimous as they were, they are all at once transformed into heroes, ready to undertake all and to suffer all for the glory of their Divine Master? O my Redeemer, I understand! This is the fire which Thou earnest to bring to earth, and with which Thou dost wish to inflame the whole world — it is the divine fire of charity. Thus, dost Thou place the seal to the admirable work of our redemption. The old Adam, our unhappy father, has tainted his entire race with self-love, one and fruithful source of sin; and Thou, the new Adam, didst bring divine charity, in order that we may establish it in our hearts, on the ruins of self-love. Ah, my Saviour, give me now this perfect charity! Behold for ten days, after the example of Thy Apostles, I have kept myself shut up in the Cenacle, to await and receive at last this fire of divine love, which is the fulfillment of the whole law — the end and abridgment of all perfection. Ah! I implore Thee, Lord, in finishing this Retreat, do not refuse me this precious gift of Thy love: it alone can seal my resolutions and help me to keep them. I ask it of Thee through the intercession of Mary, who was, as it were, the channel of the graces by which the Apostles were inundated on this solemn day, and who must be still for all Christians, and particularly for the children of Carmel, the channel of that divine charity

162

of which she is the mother and the mistress.

FIRST POINT

All the evils, whether of body or soul, which desolate the human race, have their source in the disordered love of self, which our first father transmitted to us with his fault.

Adam created in charity, in virtue of this inestimable gift which his Creator had superadded to his nature, attached himself to God spontaneously and without division, as to his principle and his end. He loved all things and loved himself in God and for God, recognizing that all comes from Him, and should return to Him. But as soon as, by the malice of the demon, sin entered into the world, self-love established itself in the degraded heart of man, who fell, all at once, from the sublime heights of charity where His Creator had placed him, into the frightful abyss of egotism. He tried to make himself his God and his end — a wicked attempt, as foolish as it is horrible, whence have come forth all disorders and crimes. From that time he commenced to seek his happiness, not in God, source of all good and of all beauty, but in the creature, in nothingness, in the flesh, and in the world. For divine love was substituted love of himself — gross and animal love, when man seeks in his senses that happiness which flies from him; diabolic love, when it places him in the esteem of his own excellence; idolatrous love, when he seeks to find happiness in the possession of some creature which he, in his folly, prefers to that of the Creator. Turn and return this truth as you will, you shall find that all the sins committed on earth have their one source in this disorderly love of self — self-love. It is the capital enemy, and inevitably the enemy of divine love.

Therefore, when the Holy Trinity take counsel for the reparation of fallen man, what is the end of the mission of the Son of God on earth? To re-enkindle there divine love — "I am come to bring fire on earth and what would I, but that it be enkindled," says Jesus Christ. He has willed that this sacred fire be not an accidental flame to be extinguished: it is the consubstantial love of the Father and the Son; it is the increated love which unites them in the Holy Trinity; it is the love which has been given to us, and which takes possession of our souls in order keep them perpetually in this sacred fire. Saint Paul teaches this in these words: "The love of God has been given to us." This love is then imparted to the Apostles to-day, and makes of them new men — men all divine. I also will be transformed by its virtue if I place no obstacle to its flame, and allow my heart to be inflamed by it.

How admirable the effects of the Holy Spirit in souls which He entirely possesses? Besides sanctifying grace which is common to all the just, He imparts the inestimable gifts of His love which become in them like certain habits or permanent qualities, communicating light to their minds, and to their wills a special strength for loving and practising virtue. These gifts are: Wisdom, understanding, knowledge, counsel, fortitude, piety, and fear, of! which the first four enlighten our minds, and the other three affect our wills. They

163

are opposed to the fatal properties of self-love: to its wisdom, carnal and diabolic wisdom, which enjoys only present and earthly things; to that understanding which has aptitude and attention only for the things of the world; to its science which inflates the heart and disappears with its object; to its prudence — prudence of the flesh, which applies itself entirely to the seeking and the acquisition of earthly goods, honors, and pleasures. After having thus enlightened the understanding with His celestial lights, the Holy Spirit penetrates even to the innermost part of the human soul — the will. He fills it with supernatural strength, enabling it to triumph over its weakness in virtue of a secret unction which gives it a taste and love for holy things, and finally, inspiring that filial fear which makes it avoid even the appearance of evil, in place of that fear, according to the spirit of the world, of which the Prophet said: "They feared where there was nothing to fear," while they had not feared sin, the only object worthy of fear.

O Holy Spirit, infinite love, ineffable bond of the Father and the Son! Come to me, unite me to my God, according to the prayer which my Saviour addressed to His Father, in order that I may be consummated in unity. Pour into my soul Thy sacred gifts, give that heavenly wisdom which will make me relish Thee in all things. Give me the understanding of Thy law and of the life and death of Jesus. Give me that divine knowledge which will teach me to rise unceasingly from the creature to the Creator; the gift of counsel to choose always the surest way of perfection; the strength to triumph over my rebellious will and my flesh always ready to hinder me in the practice of good. Grant me that piety full of unction and ardor for the things of God, and that filial fear which will not permit me to offend Thee in anything whatsoever. Ah! if I had love, I should possess all these gifts, for they are only the divine properties of charity. He who loves has understanding, fortitude, wisdom — in a word, he has all. Grant, then, at last that I may love Thee, that I may think of Thee alone.

SECOND POINT

Whence comes it that, among souls animated by sanctifying grace and honored consequently, by the presence of the Holy Spirit — even among the spouses of Jesus Christ, privileged inhabitants of Mount Carmel, there are found so few who enjoy these divine properties of love, and those gifts the price of which, according to the Holy Books, is far above the purest gold and the most precious stones? Ah! it is because of their imperfections, their infidelities — in a word, it is self-love, whose roots, badly extirpated from their hearts because of want of mortification, restrain these eminent properties of holy love and prevent the exercise of them. Thus these souls never reach that divine union, that perfect union which is, nevertheless, the object and the end of their vocation.

It is then very important that, before terminating this Retreat, I consider the summit of the sublime Mountain of Carmel to which I have been conducted by a succession of meditations that are, as it were, the development of the practical truths of Religion. Now this summit is divine charity — perfect love, the love of God obtained by immolation of self, the transformation of my whole self into the being of God, my Beginning and my End, my one and sovereign good. This is the height to which I am called, to which I should tend, and which I shall infallibly reach, if I am faithful to my vocation, that is to say, if I enter generously and perseveringly into the practices and the spirit of the Rule of this Holy Order of the Blessed Virgin Mary, Mother and Mistress of fair love, whose incomparable charity is proposed to me as the model of the love to which I should aspire.

In effect, divine love can be established in a soul only on the ruins of self-love. Thus, by a little reflection on the spirit of the Rule, Constitutions, and practices of the holy Order of Carmel, I recognize with admiration, that the spirit of God has inspired every point to make war to death on self-love, pursuing it everywhere and always, chasing it from its strongholds, in order to leave the soul wholly free for divine love. Self-love is first attacked in the flesh by the prescription of a universal and continual mortification, by that law of a fierce and constant war which the soul must make on the senses, allowing them no rest, no satisfactions except those which necessity requires, and not even taking any complacency in these. Then this Divine Spirit goes on, continuing its work of destruction, carrying its holy requirements into the most intimate recesses of mind and heart. For the mind it permits no curiosity, preoccupation, remembrance, no attention to persons or things the sight and thought of which could turn it from the one object which should occupy it. To the heart, it forbids the love of creatures, the desire of their approbation, the affection of relatives, of friends, of objects the most innocent in appearance, but which could occupy it uselessly. It goes so far as to demand entire death of the will, requiring the soul to live only to obey the Rule and superiors, to submit all its sentiments to theirs: that is to say, that she then lives in God, since the will of superiors is for her the faithful expression of the divine will. The generous soul is sustained, in the midst of these sacrifices and of this warfare, by the love which increases with her victories. She encourages herself to correspond more and more with the requirements of this sacred love; she avoids even a look, a useless word, in order not to lose the least of its favors or interrupt, for an instant, any of its holy exercises.

Ah! Lord, I recognize to-day, if I do not love Thee with that royal charity which should be found in every soul in Carmel, it is because I have not satisfied its requirements; it is because I have loved myself too much, and have not practised that renunciation, that hatred of self, which Thou hast so much recommended to those who would follow Thee, or rather hast imposed as a rigorous condition of their union with Thee. O God, my supreme good, I wish to love Thee now, I wish to love Thee at any cost; I wish to love Thee with that perfect love which will make me despise, hate, and immolate myself entirely. In this Retreat Thou hast made me see and understand the conditions of this divine love; with Thy grace, O Lord, I will fulfill them. While waiting until, by my works and renunciations, I can prove this love, let me make to-day a generous protestation, a firm act from the depths of my soul, which will influence all the rest of my life. I shall renew this act every day and prolong it by ardent aspirations, to be repeated every instant of my existence.

Yes, I wish to love Thee with my whole soul, with my whole mind, and with all my heart, O Jesus, my Saviour, O God! sovereign beauty, sovereign good-ness, O God who art all love! Ah! how can we help loving Love, when we have received the pledge of the Holy Spirit — Love itself? This Spirit, the Spirit of Jesus Himself — principle of all His life, all His acts, of all the immolations which He offered for the glory of His Father — has been given to me in Bap-tism. In Confirmation I received the plenitude of it, and an ever new and more abundant communication is given each time that I am nourished with His Adorable Body. In receiving Thee, O my Jesus, I have within me the ob-ject, the principle, the means, and the very act of my love.

Ah! how is it, in the midst of these flames, that I do not burn? Why, in the bosom of love, inundated by love, should I not love? How could I not love that beauty ever ancient, ever new, that goodness ineffable in all its gifts, that miercy ever ready to pardon and to forget, that wisdom so amiable and so admirable? How not love that Father "of whom all paternity in heaven and earth is named," and His Son, the Word and image of His substance, and that Spirit, ineffable bond of the one and the other — consubstantial. eternal, infi-nite, adorable love! O Father! O Son! O Holy Spirit! Adorable Trinity, my Be-ginning and my End; I say no more that I wish to love Thee, but I do love Thee, because I unite myself with Thee and love Thee with Thyself; for Thou alone canst worthily love Thyself.

For the future, then, my life shall be but one exercise of love. What ever I do shall be all for Thee — all my thoughts, all my words, all my acts, all the movements of my heart shall have no other end, no other principle than love. In repose as in labor, in sleep and in watching, I shall think of Thee alone, I will live only for Thee, that, possessing Thee in time by grace, I may possess Thee in eternity by glory. Amen.

LECTURE - DEVOTION TO THE BLESSED VIRGIN

Since devotion to the most Holy and Immaculate Mother of God belongs essentially to the spirit of Carmel, it is only just to terminate these considera-tions and this entire Retreat by treating of devotion to Mary. As all Christians are obliged to render to the august Queen of Heaven that special homage due to her alone, it is important to consider what I owe to her as a daughter of the Church, before examining what I owe to her as a child of Carmel.

The dignity of this adorable creature, the sublimity of her title of Mother of God, her many and singular privileges, the ineffable grandeur of her perfec-tions, the eminence of her virtues, and above all her incomparable charity, her devotion to the glory of God and the salvation of men, surpass all that can be said or imagined. Her glory and her virtues so far exceed all those of the

166

Angels and saints united, that the Doctors of the Church fail in expression when they wish to describe them. St. John Chrysostom, in particular, says that her soul contains eminently all that there ever has been or ever will be of the most sublime perfection in heaven and on earth. Provided that, in praising her, we do not exceed the just limits fixed by faith, admitting the infinite distance between the creature and the Creator, and recognizing her grace and her beauty as the work of God Himself, our praises and our homage will always be far below her glory and her merits. Far then from fearing to say or to imagine too much of this lovely Queen, let us sigh that we know so little, and can only lisp when Ave speak of her greatness and her perfections.

Although we know in general the great privileges and sublime dignity of Mary, there are few persons who really know the high rank which she occupies, not only in the work of our redemption and the esteem of the Church, but even in the thought of God. Therefore, when some privileged souls, dazzled by the knowledge which God has given them of this incomparable creature, make use of certain expressions or praise her in terms proportioned to the sentiments they have conceived, timid servants of Mary seem to take fright.

However, the Church, pillar and foundation of truth, fears not to call her our life, our hope, Mother of Mercy, Mother of Divine Grace, and to apply to her these words which seem to have been written only of eternal wisdom: "I was set up from eternity, and of old before the earth was made. The depths were not as yet, and I was already conceived; neither had the fountains of waters as yet sprung out; the mountains with their huge bulk had not as yet been established; before the hills I was brought forth." Mary was eternally in the thought of God; not as all other creatures which God had foreseen coming forth from nothingness, but in the distinguished rank which belonged to her, that is to say, as the true Eve, the Mother of all the living — the woman by excellence who was to give birth to the Man-God type of creation, that image on which the old Adam had been formed. God has not separated, in His eternal decree, His Incarnate Son from His Mother; this divine fruit is seen in His thought on the tree which was to bear it; this marvelous flower is offered to Him on its stem, because God has willed that the new Adam should come by the way of generation, that He should have a mother, in order that the family of which Jesus Christ is the elder Brother should have one; that there should be a mother in heaven — that there should be a maternity, as there is, according to St. Paul, a Paternity which is the source of the fecundity of all being. This is the place which Mary occupies in the Incarnation, and which will be hers in Redemption until its perfect accomplishment on Calvary, where uniting and offering herself in the sacrifice with her Divine Son, taking the title of our Mother, she will suffer the sorrowful travail of it, and bring us forth to a new life by the immeasurable sorrow of this immolation: truth admirably announced in the mysterious title which the Church gives her of Mother of Divine Grace. Should we be astonished, after this, that the Fathers of the Church call her the Mediatrix of our Redemption, and endeavor to inspire us with unlimited confidence in her supreme power over the Heart of God?

But this is not sufficient for our confidence. What would her ascendancy over the Heart of God be to us, if her maternal heart did not constantly solicit her to use it in our favor; or rather if God, in establishing her the mother of all men, had not given her a heart proportionate to the immense love which this function would call for — a heart the master-piece of grace, as the heart of a mother according to the flesh is a master-piece of nature? Again this comparison fails to do justice to the heart of Mary; since she received, in recompense for the sacrifice which she offered on the Holy Mountain, a love for her children that corresponds to the designs of the mercy of God, Who has placed her on a throne of love, unceasingly to implore grace and mercy for them, and to bring down upon their heads showers of blessings. Thus we may say of Mary that her goodness equals her power, and that both are in a way without restriction and without limit.

When we say of Mary that she is a mother, that she is a virgin, that she is immaculate, these titles have a meaning so profound, so elevated above our feeble lights, that we scarcely know what we say. When we speak of her Immaculate Conception, we do not sufficiently understand that this privilege is only the first trait of that purity with which God wished to adorn the soul of her whom He had eternally chosen to be the ark of the covenant, His temple and His veritable sanctuary. When we speak of her virginity, we understand well the integrity of her body exempt from all stain; but who knows, who admires in Mary other virginities far more glorious than that of her body — the virginity of her mind which permits no thought foreign to her supreme end, and the virginity of her heart, which allows no affection, forms no design, conceives no desire which has not for its end and object divine love? In one word, she had as her portion all the purity with which a creature could be endowed, so that Holiness itself, in contemplating her, could exclaim: "Thou art all fair, my beloved, and there is no spot in thee." What more shall we say to prove how little we know of the marvels hidden in Mary? That she was a virgin and a mother at the same time, reversing all the laws of nature, unique privilege given to her alone, prodigy which will never be repeated; but do we think that we have now said all that there is wonderful and divine in this virginal motherhood? It is undoubtedly a miracle, and a miracle of the first order, that a woman should become a mother without ceasing to be a virgin; but there is nothing which we cannot easily conceive with the assistance of the sovereign power of God; but the master-piece of omnipotence, of mercy, and of divine wisdom, is that this virgin, daughter of Adam, gives birth to a child who is more than a man, who is the great Emmanuel — that is to say, "God with us."

That a stem detached and planted in an arid soil bears a fruit full of beauty and sweetness is marvelous; that this fruit be not of this world but of another, not of earth but of heaven, is what passes all conception, and is the object of the admiration of the Angels; it will be eternally the marvel of heaven, and should be the subject of thanksgiving and praise on earth.

What shall we say of her fidelity in corresponding to the graces with which God prevented her and in rendering herself worthy, in so far as it depended on her, of the privileges by which she had been distinguished? If God has done such great things for Mary, what has Mary not done for God! If she was called happy for having borne and nourished the Saviour, she was much more happy, according to the testimony of Jesus Christ Himself, for having conceived in advance the Word of God by her humility, for having preserved and nourished Him by her fidelity, and for having brought Him forth anew, at the foot of the Cross, by her incomparable charity. Her crown and her glory consist far more of the admirable virtues which she practised and the part which she took in our redemption by her zeal, her suffering, and her immolation, than of the privileges with which she was enriched.

Likewise, as God willed the Redeemer to be announced by holy Prophets and prefigured by holy and illustrious personages, so Mary, His Mother, had her Prophets and her figures. The Holy Fathers are pleased to recognize her in Esther, liberatrix of her people; in the invincible Judith victorious over Holifernes. They have admired her fruitful virginity in the rod of Aaron which blossomed in the shadow of the tabernacle; in the burning bush which burned without being consumed; and again, in that little cloud which our Holy Father Elias saw shedding a refreshing rain over a land desolated by long drought.

Is it astonishing, after this, that the Church should have assigned to Mary a special cultus, due to her alone; that in her praises she seldom ever separates the Son from the Mother; that the name of Mary should constantly mingle with that of Jesus; and that if at the beginning of her Offices she implores His assistance, she terminates them by addressing her prayers to her? One cannot be a child of the Church without making it a duty, a consolation, a happiness to be a child of Mary, and paying to her each day a tribute of praise, thanksgiving, and love.

But what, in regard to Mary, should be the sentiments and the homage of the children of Elias, of the Solitaries of Carmel? We know there is a tradition in this holy Order — tradition sanctioned by several holy Pontiffs — that this Virgin Mother of the future was shown to the holy Prophet, and that her expectation became, from that time, the subject of special devotion for the pious solitaries who dwelt on the holy Mountain. Then when the world was awakened by the preaching of the Apostles, the heirs of the spirit of Elias were the first to range themselves beneath the yoke of the Faith, and on Carmel arose the first chapel built in honor of the Mother of God. They were the first to take the name of servants of Mary, who was regarded as their mother, their foundress, and their model. The Rule which they followed was the expression of the charity of that incomparable Virgin, who gave them her habit — symbol of that sublime perfection which they pledged themselves to practise — and, later on, clothed them with the signal privilege of the scapular, as the distinctive mark of their adoption.

The children of Carmel are then the privileged children of Mary, and are obliged by this title to honor her as their foundress, their superior, and their mother. It is for this reason that in this holy Order there is no abbess, but simply a prioress — the most Holy Virgin being regarded as the general Superior of the whole Institute, and the Superior of each monastery in particular.

How can the Solitaries of Carmel prove themselves worthy of the privileged title of first servants and daughters of Mary? First of all, by clothing themselves with her spirit, with her charity as with a vesture which is proper to them; this is the true habit with which they should be clothed, and of which the holy habit they receive from the hands of the Church is the characteristic symbol. They should be clothed with Mary, as St. Paul enjoins all Christians to be clothed with Jesus Christ. Since Mary has been the most perfect and faithful imitator of Jesus Christ, by retracing in their lives that of their Mother they retrace that of her Son with a particular grace which renders them still more agreeable to their Heavenly Spouse. Therefore the Queen of Carmel, the Mother of fair love, addresses to them these words, far more true on her lips than on those of St. Paul: "Be ye imitators of me as I am of Jesus Christ." In vain would one wear the habit of Carmel, without also putting on this interior habit, the veil of the modesty and the purity of Mary, the tunic of her humility, the mantle of her charity, the girdle of her fortitude, the sandals of her fidelity, the robe of her penitence and mortification.

As Mary is herself this Carmel, this holy Mountain of perfection and charity, it is to her we should have recourse, in order to ascend by its rugged paths to the summit. We should call upon her at every moment for the assistance of which we have need in our daily combats, and say to her at each instant:

"Show thyself a Mother —
　　Offer Him our sighs,
　Who, for us Incarnate,
　　Did not thee despise."

It is then by Mary that the children of Carmel should go to Jesus and attain unto union with Him. From this confidence in Mary, her true Mother, and from this obligation to resemble her, zeal should arise in the Religious soul, to profit by every occasion to prove her love and to render homage to her. She will then be happy to sing her praises, to ornament her images, to invoke her at every hour, to beg her blessing on entering or leaving her cell. She will have recourse to her in her sufferings, in her temptations, and in her discouragements; the better to receive the Body and Blood of her Son, she will try to unite her heart to the heart of Mary. She will pay to her with particular attention the repeated tribute of the salutation of the Angel, which we call the Rosary; a prayer so excellent and which would be so fruitful, if at each decade we renewed our piety, offering our fervent prayers to the Mother, in unison with her Son, to obtain some special grace; but a prayer the value of which is not known, or the fruit of which is often lost through routine.

Examen On the Lecture

Have I an esteem for the Most Holy Virgin, her greatness, her virtues, and her power, conformable to that of the saints, and in accord with my title of privileged daughter of Mary, Religious of Carmel?

In order to acquire this veneration and love for my august and holy Mother, have I taken pleasure in meditating on the mysteries of her life, and in celebrating the solemnities consecrated to honoring them?

In my meditations, at the Holy Sacrifice of the Mass, and in my prayers, have I had recourse to her powerful mediation for advancing in general in the perfection of my state, and in particular to obtain the victory over my defects, and the acquisition of the virtues most necessary for me?

Have I not limited myself to those devotions required by the Rule, in visiting her shrines or reciting the prayers prescribed in her honor, without seeking to reanimate my confidence in her goodness and her maternal love?

Have I not in particular to reproach myself with precipitation and routine in the recitation of the Rosary?

Is it not my want of devotion to the Most Blessed Virgin and to my little zeal in her service, as well as to my negligence in invoking her powerful intercession, that I should attribute my little advancement in perfection?

Prayer to the Most Holy Virgin

———

To Conclude the Retreat

O most Holy Mother of God, Queen of Carmel, in terminating my Retreat, I humbly supplicate thee to receive into thy hands the graces which thy Divine Son has given me, with the resolutions they have inspired, in order that thou mayst keep them and obtain for me the grace to be faithful. For if abandoned to myself, and left to my weakness and natural inconstancy, I will soon forget them; and in a few days will again find myself with senses as little recollected, flesh as unmortified, my mind as dissipated, and my heart as little touched by the things of God as formerly; and will fall back into the same old way — those exercises with tepidity, meditations without devotion, Communions without fruit, over which I have had so much to sigh. It is necessary then that the Spirit of thy Divine Son complete the work of my sanctification which He has commenced during this Retreat. It is to thee that I address myself, O Virgin Immaculate, in order that, by thy powerful intercession, I may obtain from God courage and perseverance. It is for thy glory, O Mary, ornament of the holy Mountain of Carmel, since although unworthy of it, I am a member of thy family, and belong especially to thee. Suffer no longer in thy house a soul so imperfect. May I die at last to myself and to all creatures that, after thy example, my "life may be hidden in God with Jesus Christ," and at the last day I may appear with Him in glory, never more to be separated from Him. Amen.

www.ingramcontent.com/pod-product-compliance
Lightning Source LLC
La Vergne TN
LVHW091257080426
835510LV00007B/298